I0796731

YEAR OF THE WATER HORSE

YEAR OF THE WATER HORSE

A MEMOIR

JANICE PAGE

PEGASUS BOOKS
NEW YORK LONDON

YEAR OF THE WATER HORSE

Pegasus Books, Ltd.
148 West 37th Street, 13th Floor
New York, NY 10018

First Pegasus Books cloth edition December 2025

Interior design by Maria Fernandez

Library of Congress Cataloging-in-Publication Data is available.

ISBN: 979-8-89710-009-5

10 9 8 7 6 5 4 3 2 1

Printed in the United States of America
Distributed by Simon & Schuster
www.pegasusbooks.com

For Zoe,

the horse who brought me home

What is true is not always convincing,
and what is convincing is not always true.

That's Nietzsche, I think. But it might just be something I made up. Or did I find it in a fortune cookie? Doesn't matter. The point is, you can't believe anyone who tells you their memoir is "mostly true" because it's only mostly true to them, and sometimes names and minor details are changed to protect the innocent, or themselves. Also, never trust a fortune that says "Everyone agrees you are the best."

Contents

CHAPTER 1

Paragon Park

The greatest day of my life happened when I was five.

I mean no disrespect to all the other great days of my life, including those that involve a child or a spouse, but my greatest day is my greatest day because of four things: surprise, unconditional love, durable life lessons, and ice cream.

It happened in a suburb of Boston on a perfect July day, which in New England means the sun was out, the humidity was tolerable, and the Red Sox were probably playing a weekend double-header at home. I woke up, as I always did, to the sound of my dad raking his metal teaspoon across the surface of his ceramic cereal bowl.

Every morning of his life, my father ate Kellogg's Raisin Bran (never Post) drowned in whole milk, a ritual that required scraping the bottom and sides of his shallow bowl no fewer than fifty times. I know this because I counted the scrapes from my bed, which was only a few feet away on the other side of a wall no thicker than a communion wafer, with a painted plywood door that hung several inches short of the floor.

We lived in Braintree, a proudly average South Shore town most infamously known for the fatal armed robbery that sent Italian immigrant anarchists Nicola Sacco and Bartolomeo Vanzetti to the electric chair in

1927, fueling many decades of ethnic profiling and name-calling (a regional specialty). In a neighborhood labeled the Highlands despite having almost no perceptible elevation, we occupied a tan, one-story ranch with a single tiny bathroom, two official bedrooms, and a small dining room that had been converted into a third bedroom to accommodate our family of eight. I was the youngest, so I squeezed into that makeshift sleeping space with my sister closest in age (Patty), the headboard of our double bed resting against that same thin wall, which backed up to a small, hardworking electric stove on the other side. There was only enough room in the kitchen for a two-person, Formica-topped café table where my father slurped his breakfast while my mother drank black coffee and chain-smoked Kents. The dining room table was in the living room.

Clink, clink, clink. Clink, clink. Crunch, crunch. Clink. That was my daily alarm clock.

But on this particular summer day in 1966, there was an added element to the crack-of-dawn soundtrack. It stood out because it didn't happen often. Ma and Dad were arguing (not so odd) and she was holding her ground (odd).

"Well, I'm not doing it," she said.

"We have to," he countered. "Already told them to come."

"*You* told them," she corrected. "I didn't tell them anything."

"Them" was a couple I'll call Agnes and Howard Patterson. My dad had been buddies with Howard since their years in the navy; Agnes came with, like potato salad. They were decent, plain vanilla Rhode Islanders who required little effort to host, and most days—with or without advance warning—they would have been welcome in our home. This time, my mother just wasn't in the mood.

"I'm not staying here to cook for them," she told my father.

"Have to. Already invited them," he said again, dismissively. "It'll be easy. I'll throw some hot dogs and hamburgs on the grill."

"*You* stay and entertain them, John," she shot back. "I'm leaving."

There are no days off when you're a woman with six kids and an Archie Bunker husband. My mom's idea of a break was when she'd escape to the grocery store and return hours later, it felt like, with little more than ground beef and a carton of Kents. None of us was allowed to accompany her on those trips; undivided attention wasn't a thing in our otherwise happy house. We generally just went along, and got along, without much drama.

Not today, though.

My dad dropped his bowl in the sink and headed out back to prep the grill, mow the lawn, clip the hedges, and enlist my two brothers—eleven and thirteen at the time—to help with the rest. He was whistling as he went about his chores, which, in hindsight, seems like a gross miscalculation. Inside the house, my mother was seething.

She fed me breakfast. Dressed me. Packed a bag. Where were we headed? I'm sure I asked, repeatedly and without really expecting an answer. "Just get in," she would have said as she hustled me into the back seat of our seaweed-green Chevy Nova. If there was a seat belt, I doubt this was the one time we made use of it. All I remember is my dad's quizzical look from a far corner of the yard as we backed out of the carport, lurched forward over the sidewalk curb, and sped off.

When my mother was a little girl, her mother would grab her by the hand and say, "Come on, YoYo, we're getting out of here."

It was the 1920s, but my grandparents were recent immigrants from the Abruzzo region of Italy by way of Ellis Island, so there was nothing roaring about their finances. They'd board the cheapest bus (or maybe several) from Boston to Hoboken, New Jersey, where my great-uncle lived. From there, they'd often venture to Coney Island, spending all day taking in things my grandfather dismissed as frivolous and my grandmother preached as vital. My mother told me how the air smelled of sugar and grease, how the sand burned her toes, how the saltwater still crusted her skin the next day. She wanted me to know that my grandmother, who died long before I was born, had been right. Life was too short to waste on obligations.

This is exactly why, after about thirty minutes of deliberate driving, Yolanda DiMartinis Page pulled the Nova into the parking lot at Nantasket Beach, our first stop on the Screw You and Your Barbecue with the Pattersons Tour.

We never went to the beach this early in the morning.

In the bathhouse, I pulled on my favorite cerulean swimsuit with the neon-lime piping. My mother slipped into a cocoa-colored one-piece, a beige terry-cloth cover-up, and a wide-brimmed straw hat. Yolanda was a babe, even at forty-four, with supple Mediterranean skin, brunette hair, dark brown eyes, and enough curves in all the right places to make a melon-baller jealous. I took after her in the expected ways of a dark, hairy, petite Italian girl, but I also had pronounced red highlights in my curls, and freckles bestowed by my father's Scottish heritage. We unfurled our blanket on packed sand close to the seawall. The next several hours were a blur of sun and surf that only ended when the last bit of beach gave way to the tide.

If this had been any other day, that would have been our cue to head home. Instead, we changed out of our damp suits and headed across the street to the frozen custard stand, where my favorite thing was watermelon sherbet with the chocolate sprinkles known in these parts as jimmies. It wasn't even lunchtime yet, and she let me order a large cone. What the *F Troop* was happening?

On the other side of the frozen custard stand at Nantasket Beach, rising out of the ground for blocks and blocks and blocks, was a white wooden monster known as the Giant Coaster. It stood nearly a hundred feet tall. Surrounding it was a legendary utopia called Paragon Park. If you lived anywhere near Hull, Massachusetts, in the mid-1960s, this was your Disneyland.

We got to go to Paragon Park exactly once every summer. My father, who worked as a boilermaker at the Fore River Shipyard in nearby Quincy, would bring home his modest paycheck and my mother would divide up the cash, slotting it into budget envelopes marked "electric," "food," "oil," "water," etc. There was no envelope marked "entertainments." So, starting about two months before the week that we all went to Paragon Park, she'd skim a little off the top of each fund until we had enough to pile into the car, sitting on laps and floorboards if we had to, and set out on a mission to have a year's worth of fun in a day. Never would I have expected to enter the park for an unplanned, unsanctioned, Mommy-and-me-only visit. But here it was, happening.

First, we played Skee-Ball in the arcade outside the park gates. That was cool enough, the lathe-turned wooden balls skipping up a long ramp before rolling down with a glorious *thump thump thump*, rattling around the pinball-like catch basins, circling and teasing until settling on a hole with an assigned point value that occasionally matched what you'd aimed for. I figured I'd go home with a Chinese finger trap or some other trinket I'd earned with my vast Skee-Ball winnings. When we actually moved toward the park entrance, I thought my mother had made a mistake.

"We're going in?" I questioned.

"We're going in," she confirmed.

It didn't seem like a dream, or a joke, but maybe I was too young to recognize the signs. Maybe we were on *Candid Camera*. I looked around suspiciously in case Allen Funt was somewhere lurking with a microphone. The stern man taking tickets motioned me through the gate. The full expanse of the park came into view.

There was the Rocket Swing, and the Beep Beep Cars. There was the Whip, the Kooky Kastle, the Tilt-A-Whirl, and dozens of other attractions. The Giant Coaster loomed above it all. People squealed from inside cars that appeared to teeter on the edge of the sky.

I wasn't tall enough to board most rides, and what I could go on (spinning teacups, kiddie coasters) I generally hated because I had a weak stomach and a kindling stack of fears that included acrophobia. The one exception was the Congo Cruise. Though it finished with a precipitous drop, I tolerated those few seconds because all that came before them so intrigued me.

To begin with, you were loaded into a precarious little boat that quickly entered a pitch-black tunnel, bumping into the concrete sides as it floated down the track. Whenever you'd glimpse light, it was because the tunnel opened up to a jungle-themed vignette, the most consistent theme being White People in Peril. There were dioramas with scale figures of humans and animals on the prowl. A man in a pith helmet faced down dangers like quicksand and fire ants. And then, suddenly, cannibals! The pith-helmeted white man was shown in a kettle perched over a fire, with straw-skirted, black-skinned pygmies dancing around him, wielding spears. One pygmy had a mechanized arm that lowered the lid on the man in the pot. *Ooga-booga* music played in the background.

In 1966, we were on the cusp of race riots that would consume news headlines and define the era in which I grew up. My five-year-old brain didn't have a clue about that, and it wouldn't have known to reject this scene as wrong, on so many levels. I was raised in a monochromatic world where casual racism happened regularly. The only times we went as a family to a marginally upscale restaurant were when my father won an unsanctioned workplace lottery called the [N-word] Pool. I have no idea why it had such a vile name, or why no one I knew thought to question it. And it wasn't until much later that any of this incensed me. At the time of my greatest day, all I knew was that something about this place, this ride, was *off*. And I found that fascinating. Maybe because my mother was also a little . . . *off*.

The finishing descent of the Congo Cruise, down a long ramp, through a spray of water that ended in a soaking splash, was the reason most people boarded the ride in the first place. Well, that and the darkness of the tunnels, which provided cover for couples making out. My mom held my hand as we felt our boat cranking up the rickety ramp, and she squealed as we plummeted in a great *whoosh*. I stifled my nausea.

My stomach didn't like me any better when we moved on to other amusements, but no amount of motion sickness was going to compromise my reverence for this place or my delight at knowing how jealous this rogue excursion would make my brothers and sisters, even the fully grown ones. My mom was as gleeful and unfettered as a trampolining toddler and seeing her let go made me less focused on my own phobias. Plus, whenever

I needed a break from the dizzying action, the concourse had games of chance—one offering ginormous candy bars as prizes—and mini golf tucked into a back corner.

We spent about three hours in the park, including a break for hot dogs, fries, and a creamy soft-serve twist, which Ma joked she should not have eaten before trying her luck at the Guess Your Weight booth. It was midafternoon when we finally exited. I think I started napping on my feet, before we even hit the parking lot.

But my mother wasn't done.

When I woke up, we were at the East Braintree home of my eldest sister, Nancy, about a twenty-five-minute drive from the beach. Nancy was nineteen years older than me. She was married already, with a one-year-old son. He already had more toys than I did (firstborns had it made).

Nancy was my second mother—or maybe my first mother, since Ma was old enough to be my grandmother and acted more like an eccentric elderly aunt. Ma and Nancy spent a lot of that afternoon deep in conversation, much of which involved the phrase "your father" in a way that did not seem very flattering. Nancy offered me more ice cream—spumoni this time—and since no one on this planet seemed to be counting, I accepted. When dinnertime rolled around, we moved on down the road to the nearest Howard Johnson's, where I ordered fried clam strips and Ma ordered a cheeseburger. She wanted hot fudge sundaes for dessert; who was I to argue? It was dusk when we left HoJo's. The local drive-in was practically across the street, and it was our next stop.

I wish I could remember the first movie we saw that night. It was probably something like *The Singing Nun* or *That Darn Cat!* Maybe it seems odd that I don't remember the exact title when I'm able to recall ordering clam strips for dinner; I think that's only because the second half of our double feature blew my mind so completely that it obliterated whatever had come before it on-screen.

In fairness, my mother probably thought I was asleep when she hopped screens between movies. She obviously didn't know that the five-year-old curled up in the back seat would be taking in every word and frame of *A Patch of Blue*, an intense drama in which Sidney Poitier befriends a white woman (Elizabeth Hartman) who was blinded at age five (!) when her mother (Shelley Winters) hurled a bottle of acid at an abusive lover and missed. The black-and-white film, for which Winters won an Oscar, features rape, persistent abuse, rough language, and numerous anxiety-provoking scenes of accidental jaywalking by the blind girl. I'd never seen people be so mean to each other, or so vulnerable. And though I was too young to appreciate the irony of watching a movie about racial tolerance just hours after enjoying a stupendously racist amusement park ride, somewhere in my nascent conscience it registered and lodged.

I remember thinking Poitier was the handsomest man I'd ever seen. And so compassionate. What I saw up on screen was ugly and disturbing and tender and hopeful all at once. Could these people be for real? Poitier sure seemed real. Though I'd only just met him, I felt certain he wouldn't ever lie to me.

Around midnight, the Nova finally rolled up our driveway and settled back into its carport cradle. My father came to the back door as my mother carried me inside. He looked stricken. However angry he may have been, it was clear even to a child that he was far more rattled, and now relieved. A new world order had been established, or at the very least threatened. I wasn't too sleepy to remember finding that pretty interesting.

I revisit my greatest day often. It taught me how to listen and observe. It taught me how to construct a priceless day of memories for someone you love, even as a collateral objective. And, maybe most useful, it taught me how to really stick it to a boyfriend or a spouse when he seems to be taking you for granted.

But there was something else I learned that day in 1966—something more disturbing and less in line with my naïve first assessment of our carefree existence. I saw cracks, deeply rooted and widening. I was pretty sure my father saw them, too.

Trained to be a dutiful wife—the kind who always had a cold Schlitz waiting when her man got home from his shipyard job, which let out every afternoon at 3:30 with a *Flintstones*-like factory whistle—my mother knew that a comfortable life isn't always a fulfilling life. From her I learned the power of picking your spots, and that feminism can be just as loud when it's whispered. Very early in my life, I started to notice that she had a quietly subversive side. Once, when I asked her why, as a devout Roman Catholic, she never went to confession but did take Communion every Sunday in blatant violation of church law, she said, "If I have a one-to-one relationship with God, as they preach that I do, then I sure as hell don't need to confess my sins through a man." It should never be underestimated how powerful such words can be to a child, especially coming from a mostly by-the-book parent.

Yolanda Page was, in her own way, a feminist. My father may have thought he was in charge, but *she* decided how much or little she wanted to be heard, and when she talked or acted, people listened. Even *he* listened because, let's be honest, she scared the crap out of him.

Mental illness wasn't something I understood in the 1960s. I simply thought my mother had light and dark days, same as everyone. Her way of dealing with them was maybe just a little more extreme. The story my siblings liked to tell was about a standard 1950s afternoon before I was born, when one child after another clumsily knocked over their milk glass during an at-home lunch of tomato soup and grilled cheese sandwiches.

First there was Patty, all red hair and freckles and gorgeous green eyes, who never got in trouble because she never did anything to which you could ascribe motive. Everyone liked Patty. So, when seven-year-old Patty, the third oldest child, knocked over her milk, it was obviously an accident.

Ditto the next glass that fell. That was Jimmy's, and Jimmy wasn't much more than a baby, so he couldn't be blamed. Besides, he was adorable, with incongruous blond hair and blue eyes that prompted my dad to quote the old joke about suspecting the milkman had played a part—a joke with an edge to it because we did have a milkman (Arnie) and my father could be jealous of a Tootsie Pop.

Jacky's drink went over next. He was the oldest boy, held to a higher standard than the rest of us, even at four. He was lanky and clumsy while also being athletic. He'd grow up to be quarterback of his high school football team and the first college graduate in our family. But on this day he was just the third kid that my mother had to mop up after, and now the Page family was on ice about as thin as our bank account.

Ten-year-old Carol, my parents' second child, had a reputation for being a thorn in my mother's side. She was outspoken, which in my house was seen as defiant and disrespectful. She got branded as a troublemaker to discourage the kinds of bold behavior that one cultivates in sons. Carol was my father, but without an ounce of validation or power. No one thinks she knocked her glass over purposely, of course; it just happened.

My mom lost it.

"Alright then, let's have a party!" she shouted, and with the dramatic flourish of a Vegas magician, she yanked one end of the tablecloth with both hands, sending the soup, the glasses, the plates and bowls and every piece of S&H Green Stamps–financed flatware crashing to the floor.

Her kids laughed at first—because, come on, this was objectively more hilarious than *The Ed Sullivan Show*—but they sat in wide-eyed silence once it sunk in that the outburst wasn't an act. *Should they clean up the mess? Make a new lunch?* wondered the eldest of the bunch, fourteen-year-old Nancy. *Go back to school?* Yolanda gave no instructions. She just retreated to her bedroom and cried.

It wasn't long after that lunch that my mother was checked into a hospital for another evaluation of her "nervous breakdowns." They pronounced her chronically depressed and in need of a course correction, the inevitable prescription for unruly women of a certain age and circumstance, whether they were truly manic-depressive, as it was known then; or postpartum/perinatal, as wouldn't be widely understood for many more years; or just not "acting normal." She received the standard electroshock therapy and was sent home a few days later.

Home. Where, on one tiny wall to the left of our tiny kitchen sink, my mother had hung a tiny ceramic plaque emblazoned with cartoon flowers and the Serenity Prayer that was her daily affirmation.

God, grant me the serenity to accept the things I cannot change,
Courage to change the things I can,
And wisdom to know the difference.

The thing is, she did know the difference, mostly. You can be bipolar and still be a strong woman. You can have a mind of your own, even when you've lost it over spilled milk. Our impromptu flight to Nantasket Beach and other uncharted territory was always characterized by my father as evidence that his wife was unstable, because it couldn't possibly be that she was just ticked off. In time, my siblings and I would come to see that these were not mutually exclusive concepts. We'd discover the lie of the dependable, black-and-white life, which lacks credibility even in white suburbia. We'd learn to cope with patches of all colors and tones, including—not least where my mother was concerned—every imaginable interpretation of blue.

CHAPTER 2

The Point

We were buddies. That's the first thing I would say about my relationship with my father.

On Saturdays, when he'd go to Chick's Barber Shop in the Quincy Point neighborhood where he grew up, about a dozen miles south of Boston, I'd tag along and observe from the wide, super-slippery vinyl chairs while he got a haircut and a shave. There wasn't much to trim on his balding pate, so that part wasn't so exciting. But the shaving process, *that* was something.

I love everything about watching a man shave.

At Chick's, it was done the way you see in mob movies—with a great lather of shaving cream applied in rough strokes by a smooth stub of a brush, the end result resembling meringue mounded onto a pie. Except that it smelled like soap and throat lozenges.

Conversation in the shop was always consistent, hearty, and fast. Chick's Saturday regulars were sharp-tongued denizens of the Point, with nicknames befitting Whitey Bulger's Winter Hill Gang—names like Tubba, Old Vic, Droopy, One Two. Here, my dad was Jocko, not John. Even Chick was a nickname; to his parents, he was Ralph. When my brain summons those characters today, as a film-obsessed arts journalist conditioned by thousands of hours spent in front of screens as big as the Braintree drive-in's and as small as the phone in my hand, their banter lands somewhere between *Goodfellas* and *Good Will Hunting*. I hear their thrusts and parries, and I'm powerless not to turn them into a scene from the running screenplay that lives inside my head.

INT. CHICK'S BARBERSHOP—MORNING

Fall (football season), any Saturday in the late 1960s. Jocko (mid-40s, already balding) has just arrived and is seated at Chick's station, where the barber is draping him in a white apron cape, preparing to groom him. The shop's other middle-aged regulars—Tubba, a portly Italian American with a disproportionately tiny head; Old Vic, of indeterminate European descent, tall, gruff, prematurely gray; Droopy, Irish American, branded by a long face that's all earlobes and eyebags; One Two, a squat Italian, former boxer, with jacked arms still capable of a wicked sneaky jab-cross combination—sit nearby leafing through magazines, smoking, and generally making themselves at home.

DROOPY

Hey, Jocko, you in for a cut or a shine? That head of yours is looking more and more like Babe Parilli's helmet.

OLD VIC

Parilli's overrated, Droopy. Washed up. Face it, he ain't never gonna be Bart Starr, and the Patriots ain't never gonna have a Hall of Fame-worthy quarterback lead them to a league championship. You know why? Because the last Babe who was a true star in this town left us with a damned curse, that's why.

ONE TWO

Here we go again. You don't really believe that bunk about the Curse of the Bambino, do you, Old Vic? The Pats are just rebuilding, same as the Sox.

TUBBA

It's been almost half a century since we won a World Series, One Two, and we haven't been near a Super Bowl. What are they rebuilding, the friggin' Great Wall of China?

ONE TWO

Try to keep up, Tubba—I know it's hard for a *paisan* with such a puny cranium. If Queen Victoria here is saying that Boston sports are totally and forever screwed just because Babe Ruth was sold to the Yankees in 1920, how does he explain the success of the Celtics? And the Bruins, for that matter? Did someone over at the Garden perform an exorcism? Douse the place in holy oil?

TUBBA

I wouldn't put it past Red to do that, honestly.

JANICE

(voice-over)

Red was Red Auerbach, the legendary Celtics coach, general manager, and chief prankster, notoriously rumored to have sabotaged opponents—maybe by ordering the hot water turned off in the visitors' locker room at the Boston Garden during a playoff game, just for example. I idolized Red because he was gruff and balding and looked a lot like my dad, except that he smoked fat cigars and had courtside seats. By "holy oil," I knew that One Two meant the stuff that sat on the altar of my church and looked just like regular olive oil except it was in a fancy bottle, which only meant that it probably didn't taste half as good as what was in your nonna's Sunday gravy. They used that anointing oil to mark babies during baptism, and to comfort sick people who looked desperate for any kind of edge. Just hearing the words *holy oil*, I could feel its slick thumbprint on my forehead.

DROOPY

You numbskull guineas do know that Red is Jewish, right?

OLD VIC

Whatever, Droopy. The fact that a mick as homely as you found somebody to marry him proves there's no accounting for most things. Just ask Jocko. Jocko believes in curses.

ONE TWO

And how do you know that, Victor Immature? He hasn't said a word this entire time.

OLD VIC

Because he's a Scotsman.

DROOPY

So?

OLD VIC

So the Scots are historically screwed before they even leave the womb. That's why they call the nine of diamonds the curse of Scotland. Even poker players believe that whole country was dealt an unlucky hand.

ONE TWO

You know what, Vicks VapoRub? That might be the only sensible thing you've said today.

JANICE

(voice-over)

Jocko remained silent under Chick's majestic mountain of shaving cream. But

```
if they could have peered deep inside
the meringue, his friends would have
seen his DNA wincing.
```

The lathering took a very long time at Chick's Barber Shop. The proprietor was meticulous about prepping every whisker, so he'd double back on his brushstrokes and let the face marinate in foam a while before moving on. Then, out came the straight razor, which, when you're a kid looking on, seems a lot like bringing a murder weapon to a bubble bath.

The juxtaposition of pleasure and danger fascinated me, as did the casual artfulness of accomplishing the task without nicking any exposed flesh. What I remember most is the image of the long silver blade gliding through those mounds of meringue, methodically clearing a path that restored my father's face the same way our shovels uncovered the driveway one row at a time after every mammoth New England blizzard. There was something magical, and so zen, about this kind of simple, linear, necessary exercise. It was order restored and reborn. It was conquering the natural world. It was empowering—or at least felt as though it ought to be.

Of course, my father shaved at home as well, and that had its own allure because whenever he was alone with his thoughts and a razor, he always sang. Sometimes it was contemporary pop: Bobby Vinton's "Blue Velvet," Tammy Wynette's "Stand by Your Man," Wayne Newton's remake of "(I'll Be with You) In Apple Blossom Time." But mostly it was hymns.

My dad was raised Protestant. While we went to Mass with our Catholic mother, he went to the Congregational church by himself on Sundays, always returning with a fresh loaf of white bread that as youngsters we thought was an official part of his religious observation—his communion. Eventually we learned it was just the result of his church being located around the corner from a bakery.

John Addley Page wasn't a notably spiritual man, but he did love to sing. The hymns he grew up on made him joyful, as they also made him weep. He could be heard whistling and humming them often, around the house and in the yard, washing the dishes, driving almost anywhere. But the only time he really let them rip was when he was in church, drunk, or shaving. Then the hymns were a thing to be belted out, and Lord help you if you needed to use our one bathroom because the shaving could take as long as a full Sunday service. Sometimes it took him two or three times just to get through "The Old Rugged Cross" without choking up. He'd pause at the onset of the chorus to steady his hand, but he'd pass it off as part of the ritual, taking extra long to swish his razor around in the basin of warm, frothy water, and then he'd dry every nearby surface with a hand towel before continuing.

So I'll cherish the old rugged Cross
Till my trophies at last I lay down.
I will cling to the old rugged Cross
And exchange it some day for a crown.

Death as reward. That's quite a thing to contemplate when you're holding a blade to your neck. No wonder it made him pause.

As a young girl hearing those lyrics, I thought, Why does my father need a crown? Where would he wear it to if he had one? And would he otherwise keep it in the closet, next to his everyday fedoras, or would it occupy a more special place, maybe on the shelf in the living room alongside my mother's precious Hummels? Later, I realized that prayers of this sort, most persuasively those set to minor chords, are really about the common man's need to believe that life is glory deferred. Something better awaits all those who play by the rules, right? It must.

I've always wanted to trust in an afterlife that included joyful family reunions, and crowns, but it went against the cynical instincts of the budding journalist I was already becoming. So, I settled for appreciating that the words my father sang were far less important than what they unleashed in him—and, by extension, in me. Above all else, the hymns were a gateway to my paternal grandparents, both natives of Scotland, who immigrated to America in the early 1900s. They were long gone by the time I came around, and I liked knowing that he could access their memories within just a few notes. When you're the baby of the family, you miss a lot—not only because you weren't there when it happened, but because your family adopted a kind of unintentional shorthand before you had a chance to catch up. So, you don't grow up knowing about the shotgun weddings, or the crazy petty run-ins with the law, or the real reason three of your aunts don't speak to each other, because those bits of gossip ran out of gas ages ago. Not that your father would have been the one to tell you anyway.

It wasn't until I was an adult that I learned, by way of a random conversation with one of my cousins, that my paternal grandfather had been a professional soccer player, lured to Massachusetts by the promise of a grubby shipyard job in exchange for playing on a nascent world-class team. I had always been a fan of the sport—swept up in the zen of its grace and magnificent geometry—so everything about this revelation enthralled me. I began researching my grandfather's considerable athletic achievements, discovering *New York Times* game reports of his team, the Fore River Shipbuilding Company Stars, including the time they'd come close to winning a national championship in 1920. I asked my dad's siblings to tell me stories that would color in the sketch that emerged from those news clippings. One anecdote captivated me, probably because it said as much about the blunt-force communication skills of the men in my family as it did about their athletic ability. It happened in the final minutes of a regular-season match played at home, when Dave Page (that's my grandpa) struck a ball that missed its mark and landed among a group of fans who crowded the edges of the field.

"Jeezus, Pagey," one of his teammates, a fellow Dundee recruit, called out. "Yi jist clobbered a kid!"

Only then realizing that his powerful kick had slammed into a spectator's baby carriage as it sailed out of bounds, Dave dutifully ran over to check out the damage on the sidelines. Muscling his way through the thicket of concerned fans, he stopped abruptly when he came close enough to the screaming, red-faced infant to see who'd been at the end of his boot.

"Ah fir chrisake," he muttered, turning quickly on his cleated heel to rejoin play. "It's jist meh *oon* kid."

My father wasn't embarrassed by this or any other tidbit of personal history; he just wasn't much for talking about the past—or the present, or the future. The closest he ever came to baring his soul was his reverence for what became known in our family as his "shaving songs." Consequently, I remember being fascinated by them even as a young girl and climbing up to stand on the lid of the toilet while he warbled.

When you have an emotionally distant parent, you learn to seize whatever access points you're granted. I knew when my dad's walls were made of brick and when they were made of glass, and I knew how to increase the chances of us seeing each other across the divide. That's why you could find me by his side most days, inserting myself into his routines, whether they were meant to include me or not.

On Saturdays, we ran errands and dropped in on family and friends so numerous and welcoming that I would not have been surprised to find out my dad was some kind of secret mayor, elected in a landslide popular vote but too humble to reveal his lofty position. On Sundays, we puttered around the house and yard; him in an unflattering threadbare undershirt and me wishing that girls wore undershirts.

A more frequent routine involved newspapers. My father read three of them a day, front to back, sometimes twice. Even though he'd dropped out of school in the tenth grade to help support his family during the Great Depression, he was a literate man and a legitimate newshound. And I was the child who stood on his shoulders—or, at the very least, sat on them.

Before I was old enough to even read the newspaper with him, I found a way to join in by perching atop the back of the living room couch, straddling his head by dangling my little legs down either side of his neck as he sat flipping pages. While he would steep himself in current events, I would pretend I was running my own outpost of Chick's Barber Shop. Every item in the kitchen cabinets was a potential part of my salon toolkit: a pastry scraper shaved his chin stubble, a rolling pin massaged his neck, an eggbeater whirred around his ears to give the effect of a blow dryer.

Sometimes, I used empty tomato paste cans as curlers for the few strands of hair he had remaining in his comb-over.

No matter what utensil or foodstuff I brought out to experiment with in my salon, my father just sat there, consuming his newspapers, acting as though nothing out of the ordinary were going on. He'd only acknowledge me when, every half hour or so, I'd lean over to comment on a photograph or a cartoon or a word that I could recognize in a headline.

"Who's that?" I might ask, pointing to a black-and-white image of a dapper man in an expensive-looking suit, standing in front of a microphone.

"Just another idiot who's ruining the country," he'd answer.

"Politishun?"

"Yeah."

"Repubicun?"

"Yeah."

In Massachusetts, politics are a sport the same way that sports are a sport. And weather is also a sport. And teasing. If you didn't learn your sports, and learn to respect them as though your life depended on it, you could expect to be left out of at least a third of the conversations that happened in your lifetime. I learned my sports—all of them, including the pretenders, like professional wrestling and roller derby—so I'd get to enjoy more time with my father. That brought us together on muggy summer afternoons, when we'd sit on webbed chaise lounges in the carport, sipping something icy (and, in his case, yeasty) and listening to the Red Sox by way of a powder-blue transistor radio. It also put me in the room the day my dad hurled his cardigan sweater at the television set to protest another ugly New England Patriots loss, and we watched in horror as his errant throw knocked down the Christmas tree, sending ornaments and tinsel flying everywhere, along with my mother's shouts and limited sanity.

I was the daddy's little girl that Al Martino sang about. I didn't even question the sexist expectations set forth in the lyrics (*"You're sugar, you're spice, you're everything nice . . ."*). I wore my daddy's girl label proudly, and I would have bet everything that it came with a lifetime warranty.

We don't consider the possibility that reality is fluid when we're children. My father and I were unconditional buddies until we were not. That decision was his, not mine.

⁂

No one called my dad by his given name, John, except for my mother. To everyone else he was Jacky or Jocko, monikers that were far better suited to his blue-collar soul. Everyone in our field of vision knew Jocko. And everyone loved him, it seemed—which was odd because he could definitely be an asshole when he put his mind to it.

When he first encountered Yolanda DiMartinis sitting with her chums in the stands of a local basketball game in 1940, he barely even acknowledged her. And she was a looker, as I've noted, while he was a scrawny, sub-five-foot-eight-inch high school dropout with crooked teeth. But he was also confident, chivalrous, funny, and street smart, so Yolanda viewed him as marriage material from the outset.

They dated for about two years. Jocko introduced her to his saintly mother, whom he adored, and to his pa, whom he tolerated and fetched from the bars most evenings when the washed-up footballer was too snockered to stumble home alone.

Shortly after John and Yolanda wed on Valentine's Day in 1942—their vows were taken in the rectory, where the Protestant groom swallowed his hatred of the petty Catholic dogma that barred them from tying the knot in the church proper—he enlisted in the military and shipped out to Corpus Christi, Texas. They had their first child, Nancy, before World War II ended without the spectacularly queasy Seaman Page—who'd meant to join the army but somehow found himself in the navy—ever making it beyond the Gulf of Mexico. Carol, Patty, Jacky Jr., and Jimmy followed at respectable three- to four-year intervals. I came along a full six years after Jimmy, a silly miscalculation of the rhythm method that passed for contraception among so many Christians, and because I was born to a thirty-nine-year-old woman, I was frequently referred to as a "change-of-life baby," which was at least better than what that crappy euphemism stood for: a mistake.

When there are nineteen years between you and your oldest sibling, you're bound to be raised by different parents, even if they're the exact same people in name. Yolanda, tamped down by her mental health battles and the shock therapies that attended them, was a young mother in a cage. Though she found a way to maintain her spirit and humor throughout her life, she struggled mightily when she had five kids underfoot. Later, when it was just me, the light returned to her eyes more regularly, perhaps simply because she could breathe. I got the mother my older siblings all wanted, the one who had far more good days than bad.

Jocko had his own hang-ups. In the early days as a parent, he was fond of arbitrary rules, always inarguable and very often sexist. My sisters were allowed to go out one weekend night each week; my brothers, though younger, could be out every Friday and Saturday without a quota. Girls had a curfew of 10:30 P.M.; boys, a full hour later. With fewer kids came fewer rules and less micromanaging. I don't recall having any set curfew or being told to stay in on a weekend just because. What I do recall is a father who had mellowed with age but remained governed by the limitations and fears he knitted as armor.

He was terrified of water and unfamiliar surroundings and cancer, the latter of which had claimed his beloved mother at fifty-two. He avoided airplanes and boats and most things that moved, on account of his severe motion sickness but probably also because they were headed to parts unknown. The full list of aversions is long and varied and sometimes nonsensical (short pants are on it), but the greatest of his fears was menstruation. He refused to buy feminine hygiene products. In fact, he openly made fun of his girls for needing them.

"They can buy their own Mickey Mouse pads," he told his wife when she gave him a drugstore shopping list that included sanitary napkins.

"John, be serious," she pleaded. "You're going to be in the store."

"I'm not going to be in *that aisle*," he insisted.

All of this was just a cover, of course. Sanitary napkins were not the problem, even if he henceforth blamed every toilet clog on products that none of us were flushing. The real issue was puberty. It was one thing to have daughters and another thing entirely when those daughters became little women.

I've always wondered why this is not a topic explored much in literature. With all the books written about fathers and daughters, you'd think there'd be a sizable catalog—instead of just a few notable works with "Ophelia" in the title—on dads who withdraw when their girls start developing the hallmarks of sexual beings. It's the flip side of incest, I suppose—men so afraid of even acknowledging that taboo, they shut down well before the door has a chance to crack open.

There's no exact day or precipitating event in my memory. I couldn't tell you what age I was when it happened. I remember that he used to chase me around the house as a kind of game when I was little, and I would get excited and terrified all at the same time. I never felt unsafe or unsettled by the tickling that would result when I was captured; just elated.

But maybe Jocko was the one who was afraid? Maybe repression makes you wonder whether you even know all your demons. Maybe the harsher curfews he imposed on his oldest daughters were attempts to keep them safe from predators who sometimes looked and acted just like him. Maybe the cruelest part of being a man is not knowing, or not trusting, that you're better than your basest animal instincts.

Whatever the reason, the tickling stopped—along with anything that might be construed as intimacy—right around the time I started developing breast buds. I didn't notice at first, but when I did, I realized that my father had left me, even as he remained physically present. The sense of loss and confusion that followed has been with me ever since. Psychologists would undoubtedly tie it to my anorexia in college, my indiscriminate need to be adored, my trust issues with men in general.

And this was before I even knew they could propose to you naked.

CHAPTER 3

Mandarin Garden

My greatest day was an anomaly, which is undoubtedly why it remains such a vivid event. After that marathon July playdate with my mom in 1966, we went straight back to our once-a-year family visits to Paragon Park, and we never did add an "entertainments" envelope to the family budget.

But that didn't stop me from being raised at the movies.

From about 1967 until at least 1975, I spent as many Saturdays as I could—and virtually all my modest weekly allowance for doing random household chores—inside a large, generic movie theater that stood adjacent to the local shopping mall, where I would eventually land my first real waitressing job slinging patty melts and malted "frappes" for tips doled out in never enough coins to fill a sixteen-ounce takeout cup. Pulling doubles in those preteen days didn't mean back-to-back work shifts; it meant hoovering up cinematic double features that ranged from musicals and Disney comedies (*Chitty Chitty Bang Bang*, *Bedknobs and Broomsticks*, *The Computer Wore Tennis Shoes*) to the films of my nightmares (still), including *Planet of the Apes* and *Soylent Green*. I wasn't old enough to see most of the really good stuff of that incredibly fertile cinematic era in a theater, but I was aware that some of my friends' parents were holed up in adjacent screening rooms, taking in such future classics as *Rosemary's Baby, The Graduate, Midnight Cowboy, Easy Rider,* and *A Clockwork Orange* while they waited for their kids to be released into the sunlight. Curiously, I never really wanted to be in there, with the adults, having what they were having. I was happy consuming whatever was put in front of me—*(Herbie) The Love Bug; With Six You Get Eggroll; Yours, Mine and Ours; Oliver!*—unsuspecting that it was more insidious than anyone was letting on.

INT. CINEMA—DAY

Braintree, winter 1970. Rows of unchaperoned children sit mesmerized by a scene from *The Aristocats*, a feature-length Disney cartoon, in which animated felines jam out to a musical number called "Everybody Wants to Be a Cat." All the cats in the movie are clichés, but none more stereotypically so than Shun Gon—a buck-toothed, tan and brown Tonkinese who swings like a madman on drums and piano. The camera zooms in on Shun Gon pounding the keyboard with two pairs of chopsticks jammed between his paws, sing-saying a heavily accented non-sensical rhyme that goes: "Shanghai, Hong Kong, Egg Foo Yong; fortune cookie always wrong." The voice is familiar to anyone who has watched *The Banana Splits Adventure Hour* on TV, because Shun Gon is voiced by the same actor—Paul Winchell—who plays Fleegle the Beagle on that show, and who will later find a more iconic fame as the voice of *Winnie the Pooh*'s Tigger. Winchell's Shun Gon is a goofy, obnoxious caricature, as racially insensitive as anything of its time, including Mickey Rooney's infamous turn as Mr. Yunioshi in *Breakfast at Tiffany's*.

```
And this audience is as clueless as that found
in any bucolic, predominantly white New Eng-
land town. Cut to two wide-eyed nine-year-olds
seated near the front of the cinema, spellbound
and smitten.

                CHILD #1 (Janice's friend)
      We should go for Chink food after this.

                    CHILD #2 (Janice)
                    (enthusiastically)

      Sure.
```

It's a composite memory of something that happened, more than once, during and uncomfortably far beyond my childhood years—the kind of dialogue and scene that unfolded all the time and still clicks through my noggin like snippets of a film strip being put through a splicer. On that same quirkily edited reel would be my father's standard response whenever anyone would ask what he did in the navy, since he was never once shipped near a front line. "I kept the Japs out of Texas," he'd always say. And we'd laugh and laugh.

I heard no malice or harm in such slurs; they seemed of a piece with the chatter around our Thanksgiving table, where sarcasm and ridicule were as expected as the wiggle of a Jell-O mold. So of course I failed to question the pale, simplistic ideology presented by movies like *The Aristocats* and so many of my other early favorites, even when their candy-coated agitprop was occasionally interrupted by glimpses of something harder to digest, like the aforementioned *A Patch of Blue* or a snarling, combustible trailer for *In the Heat of the Night.* I can only wonder what I might have seen at an earlier age if my eyes had been encouraged, never mind trained, to value skepticism and scrutiny, to look beyond the frame. Would I have noticed, for example, how few heroic women existed outside the shadow of a man on-screen? Would I have balked at demeaning caricatures like *The Aristocats'* Shun Gon, or the dancing pygmies of the Congo Cruise ride, or every "Injun" in every Western I'd ever encountered? Would I have discerned on-screen nods to conflicts I was actually living through—as far away as Vietnam and as close as the streets of Boston—but rarely engaged with as anything more than compartmentalized headlines? And would the teenage me have then had the courage to correct my mother the time she tried to impose her own biases on whatever it was I was feeling for a boy in my class who was "different"?

"Are you going to the dance?" she'd asked me, hopefully.

"I'm not sure," I answered, not yet hope*less* but hardly confident with the big event just days away.

"Well, is there anyone you'd *want* to go with?" she pressed. And even though I didn't want to be having this conversation, I heard myself telling her "Steven," because she was clearly trying to relate to me, as a girlfriend if not as a mother, and shutting her out felt mean.

"We have a lot of fun together," I added.

She didn't respond.

"But he's . . ." I started to say.

"I know," she said then, in a way that reminded me of countless scripted mother-daughter bedside talks I'd seen on-screen, where the parents were uncommonly wise and the children almost always felt heard. I knew what her "I know" meant; it meant, "I know that's what you think you want." "I know it's a difficult thing to say." "I know it's never going to happen." "I know, because he's Colored."

She didn't know anything.

What I was going to say, before her misguided assumption intruded, was "But he's never going to ask me." Not because he couldn't see past my race, but because I was pretty sure he didn't even see me as a girl. We were nothing more than friends who hadn't once hung out apart from school, probably because he lived at least a thirty-minute bus ride away, in a part of Boston that I had no known reason to visit. Steven was part of a METCO program that promoted voluntary desegregation at my high school; he was the only Black boy in my class of more than seven hundred.

We almost never talked about what that must have been like for him. I'm sure I was too self-involved and conflict-averse to ask. He was smart and gregarious, with a warm smile and ready sense of humor that made you happy just to be in his company—and so I was, as often as possible between 7 A.M. and 2 P.M. on non-summer weekdays. I felt the sparks that undercut our conversations, but did he? I'd have bet whatever was left of my allowance on no.

I wish now that I'd said any of this to my mother. I didn't. I think I just shuffled the two or three steps from our kitchen into my bedroom and started in on my homework. Whatever she thought when I didn't go to the dance was left unspoken. *See something, say something*, they teach people living in the crosshairs of terrorism. But we almost never did in my house. Or anywhere in the place where I grew up.

I was raised to be non-confrontational. To keep my head down and my ambitions modest—a quintessentially New England thing. To value what is simple, controllable, easily contained.

But the messaging was mixed, and not just within that one day when I was five and my mother flipped the script on my dad. Like a lot of American kids birthed into the deep end of 1960s and '70s divisions, I saw and heard a great many things that challenged my worldview long before I'd experienced much, or any, of the actual world. What was so controversial about two Black men raising their fists from an Olympic podium, toward no one but God?, I wondered at age seven. Was I right to see antiwar messaging and what looked like the outline of Ho Chi Minh's long beard in Sister Corita Kent's rainbow-colored swashes of paint that came to adorn the iconic Boston gas tank in the early 1970s? And how was I to process Stanley Forman's Pulitzer Prize-winning 1976 photo of a white teenager assaulting a Black man with a flag during a busing demonstration on City

Hall Plaza? How did that square with what was (or wasn't) happening in my own high school less than thirteen miles away, where my friend Steven was undoubtedly being just as otherized, amid smiles?

It's probably not unusual for your earliest cultural touchstones to be viewed as reinforcing the stereotypes and myopia of your inherited ideology. But eventually, if you're lucky, the aperture opens wider and you start envisioning the components of what feels more like you, with a corresponding voice that isn't just singing along. I was lucky. I had an impressive range of pop culture obsessions in my youth. Some were handed down unintentionally by my much older siblings, who had vinyl record collections bursting with Motown and Brill Building earworms, sultry soul, lived-in blues, and incendiary anthems. Others were cultivated by endless hours spent with Top 40 radio, network television, mainstream movies, stacks of comic books and *Mad* magazines, and weekly trips to the library. While I'll admit that way too much of what I checked out on my first library card mirrored my own limited purview, primarily as captured by Beverly Cleary and Judy Blume, I was also drawn to a range of age-appropriate literary classics, which were as much a part of our daily diet as gallons of sugary Hawaiian Punch.

I think I was around eleven years old when I decided to read Pearl S. Buck's *The Good Earth*. Up until that time, my main reference points for Asian culture, aside from that darn cat Shun Gon, were Hop Sing—the lovably temperamental ranch cook on one of my favorite shows, *Bonanza*—and Bruce Lee's kick-ass turn as Kato in TV's *The Green Hornet*. Buck's epic 1931 novel was a revelation, even if I didn't pause to question its role in the spread of Orientalism. Her perspective as a white woman—earnest and informed if inevitably insufficient—wasn't something I thought about then, but I'm sure it made the book more relatable. It was Buck's voice that expanded and reshaped my notions of China and all things Chinese, the first of many times this would happen.

I was initially drawn to the book's dust jacket, with its earthen tones and hypnotic pattern of thick vertical lines denoting a freshly plowed field that stretched upward, into the horizon's low-hanging sun. That evening, a few chapters in, I was already on my way to being deeply moved by Buck's tale of the noble farmer, Wang Lung, and his long-suffering wife, O-lan, who slog like resilient oxen through the turbulent, feast-and-famine history of rural China in the late nineteenth and early twentieth centuries. When I later saw the 1937 movie version starring Paul Muni and Luise Rainer, I couldn't believe it. Not because white actors played all the lead roles—though there's that, and it's as tone deaf as anything cast by the studios in that era—but because the screenplay was so outrageously romanticized. In Buck's book, the only steadfast and truly worthy love is for the land. It is the simplest of equations: We reap exactly what we sow, and only as the elements allow. *The Good Earth* portrayed China as a country where intelligent creatures step gingerly and respectfully, so as not to unleash any malevolent supernatural forces. A man can be ambitious, but he must know his place. This is infinitely truer for a woman, naturally.

The seismic shift in power I'd observed during the denouement of my greatest day with my mother was now something I kept an eye out for, even in amusements. Part of my attraction to *The Good Earth* was that I wasn't just learning about Asia; I was learning about agency. And not just about agency for young women who looked like me, which is what I got from Blume and Cleary, but empowerment that sometimes didn't read like empowerment, in places that recalibrated my idea of oppression, and triumph.

One of those places was China—at first just in book and celluloid form, but eventually embodied in a few key people who would come into my life. I met them when I was most ready to appreciate their stories, which I think is no accident. As a savvy businessman among them would tell me, possibly hijacking the words of a philosopher I should know: *It's hard to become wealthy if you're always closed.*

❧

It was the summer of 1979. I'd just turned eighteen, the start of college was a little more than two months away, and I needed money. Fast.

My father, who'd been a shipyard worker for most of his life, was enjoying a brief second career making even less as a HUD inspector for the city of Quincy. My mom had never had more than a part-time job (retail, mostly) outside the home. They were middle-class Americans, I was the last of their six kids, and it was simply understood that whatever part of my Rutgers University tuition and expenses wasn't covered by scholarships and government loans was on me to come up with in real time. I already had waitressing jobs at two restaurants that summer. I was in search of a third.

The classified ad was no more than a couple of lines that read something like: "HELP WANTED. Experienced waitresses to work at exciting new restaurant on the South Shore." It gave an address and a phone number. I called.

"Hello?"

"Hi. I'm calling about your ad for waitresses?"

"Okay. You come Saturday. 10 o'clock."

Click.

The man had an accent that wasn't any of the dozens of standard iterations of suburban Bostonian that treated spellings as suggestions, like traffic lights. I had no idea where he might be from.

I had lived my whole life in Braintree, a town with distinguished colonial roots, dutifully preserved. There you could dip candles at the 1720 home of General Sylvanus Thayer, the father of West Point, and engage in debates about whether the Adams family that yielded two presidents was really from Quincy, as most people think, or Braintree, which stupidly relinquished the land containing their birthplaces in 1940. Our high school mascot was a Native American caricature known as a "Wamp" (short for "Wampanoag"), whose cartoon image—right up until 2020—inspired legions of unquestioning not-Native kids to slap on feathers and warpaint and canoe across nearby Sunset Lake for pep rallies.

The South Shore, which roughly stretches from just south of Boston to the Cape Cod Canal, was a mostly suburban and rural tract, with a mostly middle-class mix of folks defining it when I was growing up. Braintree was considered a step-up town for those of European immigrant stock coming by way of the hardscrabble Dorchester section of Boston. If you were *really* upgrading, you also had a modest cottage in Hull or Scituate or Plymouth or any of the beach communities along our Irish Riviera. On my street (not remotely beachfront), our family of eight was considered small; there were several families of ten or more, not counting live-in grandparents. We knocked on each other's doors to see which kids might be home (all of them, usually), and we played kickball and hockey in the road just about every day until the streetlights came on or the plows couldn't keep up with the snow.

I knew exactly one Jewish kid in all of grammar school. Everyone else was either Catholic, like me and my mother, or Protestant, like my dad. Everyone was white and liberal—not always politically, but reliably when it came to dropping letters that were actually in words and adding letters that weren't (e.g., "Is the waahdah wawm?" "Yahr it is."). Things were a bit more multicultural in high school, thanks to the METCO desegregation program that blessed us with Steven, but no credible analysis would have called my community diverse.

The restaurant owner waiting for me that Saturday in June 1979 was named Benny Wu. He was the first Asian man I ever had a real conversation with.

"Okay. So your name is Jan-ee-shee, right?"

"That's right," I told Benny Wu. (Close enough.)

"And you have waitress experience?"

"Yes. Two years, part time."

"But not in Chinese restaurant, correct?"

"Correct."

"Okay. Because my restaurant is Chinese restaurant."

"Right. I see that," I said, dropping my gaze to the pile of paper takeout menus he'd been folding into vertical thirds when I walked in.

"You know Szechuan food?"

"No. Sorry."

"Hunan? Mandarin?"

"No. Sorry."

"No problem," he said.

"I really don't know much about Chinese food at all," I admitted.

"But you know pu-pu platter, right? Chicken chow mein? Egg foo young?"

"Sure. All of those."

"I figured," he scoffed, affably.

I started at Mandarin Garden a few days later.

The place was a true mom-and-pop, only about seventy-five seats, and it sat close in on the corner of a very busy East Braintree street where parking was tricky and noise was constant. The new owners had poured all their savings into trying to spruce up the dining room, but it was still dingy and cramped. The narrow basement, where you had to go to fetch supplies and mix the duck sauce in a big plastic bucket (two gallons of applesauce, two gallons of plum sauce, a gallon of white vinegar, half a ladle of thick soy sauce, and a five-pound sack of sugar), was right out of a slasher film, dank and cavelike, its cement floor splotched with stains of indeterminate origin.

Benny Wu was a charming, enthusiastic entrepreneur. My best guess placed him in his early thirties. He was steady and lean and wore his black hair parted to one side, like Bobby Sherman in the teen idol poster that used to hang in my bedroom. Only Caucasians were brought on to be waitresses at Mandarin Garden. Benny strategized that suburban Bostonians might be less intimidated by his "new" cuisine if it was served by white people, even ones who didn't know what they were doing.

We began our training by sampling dishes. I'd never tasted things like yu hsiang scallops with blistered chili peppers, or crispy batter-coated shrimp bathed in a strange neon tomato sauce that someone should have thought to market as a shade of lip gloss, because who wouldn't want to wear Crispy Shrimp Lip Gloss? I learned how to carve wispy brushes out of scallions and steam thin flour crepes to serve with the roast Peking duck.

Benny Wu was right: This was definitely not pu-pu platter territory. It probably also was not authentic Chinese territory, but it was plenty exotic for a young woman whose idea of fine dining was HoJo's clam strips.

There were four chefs, none of whom spoke much English and all of whom had a quick temper. We were supposed to order by menu item number, which sounds easy enough except when a customer wants to make a "little adjustment." A simple soup substitution or an additional spring roll at lunch is one thing; a skilled waitress can employ ingenuity and surmount basic language barriers when necessary. But imagine trying to communicate, by some combination of gestures and Pictionary, that a diner wants their chicken dish made with breast meat instead of thigh; their roast pork lo mein light on soy sauce, with extra noodles and no scallions; and their "family-style" tofu with the semi-firm soybean curd cut into precise one-by-three-inch rectangles instead of randomly sized triangles. Benny Wu was not prepared for such inevitabilities, nor did he prepare his waitresses to confront them. Mercifully, though, we wouldn't know that for a while.

That's because the first day I went to work at Mandarin Garden, we had two customers. They came in just to pick up takeout menus. The next day, we had four people actually sit down, but they left when they found out they couldn't order the lunch buffet at dinner. In the entire first month of business, I think maybe a few dozen people actually ate there.

Every time someone walked through the front door, Benny's business partner, Mike Chin, would jump up and greet the party as though he were being paid by the word. It wasn't enough to welcome them warmly and usher them to their seats. Mike had to unleash every English greeting he'd ever heard, in one long, run-on sentence of hospitality and commerce and nerves.

"Hi hello good evening how are you nice seeing you what's new how's it going you lose weight looking good come in sit down enjoy—something to drink?"

It was breathless, and breathtaking. I was told that Mike had been running his own wok-and-fry restaurants for decades, the kind of places where white bread and french fries are on every table alongside the spareribs and chicken fingers and piles and piles of Wet-Naps. Now, having bought into Benny's culinary reinvention, Mike was sort of like a guy coming out of retirement to be a Walmart greeter. No matter who came through that door, he was going to pour it on like a Chinese Butterfly McQueen.

Among our few loyal customers in those early days was a lovely middle-aged couple who came in at least once a week. I don't know their real names. I do know that we, the immature waitstaff, referred to them out of earshot as Billie Jean and Martina, after the tennis legends Billie Jean King and Martina Navratilova, neither of whom had yet spoken in public about their sexual orientation. I have no defense for this nicknaming; I'd gotten better about spotting casual racism but not, apparently, casual homophobia.

Our Billie Jean and Martina liked their food spicy. Every time they came in, they ordered the hottest dishes on the menu, and then they asked for "extra spicy" on top of that. We waitresses always obliged, of course.

This one night, I took their order and walked it to the kitchen. *"Tài là!"* (太辣) I said as I put in the ticket. *Very spicy!*

The head chef nodded (I was learning; props for me), and the sous chef began assembling ingredients on a plate. Wok cooking is performance art. It's not the kind of cooking I grew up with, where you push a whole chicken into the oven or let the pasta sauce hang out on simmer all day while you do laundry. First, there's an impressive hissing as 100,000 Btu worth of flame rise up to meet the wok, which is followed by the sizzle and crackle of peanut oil (or, nowadays, some allergy-friendly substitute with a similarly high smoke point). Veggies and proteins tumble around in the concave pan while sparks fly off the edges of the collar that helps contain the fire. Sauces and seasonings are added inexactly and with great flourish. I felt like I should applaud every time.

Within a few minutes of ordering, Billie Jean and Martina had their entrées. But when I went to their table to check in, they weren't pleased.

"Not really hot enough," they said. "Could you ask the kitchen to add more spice?"

"Of course," I obliged, and back I went with the two dishes that were already flecked with red and smelling of chili peppers.

"Tài là!" I said again when I got to the kitchen, this time adding demurely, *"Qǐng"* (请, *please*).

The head chef looked at the plates, then over at me, then back at the plates. He grumbled loudly in Mandarin. Then he recooked each dish with a modest extra portion of hot sauce. I got out of there as fast as I could.

Back at the table, Billie Jean and Martina each took a bite.

"Better now?" I asked, praying.

"Better," Billie Jean said. "But . . ."

Shit. Please don't say but. *No* but*s. Just eat.*

"But I still can't really *taste* the spice," she concluded. "Could they maybe add just a touch more pepper?"

I should have just told them no. I should have offered to bring them a side dish of chili oil or a whole fleet of ghost pepper enemas if that's what they wanted. But I never should have done what I did: pick up their dishes and walk them back to the kitchen to be remade a second time.

"Umm. *More tài là*?" I said to the chef once again. *"Duì bù qǐ"* (对不起, *sorry*), I added.

He happened to be holding a cleaver, which he'd once or twice thrown in the general direction of his fellow chefs when irritated. No joke. He slammed the knife handle hard on the stainless-steel counter. I would have stepped back, but the narrow kitchen offered no room to retreat.

Unleashing a torrent of Mandarin curse words, some familiar and others I could only guess at, the chef threw the contents of each dish into a separate wok. He then grabbed his ladle and tossed in a full scoop of chili paste—each. The cloud of smoke that resulted was so acrid, I closed my eyes and coughed into my Izod shirt collar.

He emptied each wok onto a fresh plate. Now the dishes weren't just flecked with seared chili; they were swimming in it.

Billie Jean and Martina looked delighted to receive their new entrées. I scurried off before they picked up their chopsticks, afraid of being called to the witness stand later. When I went back to check on them, both were flushed and perspiring, and neither was eating.

"Everything okay?" I said cheerily.

Silence.

"Can I get you anything? Would you like me to pack this up to take home?" I offered.

More silence. Then, at a volume just above a whisper . . .

"No," Martina said, her voice now labored, as though she'd been placed on a ventilator. "We're definitely not okay."

"I know we said hot, but . . ." Billie Jean's rasp trailed off as she shook her head.

"I'm so sorry," I said. "Let me grab more water."

I brought a pitcher. And a bowl of white rice. Then I fetched a carton of milk and a pint of vanilla ice cream that was hanging out in the back of the walk-in freezer, left over from somebody's birthday celebration. More rice. Finally, I brought toothpicks and a dish of canned pineapple, which may or may not be the best thing for cooling scorched taste buds but at least it suggests the possibility of a festive ending.

"Is there anything else I can get for you?" I asked, knowing how perfunctory that sounded. It's like saying to the grieving, "How can I help?" Good intentions notwithstanding, you're mostly just shifting the burden instead of acknowledging there is no remedy.

"Just the check," Martina replied softly. "And maybe an ambulance."

It was a joke, but it came with a scowl, which told me that the danger had passed but not the anger.

What would Benny Wu do, I wondered? I could only try to channel the answer, because it was his one night off.

"There is no check," I suddenly found myself saying out loud, feigning the authority that would allow me to make such a decree. "Your meal is on the house. And again, I'm so sorry this happened. Please come back and let us make it up to you."

I didn't care whether I would get in trouble or end up paying for the comped dinner myself. This wasn't a moment to hide behind my apron and shelter passively in place. My mother had inadvertently preached the value of autonomy exercised on impulse, and I'd gladly imbibed that sermon. Besides, you know in your gut when you have the power, and therefore the duty, to influence an outcome for the better. Seizing those moments can be the antidote to accepting what can't be altered—so much more of which awaited me, just ahead.

For the record, Martina and Billie Jean did come back to the restaurant, regularly and for many years, but they never again sent a dish back twice. (Neither did I.) We had all learned this valuable piece of fortune cookie wisdom: *The voice that gives orders is never as mighty as the hand that carries them out.*

Put another way, know this one thing about Chinese restaurants, above all else: *If you can't stand the heat, don't piss off the kitchen.*

CHAPTER 4

The Tao of Three Wishes

Within a few weeks of Mandarin Garden's opening in 1979, most of the original waitresses had quit, unable to relate to the quirky owners and temperamental kitchen help and tired of being laughed at, or screamed at, in multiple Chinese dialects while also collecting few tips. By summer's end, I would be the only Caucasian employee still standing, the only reminder of Benny Wu's bold multicultural experiment.

But I wasn't sticking around just to prove a point. I recognized that this tiny, unassuming restaurant was rapidly expanding my world, preparing me for the inevitability of leaving home and all the comfort zones I'd constructed there.

To communicate with the kitchen, I did my best to absorb the complex tones of some basic Mandarin phrases—food terms and instructions, mostly, so that I could order soup (*tāng*, 汤), though it always came out sounding like the word for sugar (*táng*, 糖) or scalding hot (*tàng*, 烫). Every time I ordered dumplings (*shuǐ jiǎo*, 水饺), the cooks would crack up—laughing so hard that the long ash of their cigarettes nearly fell into their woks, which did happen on occasion—because the way I said it sounded like sleep (*shuì jiào*, 睡觉).

I learned how to write simplified Chinese characters to scratch out a shorthand version of moo shu chicken (木九, still useful, though I think I may have partly confused it with the character for "nine"). I learned that ketchup is the secret ingredient in a plethora of Chinese restaurant dishes served in America. I also learned to be resourceful and not take myself too seriously. I discovered that if you do what you can, with sincerity and a sense of humor, people will usually meet you at least halfway, and almost always when you are in their world and showing them the respect they deserve.

In the afternoons, when there were long stretches with no customers, I played Battleship with Benny Wu ("You sank my aircraps carrier!!!" he would whine, deliberately conjuring his most cartoonish syntax) while we engaged in spirited and revealing discussions about history, politics, and culture. He told me how his family had fled to Taiwan during China's civil war. I'd never heard of such a thing; it sounded scary, but also fabulously cinematic.

In the evenings, he would work the dining room, checking in on every table to be sure their meal and experience had been worthy of a return visit. And at the end of each night, he would clean the two closet-sized restrooms himself.

This floored me.

When I asked why he didn't just delegate latrine duty to one of us lowly staffers, he told me flatly, "Because it's my job." He viewed this as the right thing—the *Chinese* thing—to do. What's more, he understood the strong message it sent to his employees: *I'm no better than you. We succeed, or fail, from the bottom up. Cleaning the toilets properly is as important as great service and fabulous food.*

Some variation of this should be the motto and standard practice of every manager at every company in the world.

About halfway through that first summer season, as our friendship deepened and my understanding of the Mandarin Garden business—or lack of business—sharpened, I told Benny Wu that he could defer payment of my salary until I left to start college. This wasn't nearly as generous as it sounds. First, it was a relatively small sum—minimum wage for waitresses in those days was less than $3 an hour—and second, it all had to be saved for school anyway, so it really wasn't important for me to have the money before late August. I don't think you could even call it a sacrifice; it was akin to giving up eggnog for Lent.

Still, the gesture spoke volumes to my boss. He accepted my offer, with a warm smile that didn't even attempt to conceal his paternalistic pride. And that affection really came in handy when I backed his brand-new passenger van into a telephone pole one afternoon while attempting to make a Dunkin' Donuts run.

"You did what?" he asked.

"Hit the stupid telephone pole," I said again, mortified. "I'm so sorry, Benny. I'll pay for it."

"And they say Chinese can't drive," he snickered.

"Very funny. Seriously, I'll pay for it," I reoffered. "Ugh. I'm so mad at myself."

"Nah. It happens," he said. "Don't getta piss off."

I laughed.

"Okay. I'm not pissed off," I said. "But I do feel like an idiot."

He shook his head.

"Idiot? I don't think so. Just young," he said. "Later, if you *still* do stupid shit, then okay, maybe 'idiot.' Right now, come show me what kinda damage you can do at eighteen."

Outside, as cars whizzed past without so much as tapping their brakes to consider his restaurant, Benny Wu surveyed the scraped paint and plastic reflector bits splayed on the pavement. He bent down to examine the undercarriage, kicked the tires perfunctorily, and shrugged at the large dent above the rear bumper.

"Still can drive," he said.

Then he flipped me the keys and sent me on my way again, to fulfill my sacred mission of getting the Dunkin'. No hesitation. No trust issues, even with a visibly rattled eighteen-year-old. He insisted I get back in the saddle immediately. ("Go back. Get a horse," I think he said, but I knew what he meant.)

A week or so later, I noticed that the van had been completely repaired, though he never took any money from me for it. If that had been my dad's car, I'd have been on the hook for every last nickel, including insurance surcharges, less for financial reasons than as a matter of principle. In my house, parenting was focused on accountability, not forgiveness. Benny's more nuanced approach allowed for both, which was probably un-American.

Just before Labor Day, I handed in my Mandarin Garden apron and headed off to my freshman year of college in New Brunswick, New Jersey, with all my wages recouped. When I returned home at winter break, there were lines out the door; the restaurant had received a glowing review from Anthony Spinazzola in *The Boston Globe*, and it was impossible to get a table on a weekend night.

I came back to work at Mandarin Garden every summer and winter break throughout my college years. Suddenly, it was a lucrative place to be employed. More important, it felt like a refuge, which became increasingly necessary as time went on.

I once read an article in *The Atlantic* about a study done by the folks at Hewlett-Packard. They were trying to diversify their management ranks, and they wanted to know why more women weren't applying for the top jobs. Sifting through the company's personnel records, they discovered that women said they felt comfortable applying for promotions only when they "believed they met 100 percent of the qualifications listed for the job." HP men, on the other hand, felt confident enough to apply when they "thought they could meet 60 percent of the job requirements."

Is it hard to understand, when you read doctrine like this, why so many women twist themselves into circus-grade balloon animals trying to justify their existence in the workplace? Impostor syndrome may bedevil men and women in equal numbers (so the experts say; anecdotally, I find that hard to believe), but there's no refuting the so-called confidence gap—our vastly superior feminine talent for demanding perfection as a prerequisite to advancement, on and off the job.

I blame the 1970s for this.

Even if you accept the possibility that women were perfectionists and control freaks long before Post-it Notes were invented, the seventies was also when the "girls can have it all" myth really took root. I was eleven when Title IX was passed in 1972. I remember it the way my parents remembered V-J Day—as a triumph of justice and liberation and sailors kissing nurses on the street, though I could be wrong about that last part. Title IX was most immediately felt in athletic arenas, but every female of my generation took it as a sign that widespread equality of opportunity was close at hand.

We were the privileged class of feminists poised to take the torch from the likes of Betty Friedan and Gloria Steinem. We would be the ones to have it all: good educations, satisfying careers, sexual freedom, and, yes, marriage and motherhood, too. And we would make no qualitative compromises to get it. That was the money clause: *no qualitative compromises.* In other words, be all that you can be, ladies; just find a way to be perfect at all of it.

Do you know what happened in 1980? In 1980, "body image disturbance" became an official diagnosis in the American Psychiatric Association's manual of mental disorders. That's the umbrella heading for eating disorders such as anorexia nervosa, an affliction that goes back several centuries, though most people had never heard of the term before the 1970s. Suddenly, just as I entered my teens, anorexia was a thing—and I was its exact target demographic.

We can blame the rise of eating disorders (see also: bulimia and binging) on an explosion of fitness and beauty products designed to create an ideal you, presumably because the factory-issued you wasn't you at your best. We can blame "the media." We can fault fad diets and a rising divorce rate and probably a hundred other sociopolitical factors. But really, how coincidental do we think it is that any psychological disorder rooted in control and perfectionism bloomed during a campaign to sell young women on boundless success through self-determination?

So, yeah, I was anorexic. I dropped fifteen pounds during my freshman year of college; the square, white metal scale in my dorm room registered eighty-seven when I stepped on it naked in the morning, which felt like winning the Willpower Olympics, if you want to know the truth. I would eat one meal a day, which was almost always a humongous green salad and some form of unadorned bread. It was the Fat-Free Everything Era, when sugar and gluten had an unrestricted hall pass, but God forbid we ingested a drop of butter or oil. I was also up at dawn, running eight to twelve miles most mornings. My toenails fell off and my periods stopped. Then, something *really bad* happened: Karen Carpenter died.

It was the winter of 1983; a Friday when I was home from college. Most New Englanders heard about it on the evening news, just as they were sitting down to dinner.

I identified with Karen Carpenter. She sang contralto; I sang contralto (kind of). We both had dense, pelt-like brunette hair and nonexistent cleavage. My Gunne Sax high school prom dress intentionally looked like something she had worn on one of her schmaltzy Christmas specials with her brother, Richard, where they would sing and clown around with other peppy white people and puppets, like Kukla and Ollie. But I had no idea that Karen Carpenter was terminally anorexic until she died, and I saw her emaciated, unsettlingly cheery photograph on the cover of *People* magazine. This was body image disturbance? This was madness. This was obsession and deprivation forged into chain mail, and this was what women did to themselves in the pursuit of perfection.

"There is no way I look like that," I told my reflection in the mirror. It wasn't a magic mirror, so it couldn't summon feedback from Oz-like mystics or evil queens. It was just a regular old medicine cabinet in my parents' no-frills bathroom, where you had to stand on the lip of the tub to get a view of your midsection in the cabinet's sliding glass doors.

No anorexic sees themself the way that others do. Where you see lean, we see fat. Where you see gaunt, we see strong and chic. But I did, in that moment, glimpse a few bony corollaries that made me shudder at the fate of poor Karen Carpenter, whose heart had reportedly failed while she was actually in recovery, struggling with weight *gain*. Imagine. She died in the act of surrendering herself to getting well.

"You just can't win," I whined to the mirror. Even as I said it, though, I knew that I would nonetheless keep trying. I would keep deluding myself that winning was fully within my control. And I would do this with irrational conviction until someone, or something, set me straight.

Patty and I had shared more than a bed growing up. As my sister closest in age (there were twelve years between us), she was the one I studied for guidance on fashion and boys. She was cheerful and easygoing and delightfully wacky. She was also the one who made me try smoking, at age four, so her friends could have a hearty laugh. I got a chocolate bar out of it, and the good sense to swear off tobacco for life.

When I was an adolescent and Patty was beginning her career as a hairdresser, I would hang out with her at the salon some days after school and on weekends, cleaning combs and restocking products. My favorite unpaid job was sweeping the hair that collected on the floor.

People don't think much about their hair clippings, but as I would pilot the wide push broom and watch those clippings mound into a shag carpet the size of a small dog, I'd sometimes wonder why this was any less creepy than a pile of toenails, or teeth, or limbs. Then I'd imagine what might happen if a supernatural wind swirled in through the back door and spun this entire collection of discarded DNA into a composite new life. Would it be a monster, made up of split ends and all the ugliest qualities we pretend not to see when we look in the mirror? Or would it be a superior, protein-fortified, pH-balanced version of ourselves, one who would never age or get sick or let anyone down?

By the middle of my freshman year at Rutgers, Patty had begun papering my post office mailbox with literature about the perils of anorexia. I was incensed. How *dare* she. I tossed it without reading, of course; it didn't apply to me. Anorexics are very good at lying to themselves.

While I knew next to nothing about eating disorders, I knew everything about self-discipline. I was taking five or six courses a semester plus working part time in the office of the School of Communications. I did two hundred sit-ups a day and ran at least forty miles most weeks. I had the flat-chested, no-hips build of a ten-year-old boy. Was that to mimic the models I saw in magazines or to keep the college men at bay? Perhaps it was to try to win back the father of my childhood. Maybe all of the above.

I'm a control freak. I grew up with a mother who had no control over her own sanity, so I learned to take charge of whatever was there for the taking. Saying no to food is a power trip, however warped; the skinnier I got, the more the mirror showed me a winner. Then, in 1982, cancer took up permanent residence in my family and my perspective on winning, among other things, changed considerably.

&

My sister Carol, the determined second-oldest of our brood, had left home at twenty to marry a man I adored. His name was Jan Ostrum. He looked like the singer Glen Campbell, but more of a Beach Boys / Docksiders version. He was blond and beefy and hilariously goofy.

Jan was a junior high school teacher and coach, which meant that he understood how to connect with kids, but he didn't make it seem like part of his job. In a persistent memory so vivid that it could be a dream, I'm standing on our living room coffee table—probably I'm four or five years old. My parents are having a party, and I've decided that I'm the entertainment. So, I climb up on the coffee table that is made out of maple and has an oval top covered in waxy white rings because we don't own a single drink coaster. I'm in a red and black plaid party dress, black tights, and shiny patent leather Mary Janes. I'm very sure that I look adorable, undeniably so when I begin belting out *"I'm 'Enry the Eighth, I am. 'Enry the Eighth, I am, I am"* in my best imitation of a British accent, à la Peter Noone from Herman's Hermits. My mother looks delighted. My father looks proud. Jan looks concerned.

As I hit the chorus, I launch into a rough approximation of a Shirley Temple tap dance, and it's then that my Mary Janes begin to slip. I can feel my legs going out from under me, up into the air, and off the edge of the table. I know I'm just seconds from crashing to the floor, which luckily is covered by a giant oval braided-wool rug, but not one expensive or substantial enough to soften the blow to my pride. I brace for impact. Only, before I can get there, I feel a large pair of hands gathering me up and into a sturdy chest. It's Jan, who has caught me in midair and is now laughing, in deep appreciation of what will go down as a perfectly executed pratfall.

The room applauds. We're a hit. Jan Ostrum to the rescue, not for the last time.

He drove a silver Corvette convertible, with a red leather back seat just big enough for me. Once, I remember crying over a balloon I'd lost hold of as we zipped down the expressway; Jan went and fetched it, dodging oncoming cars just to stop my wailing. That may or may not have been the same day that he and Carol took me to the Bay State's final Beatles appearance, at Suffolk Downs. I was five (the same summer as my greatest day), and yes, that means my first live concert was the Beatles, which is a mic-drop party game winner and almost makes up for my adolescent crush on Bobby Sherman.

I considered Jan Ostrum my surrogate father, all but legally once my real father started keeping his distance. Jan taught me how to tie my shoes; then he taught me to run like a track star in them—not for the medals (there were none), but for the joy of it.

In the fall and early winter of 1981, my junior year of college, I enrolled in a study-abroad program in England. Carol and Jan flew over to visit me while I attended the London School of Economics and interned as an assistant to a member of the House of Commons—the honorable Sir Neville Guthrie Trotter of Newcastle upon Tyne. This was just after I'd had a gas stove blow up in my face while attempting to cook moo shu chicken (木九) for my flatmates in London's Maida Vale district. I lit a match to spark the pilot light, and a ball of fire blew open the oven door. I saw flames, felt a rush of hot air on my cheeks, and heard the metal door slam shut before everything went quiet. When I reached up to feel my face, my eyelashes were gone and a crumble of singed eyebrows and bangs broke off in my hand. I was lucky that the injuries ended there, and luckier still that it was the height of the punk era, so a quick trip to Carnaby Street turned my charred locks into a trendy fashion statement. My new, close-cropped hair went over well with everyone except the tall, imposing, buttoned-up Tory MP Neville Trotter, who remarked when he saw me the next day in the House of Commons canteen, "I take it there has been an outbreak of lice in your flat?"

Carol and Jan loved my chic new hair. And their visit gave me an excuse to play tour guide for a few days.

Working at Mandarin Garden had opened my eyes to the wider world; living in Europe bathed those visions in Technicolor. Every corner I turned held something new and, therefore, exciting. I wanted to show my big sister the dozen or so pubs just in my little neighborhood; the Regency-style houses and wooden-boat-lined canals of nearby Little Venice, where I strolled and ran with an enormous grin on my face because the whole thing was just so darling; the halls of Parliament, where I sprinted to keep up with Neville's wide, impatient stride; even the local bank, where the reedy man with glasses cheerfully took my traveler's checks and wrote me deposit slips, *in pencil*.

I suppose I wanted Carol and Jan to see me as the person I was becoming: a woman capable of making her way, not just in New England but in actual England. A woman who worked and drank and exercised and banked. A woman who would return to the States with everything she needed to make a life that included, at last, hanging with her siblings. No longer the baby. An adult.

We covered a lot of ground during that London visit, including all the usual tourist landmarks. We also drove in a rented car out to Canterbury and Kent, where we bought chunky hand-knitted wool sweaters from a lady who invited us off the street into her living room "shop." Then we hopped a train to Scotland, where my father still had relatives eager to show us a good time in Dundee and Edinburgh. It was a blissful ten days with two of my favorite people, but Carol and Jan were harboring a secret that now colors my memory of Europe the way a single grain of sand recalibrates everything you think about the chowder.

❧

It was October 1981 when Patty felt the lump in her chest. Truthfully, though, that wasn't the first time. About a year earlier, while showering, she'd felt something small and hard that slid around under her skin when she pushed at it, like a pebble caught in the fibers of her sock. She thought about consulting a doctor, but it was too easy to talk herself out of concern. She felt fine. It was probably nothing. So, telling no one, *she waited*. That was her first mistake.

When the lump came back the following fall—or rather, when she noticed it again in a way that could no longer be denied—she dutifully scheduled a doctor's visit, though still not infused with appropriate urgency. Many days later, she arrived at the clinic to find patients stacked up for appointments running more than an hour late. It shouldn't have mattered, of course. Patty should have stayed put and waited however long it took to be seen. But she had something or other to do with her two young daughters that couldn't be covered by her husband, so she left and rescheduled when they had another opening, more than a month later.

That's the kind of thing you wonder about for the rest of your life. What if Patty had called in mommy backup and kept the original appointment? Better yet, what if she'd made that appointment twelve months earlier? And what if, upon diagnosis, she'd opted for mastectomy instead of lumpectomy? What if I wasn't in London, having the carefree time of my life traipsing after some speed-walking, XXL-sized Tory backbencher instead of being home and on top of the situation? What if the what-ifs didn't hurt almost as much as the what-the-fucks?

I learned about Patty's illness the night I returned to Massachusetts in February 1982, after nearly a month of backpacking across Europe post-internship. The diagnosis was stage 3 breast cancer.

Some people like to say that God never gives you more than you can handle. I'm not one of those people, because it's an illogical concept when you consider suicides and psychotic breaks and because in 1982 someone absolutely gave my family more than it could handle; we just weren't in a position to file a formal complaint.

Eight months after Patty was diagnosed with breast cancer at thirty-two, Jan, who had been cancer-free for four years after a melanoma was removed from his neck, was told that the disease had spread through his blood into dozens of subcutaneous nodules. He was forty years old.

I don't know how to describe the double-barreled whammy of that kind of news. Maybe it's something like the one time I went body surfing at the infamous Wedge in Newport Beach, California, where wave after wave pulled me under and tossed me around like a cheap bra in the throes of a front-loading washing machine. There was no catching my breath, no taming the swells, no one around who could wade in deep enough to save me; all I could do was surrender to the current, swim parallel to the shore, and try not to drown.

In the two years that followed Patty and Jan's grim diagnoses, armies of friends and relatives mobilized on our behalf. After surgery, the first level of treatment for Patty was chemotherapy and radiation. Jan was accepted into a clinical trial of the potential wonder drug interferon, which required him and Carol to drive three hours each way to Yale University Medical Center five days a week for an entire month in 1982. Sometimes they'd come down on Sunday and stay over in a hotel, to avoid the Monday morning traffic on I-95. Since I was now in my final semester at Rutgers, I traveled up from New Jersey to meet them. We ate New Haven pizza and bet on jai alai games as though an insatiable appetite for perfectly charred crusts and men with baskets on their throwing arms was what had brought us to this place.

Patty did okay for a while. Or at least well enough that when *Terms of Endearment* came out in December 1983, I didn't shy away from seeing it. How could I stand to watch a big-screen tearjerker about a young woman with breast cancer, my friends wondered? Easy. Because in a Hollywood script, the patient's crazy mother (Shirley MacLaine) is only outwardly unhinged. When the going gets tough and her daughter (Debra Winger) needs an advocate to procure sufficient pain meds, MacLaine's character has the inner strength to wield her crazy as a weapon. "GIVE MY DAUGHTER THE *SHOT*!" she screams at every nurse on duty. And she gets the result she demands.

In real life, the breast cancer patient's unstable mother, having recently flushed all her lithium pills down the toilet (again), has a dream about her new bifocal glasses. She imagines they're evil. They're making her sick. In the middle of the night, while her perpetually exhausted husband sleeps soundly, she gets up from their queen-sized mahogany bed and smashes the spectacles to bits. Her family wonders if they have enough fingers to tally the many metaphors loaded into that conveniently telling scene.

This is the difference between scripted movies and actual drama.

There were no Hollywood screenwriters present when spring came in 1984 and Patty lay in a hospital bed, her condition deteriorating rapidly. Her fragile mother, Yolanda, was not by her side keeping the medical staff in check; instead, she was being admitted to a psych ward in a different Boston area hospital, bound for yet another electrically enhanced reboot. Yolanda was also not there when the priest administered last rites, or when Patty survived that episode ("What?" she deadpanned as she rose like Lazarus) and became thoroughly pissed off at us for counting her out prematurely, or when it happened again a few days later and this time she didn't survive.

I don't blame my mother for any of that. Nor do I blame my dad, who instinctively threw up his walls when my mom again scurried down the rabbit hole. Not that we didn't have words about it.

One time, when he felt that some of his girls were being disrespectful for questioning their mother's sustained inability to hold it together amid crisis (we may have called it a "knack for checking out"), he told us we would regret our uncharitable words. "You'll think about this when we're gone," he said, not in the ominous, booming baritone of Vincent Price, but that's how I heard him. I thought he was being a big baby, and no way would I ever regret making him confront the harsh truth, which was that the line between empathy and indulgence is very often overprotective husbands.

I was wrong. I do think about that conversation, even now, some forty years later.

What would have been the harm in letting both my parents skate in this situation, just having their backs as they retreated to whatever felt like a safe place? Isn't that the nature of the parent-child relationship anyway, if all parties survive long enough to reverse their caretaking roles? In the end, my folks did the best they could, and watching your child die should never be on the list of things you're required to cope with. It should never even happen. It's more than any God should ask any human being to "handle."

So, if the rest of this story sounds too over-the-top even for a Hollywood script, that's the best way to know that I couldn't and wouldn't make it up.

In the same hospital ward where Patty lay dying, Jan was clinging to life. My family toggled back and forth between their two rooms, located just down the hall from one another. We didn't have to hear the nurses' conversations to know what they must be saying.

"My God. That poor family. How are they coping? How are they not falling apart?"

Suddenly we were *that* family. The Cancer Family. The one that people pity, which is an understandable but also life-sucking form of compassion that no proud human covets. And so, eventually, you begin telling only a tiny fraction of your troubles, until your history sits under an inch or more of varnish, because to expose it all would just bring everybody down.

But here's what else happened in 1984, just to get it all out there.

Three months after we buried Patty, my thirty-one-year-old brother Jacky, our parents' exalted eldest son, was in a freak car accident—an improperly secured boat trailer disengaged from an oncoming vehicle and slammed through his windshield, the bow of the boat hitting him square in the forehead. He had multiple surgeries and was in a coma for weeks. When he finally regained consciousness, he'd lost significant brain function, including speech and memory. He remembered Patty, but he didn't remember she'd died. He also had no idea that Jan, who'd briefly rebounded enough to spend the summer months at home, was declining again and about to enter the hospital for the last time.

I was in the room when my brother-in-law died. Carol had just taken her two young teenagers to the hospital cafeteria for a quick snack. They'd only made it a few steps down the hall when I looked at Jan—a hairless, gaunt whisper of his former Tank McNamara self—and noticed that his chest had stopped heaving. I waited to see if the laboring would resume, but there was no sound or movement; the familiar death rattle was gone.

I leaned forward in my chair and reached for his hand, which returned nothing. There's no good excuse for why I hesitated at that point. I knew he was gone, and I knew I should be alerting other people to that fact—not for resuscitation purposes (we were way past that) but because these moments weren't mine to own.

It's odd what you feel guilty about in the end. After Patty died, I would cry every time I thought about the afternoon she invited me to go see *The Way We Were* and my horny twelve-year-old self was so excited by the prospect of Robert Redford in track shorts that I moped like a spoiled preschooler when we didn't get into the sold-out screening. Seeing my disappointment, she offered to take me to lunch, but I told her I just wanted to go home, which is what we did—in silence. Such a minor self-indulgence, and yet the memory of it makes me inconsolably ashamed.

Months before Jan entered the hospital for the last time, he had taken me aside, out on the back deck of his house, to tell me that he was prepared to die. Not that he *wanted* to die, but that he was ready if it was his destiny. "Everything's taken care of," he said. "The house, the insurance policy . . . Carol won't have to worry. I just wanted you to know."

I don't know why it was important to him that I know this, or why he elected to gloss over the many accounts that my sister would indeed have to worry about reconciling, along with finding a way to put their children through college. I only know that the moment affirmed what I already felt: that he was asking me to be sturdy and at peace with whatever was about to happen—this death scene, for example.

Whether or not that gave me license, I took my time—probably no more than a few seconds—to process his last breath and hold it for myself. Then I ran, like the track star he coached me to be, to catch my sister before she took the elevator down.

There are so many ways that loss can change your life. It can make you bitter and unfathomably sad, but it can just as easily make you determined and philosophical.

"Don't getta piss off," I hear Benny Wu advise me, perhaps as he's pushing a heaping plate of something stir-fried in my direction, encouraging me to eat my feelings if that's what it takes to fatten me up. Or maybe it's Jan Ostrum I hear, telling me in his junior high school teacher/coach voice, "Don't sweat the small stuff."

Which leads me to the Tao of Three Wishes.

Imagine that a genie suddenly appears and offers you three opportunities to alter an event that has already happened. You can't wish for wealth or fame or success, but everything else is fair game. You have the chance to change the outcome of any three things, on a global or personal scale. Now ask yourself, how many of the things we complain about daily would be worth spending a wish on? Would anything in your current life rise to meet this bar?

When I examine most things through that prism, they don't even make my Top 1,000, let alone my Top 3. I would probably save all my wishes for things that could benefit the planet, but if we're taking it down to a more personal level, the things I would change aren't in the arena of workplace dysfunction or poor customer service or the mounting annoyances of aging. They're the day my sister found a lump and didn't act immediately. The day my brother-in-law first decided to sunbathe using a melanoma-friendly marinade of baby oil and iodine. The day my mother took up smoking to calm her nerves. All seeds of the worst days of my life.

My Tao of Three Wishes is a mental game I use to remind myself that the one true upside of loss is perspective. The deeper the loss, the more perspective you stand to gain. Or, as the Chinese like to say: *Bú jiàn fēngyǔ, zěn jiàn cǎihóng* (不见风雨，怎见彩虹). Loosely translated, that's "No rain, no rainbow." Or, if you're Christian, "No cross, no crown."

CHAPTER 5

Braintree

If you want to learn some world-class curse words, work in a Chinese restaurant.

When I first started waitressing at Mandarin Garden in 1979, I didn't know enough of the language to understand just how many obscenities were being batted about the kitchen. In some cases, such as the Chili Pepper Incident, I just assumed the chef's demeanor and tone meant he was using profanity to vent. But the longer I worked there, the more I noticed the same phrases popping up regularly, and the bolder I became about asking what they meant.

Let's start with the fact that everything sounds like a curse word in Mandarin. If your native language is English, even if you're half Italian and you grew up in a house with six noisy children, all Chinese conversation sounds like yelling. I had *"diàn huà!"* barked at me dozens of times before I realized I was not in trouble for taking a personal phone call on the job. *Diàn huà* (电话) simply means "telephone"—as in, "the telephone is for you." Other times, though, I really was being admonished, and I'd grown so used to the volume that I no longer questioned its intent.

"Tā mā de" (他妈的), the cooks would say a hundred times a day. It's arguably the most common profanity in China; some have suggested it

should be the national curse word, perhaps with its own holiday and shameless marketing campaign. Its mildest application is "dammit," but it can also ratchet up to *s*-word and *f*-word territory, which makes it mighty handy. Literally, it means "his mother's." His mother's what? Use your imagination.

I've heard many foul expressions in Mandarin and other dialects involving turtle eggs (shorthand for bastard) and dog farts (bullshit). I also quite like the euphemisms attached to tofu, as in "selling tofu" (prostitution) and "eating tofu" (acting like a pervert). I don't love that a woman judged to be promiscuous is apparently called a "public bus" (*gong gòng qì chē*, 公共汽车) because everyone gets to ride.

And then there is the mother of all curses, the one that will get cutlery thrown at your head in just about any Chinese kitchen around the world: *cào nǐ zǔ zōng shí bā dài* (操你祖宗十八代). *Fuck your ancestors to the eighteenth generation*. Why eighteen? Presumably because the seventeen generations wouldn't be bad enough. The curse has to extend all the way back to your great-great-great-great-great-great-great-great-great-great-great-great-great-great-great-great-grandfather. That's when you know you've really been fucked.

I thought I'd made the biggest mistake of my life when I finished my college classes in December 1982 and nobody—at least no one in a position to hire me—seemed to care. A communications degree is apparently the three-dollar bill of diplomas, generally not worth the paper it's printed on. I also had a second unmarketable major in international relations and a darling little silver Phi Beta Kappa key that said more about immoderation than intellect. Still, I spent my days scanning the want ads for any kind of entry-level writing job that might have me.

Meanwhile I had loans to pay, so I returned to working part time at Mandarin Garden. Freelance local journalism—wherein a typical rookie assignment was covering a three-hour meeting of the Water and Sewer Commission and collecting $15 before taxes—made waitressing look extremely lucrative. Even when, at twenty-three years old in the summer of 1984, I landed a fulltime gig as assistant managing editor at the *Old Colony Memorial* (a weekly newspaper, not a funeral home) in Plymouth, Massachusetts, I held on to that second job just to make my car payments. For the next year that's about all I did—work and play soccer in a recreational women's league that didn't care if I sucked—until one Saturday in 1985, when I was setting up for the dinner shift at Mandarin Garden and the new manager, with whom I'd become quite friendly, asked if I would ever consider dating "a Chinese guy." I chuckled.

"Why would his race matter?" I said.

"He's also short," she replied. "Like, your height."

"Also not a problem," I said, fully at peace with my five-foot-two-ness and any potential mate who was at least eye level. "Anything else?"

Assured that he was neither a convicted felon nor a gym rat with a fondness for muscle shirts as streetwear (my two deal-breakers), I agreed to let the setup happen. His name was Kao Shun (Guó Xióng, 國雄). According to his sister, Chin Chin (née Zhēn Zhēn, 貞珍), he'd recently moved from Taiwan to a suburb of Boston, where he was learning the management ropes at Benny Wu's newly opened second restaurant, Mandarin House, located about thirteen miles west of Mandarin Garden.

Kao Shun (pronounced *gouah-shuhng* in my tone-addled, Pinyin-guided approach to phonetics) was twenty-six, two years older than me, and was working on getting his green card with the help of Chin Chin, who'd become a US citizen after marrying a California-born electronics technician she'd enchanted during his six months of navy contract work in and around her island hometown. Chin Chin wasn't looking to marry off her little brother; she just wanted to expand his social life and vocabulary.

"Do you have time?" he asked nervously when we were introduced a few days later.

"Time?" I repeated.

"If you have time, we can go out somewhere," he said.

Ah.

"Sure. I have time," I said. "Monday night?"

He smiled. We were both working in restaurants, so weekends weren't generally going to be an option. I think he liked that I was already making it easy on him, perhaps contrary to what he'd heard about American women in general and the single ones in particular.

Kao Shun was slight in stature, as advertised, but no less handsome for it. He had stylishly moussed, jet-black hair and dressed like a model—sharp suits, crisp shirts, colorful ties knotted in the way of an Italian hit man. He haunted Filene's Basement in downtown Boston for Armani, Valentino, and other high-end designer bargains. No man I knew did that.

He had a wide smile and a nervous, full-throated laugh that punctuated most of his sentences. His English was limited and highly influenced by John Wayne movies and the catchphrases of American TV. If I tripped on a crack in the sidewalk, he might say "Easy there, Pilgrim."

MTV and VH1 were his faithful study partners. They played on the Mandarin House bar televisions in between sporting events, so he picked up random Billy Idol–isms ("*hey little sister, shotgun*") and the wisdom of Cyndi Lauper ("*she bop, he bop, and we bop*"), which he employed liberally as he worked the front of the house. Eventually he'd make his way to a job in the restaurant's kitchen, where his talent for cooking would blossom and grow, but in his first years in America he was all about absorbing—languages, food, cocktails, culture, girls . . . I got the sense that the world was his pu-pu platter, which isn't a criticism.

On our first date, Kao Shun took me to a smoky jazz club (good start), where somehow we communicated well enough to sense how much we had in common and how much we stood to learn from each other. Plus, if nothing else, I thought our conversational fumbling would be good for a few laughs. I desperately needed laughs.

Sometimes when you meet a person, you present the very best version of yourself. That wasn't me in 1985. I was broken in places and incapable of pretending I was whole, which means I needed the rare man who does not need a woman to stroke his ego. I needed a man who put friendship before courtship, and compassion before everything. Being with someone who literally spoke a different language meant that neither of us could hide behind pleasantries and hollow chatter. We showed all our cards from the start; it was challenging but also incredibly liberating. He needed to learn English; I needed someone to lift me out of a worldview that had become narrowed and darkened by too much personal tragedy.

Kao Shun had layers that made him unlike anyone I'd ever met. His CD collection contained as much Beethoven and Bach as it did Pink Floyd and Eagles. He'd learned to waltz, foxtrot, and cha-cha in Taiwan, guided around his childhood living room by the arms of an older brother who insisted it was the only way to "get girls." And of course he knew food—how to eat it, how to treat it, how to make it sexy as hell. We soaked up each other the way one bathes in a Kurosawa marathon—in fact, it was Kao Shun who introduced me to the mind-blowing films of Akira Kurosawa, on one of our first dates. The white-bread American guys I knew were a Buddy Hackett marathon at best.

Eventually, many weeks into the relationship, it became time for him to meet my family. But first, he had a decision to make.

"Let's talk about your name," I said.

A Chinese man is most often addressed by his last name, with the salutation of *"xiǎo"* (小, pronounced *shaow*) or *"lǎo"* (老, *laow*) depending on whether he's younger or older than you. His given name is reserved for family and other very close relationships. I was allowed to use Kao Shun. Most everyone else in our restaurant-centric friend circle called him Xiǎo Tseng, meaning "young mister Tseng."

"Do you want my family to call you Xiǎo Tseng?" I asked. "I just need to know what to tell them. Whatever you want is totally fine, of course; formal or informal, they'll be good with whatever you prefer. The only thing is, I have to warn you, they're definitely going to butcher the pronunciation of Xiǎo Tseng.

"Maybe a few will get it right [*shaow-tzen*]," I added pessimistically. "The rest will just call you Sheldon, if you're lucky."

He smiled and exhaled a laugh through his nose.

"I'm only bringing this up because you've talked about taking a Westernized name," I said. "Is that something you're still interested in doing? If so, have you got one in mind?"

We were sitting in his car, a candy-apple-red Porsche 924 that would later be repossessed when he defaulted on the payments but for now looked great on both of us. He pondered the question. Then he cocked his head and said with a straight face, "James. James Bond."

It didn't matter that he got the quote twisted (spy fiction fans know it's "Bond. James Bond."). And maybe that was intentional anyway. I cracked up.

"Okay, James, James Bond," I told him. "See you at my sister's house for dinner on Sunday. Six o'clock sharp."

He arrived bearing a fruit basket.

And I don't mean some wimpy collection of tangerines and kiwis and other frou-frou citrus. This was a FRUIT BASKET—the size of a funeral spray, with apples, pears, oranges, grapefruit . . . the total haul approximated the yield of a small orchard. It was wrapped in a tunnel of cellophane and tied up with yards of red ribbon. When I saw James, James Bond coming up the walkway, it just looked as though the fruit basket had sprouted arms and legs. His body and head were completely obscured by the bounty of produce he was carrying.

Carol owned a raised ranch in the town of Hanover, about twenty-five miles south of Boston. I'd pretty much lived there since well before Jan died, and once he was gone I moved in full-time to help with her bills and two kids, Kristen and Jeff, who were fourteen and almost fifteen (Irish twins, in Caucasian parlance), respectively. They all knew I'd been dating some guy from Taiwan who worked at one of Benny's restaurants. James presented the fruit basket to Carol, bowing slightly as they shook hands.

"Nice to meeting you," he said. "My name is James."

Then he laughed. Loudly. Like a Chinese Santa Claus. "Ahhh-ha-ha-ho-ho-ho!"

It was a strange and adorable beginning, exactly as expected.

Carol knew how to cook, which James appreciated. They were instantly able to connect over sauce components and the best way to roast a chicken, which was good for at least twenty minutes of small talk once we sat down at the table. With two teenagers in the house, the conversation naturally turned next to pop culture.

"Did you have American TV shows in Taiwan?" the kids wanted to know.

"Sure," James answered. "Do you know . . . Uh . . . Sunday, Monday . . . Something like that?"

No sign of recognition from us.

"Saturday, what a day . . ."

"Wait. *Happy Days*?" I asked.

"Right, right," he said. Then he leaned way back in his chair and offered a double thumbs-up. "Ayyyyyyy!"

Jeff and Kristen stifled a spit take.

"Also, in Taiwan we love *Three Company*," James continued.

"You had *Three's Company*?" I said, incredulous. "Why on earth would we export *that*?"

Ignoring my snark, Carol asked about his favorite movie stars. There was John Wayne, of course. He mentioned Marlon Brando and Al Pacino, continuing the tough-guy theme. A few comics made the list. "And Mary Lemon Rose," he said with certainty.

We looked at each other. I considered the possible combinations.

Did he mean Mary Tyler Moore? Mary Ann Mobley? Mariel Hemingway? Maybe he'd combined Rose Marie and Jack Lemmon, in a sort of precursor to Brangelina? Nothing quite added up. Until, eventually, it hit me.

"Marilyn Monroe!" I declared.

Carol roared. Jeff and Kristen giggled. James let out another booming, involuntary "Ahhh-ha-ha-ho-ho-ho!" And I was suddenly acutely aware that our dinner table hadn't seen this much laughter since Jan died, more than a year earlier. As much as we'd tried not to live in the past, it kept reviving and filling every cranny of the house. From my chair, I could look out through sliding glass doors onto the back deck, where my personal superhero had revealed that he wasn't immortal. So, it felt good to be howling again now, without reservation. More than that, it felt as though we might actually be moving on, into some kind of new chapter that made room for unexpected delights like James (Bond) Tseng. His arrival had given us permission. That and an abundance of fruit.

❧

New Year's Eve, 1986.

It was rare—like, Halley's comet rare—that my parents spent a whole night away from home. But that is what they did as 1987 dawned. My mother's mental health and outlook on life had restabilized after Patty's death, thanks to Big Pharma, and my father was motivated to keep her happy, so they agreed to attend a party and sleep over at a friend's house on Cape Cod, which meant that my childhood home was going to be empty.

At twenty-five, I was still living with my sister and her two kids. James, twenty-seven, had a room in a small house littered with his restaurant colleagues and their laundry. Privacy was not something we came by easily, so of course we planned to make use of my parents' place while they were gone. I had a key. My old room had been preserved as a shrine, with my desk still covered in "Wacky Pack" stickers and my *Saturday Night Fever* album preloaded on the turntable. What further consent did I need? As James might put it: She bop, he bop, and we bop so, hey little sister, shotgun. Translation: Don't overthink it.

Anyone employed by a Chinese restaurant works on New Year's Eve. It's the busiest day of the year, sometimes by two or three times the volume of the next biggest days (Mother's Day, Christmas Eve, Thanksgiving Eve, etc.). James and I would both be ending our shifts by elevenish. We'd meet at my folks' house shortly before midnight and watch the ball drop in Times Square—just us and Dick Clark.

I arrived at 11:40 P.M. Unbeknownst to me, my brother Jacky was already there. He walked out of my bedroom as I was lighting the jasmine- and ylang-ylang-scented candle I'd brought, to set the mood but also to mask the fact that I smelled like chicken fingers. We stood there in our parents' living room, just looking at each other.

Now thirty-four, Jacky had regained a good deal of brain function since his car accident, and he had most of his motor skills back, though his right arm remained partially paralyzed. He could talk, communicating largely in words and phrases rather than sentences. But he was plagued by terrible seizures that came without warning and plunged him into a trance, after which he'd be sapped of energy for days.

The accident had remade my brother's personality in at least two significant ways. He was gentler and more emotional than I'd ever known him to be—less the narcissistic former high school quarterback; more the empathic, protective sibling and family man. But he was also angrier and darker.

A fight with his wife—the woman who'd been with him since his college years—had brought him to my parents' house. She struggled to cope with his frequent mood swings and myriad frustrations, and with three kids under the age of seven, she probably had about as much patience on this night as my mother had with the cascade of spilled milk all those years ago. James walked in through the back door as my brother's explanation was unfurling. He was wearing a virgin wool Emanuel Ungaro suit and carrying a bottle of Dom Pérignon.

The accident had taken a lot from Jacky, but he wasn't oblivious. He knew what kind of evening he'd crashed. Even when James tried to cover his initial double take with a breezy "Hey, brother, what's happ'nin'?" the dynamic remained awkward. If I could, I might use my Tao of Three Wishes to alter the path of Jacky's car the night he was driving down a country road, minding his own business when he got hit in the head by a boat. But if I couldn't do that, I would at least use it to change the way I handled this one New Year's Eve at my parents' house.

James invited him to ring in the New Year by joining us for a glass of champagne. I said nothing. Jacky (who no longer drank alcohol anyway) said thanks, but no thanks. I was relieved. In my defense, the whole thing was just too awkward. Plus, I wanted to salvage what I could of our romantic plans. So, when my brother excused himself and went to bed, I thought it was just about the best way this unscripted scene could have ended. James and I cuddled up on the sofa, toasted to the New Year, and kissed as the ball dropped and "Auld Lang Syne" blared out of the television. I didn't have a clue what the year ahead would bring. I just thought it was off to a comically rocky start.

❧

For a long time, I didn't actually have a bedroom at Carol's house. I slept on a couch in the family room, which occupied a portion of her finished basement. It had psychedelic, *Yellow Submarine*–inspired wallpaper and a back door that was almost never locked. That's how my oldest sister, Nancy, and her husband, Joe, entered on March 22, 1987, the night they came in to tell us the news that Jacky was dead.

They woke me first, since my couch-bed was right there. I remember shaking my head and rubbing my eyes a lot, to try to either gain some clarity or discover that I wasn't awake at all. I told them I didn't believe them. Then I told them I "couldn't take it," so it couldn't be true. But it was true.

Jacky had had a seizure while his wife was visiting with friends at a house nearby. She's the one who phoned Jimmy to relay the tragic events that had unfolded hours earlier: Jacky's seven-year-old son, awakened by his dad's labored breathing in an adjoining bedroom, was reassured by my brother and ordered back to bed. He couldn't have known the magnitude of the seizure that was coming. EMTs were called to the scene when my sister-in-law arrived home around 11 P.M. to find Jacky unconscious. They managed to resuscitate him, then lost him again. A more thorough examination of hospital records could help fill in the timeline, I was told, as though those details mattered.

"Should we wake up Carol?" Nancy asked me. It was around 4 A.M.

"I think . . . I don't know," I said. "Maybe let her sleep a while longer? There's nothing we can do right now, right?"

"Right," Joe said. "When Jimmy called, we said we'd pick him up at six and drive over to Ma and Dad's to tell them. They'll be up by then. We should deliver this message in person, together."

I nodded. Then we sat for an hour in stunned silence before venturing upstairs to break the news to my prematurely widowed, couldn't-catch-a-break, extraordinarily resilient sister who'd already learned whatever lessons we're supposed to take from the tribulations that try us most. You can careen through a lot of emotions and memories in an hour. Or you can fixate on one small thing, like a yellow Post-it Note stuck to a kitchen cabinet by a teenager with impressive voicemail editing skills. Scrawled in Kristen's cartoony handwriting, this one read: *JP: Uncle Jacky called. Call him back.*

Lord knows, I meant to.

The message was at least a day old; somehow I just hadn't found time to heed its simple directive. And now I couldn't, I realized with a suffocating heaviness. Not ever.

Ignoring my brother's landline voicemail was another immutable regret that I would need to add to a pile of personal shortcomings. It probably ranked somewhere above prioritizing Redford's hunky screen scenes over my sister's feelings, though the exact hierarchy didn't much matter. Both were sins for which there was no atoning.

And the day was still so young.

❧

You don't rehearse a speech you never expect to deliver. Not that practice would make much of a difference. There's no good way to present bad news, which is all any of us were thinking about as we loaded ourselves in the car and drove back to the little brown ranch of our childhoods.

The sun was just coming up. I remember it as a clear and beautiful morning, much like the one that had dawned in July 1966 and went on to become the greatest day of my life. As the car carrying me and all three of my living siblings motored toward its destination, I couldn't know if this would be the worst day of my life, but I did already recognize that it was in the running.

I was shaking with anxiety when we approached my parents' street. We parked at the curb, so as not to alarm them, and as we climbed the driveway,

I noted how small and vulnerable the house looked. Despite its modest size and the ridiculous ceramic donkey lawn ornament that stood guard out front, pulling a cart that in warmer months would be filled with pink petunias, this had always been my fortress. I'd come here during college to pig out, guilt-free because it made her so happy, on my mom's chicken-fried flank steak and buttery apple pie. In high school, it was where I consoled myself with mint chocolate chip ice cream and romantic comedies when the boys I liked didn't like me back. Now, it was no better than a teepee in the path of a tornado.

We approached through the carport, inching past whatever model of Chevrolet had most recently replaced the seaweed-green Nova. In the kitchen, my father was in his overnight underwear, halfway through his bowl of Kellogg's Raisin Bran. My mother, in a housecoat and slippers, had just poured herself a second cup of coffee.

At first, when they saw us all standing at the back door, they had that look of delight that parents have when their grown children show up unannounced and not bearing laundry. They might have been just about to say, "What a great surprise! What are you doing here?" when it must have dawned on them that no good news comes at this hour of the morning, not by telephone and definitely not by a committee arriving at your door. Their faces fell.

"It's Jacky," someone said. "He's gone, Dad. Jacky's gone."

What happened next is an image that I will never be able to chase from my brain. It's burned on the insides of my eyes, the way my mother warned me would happen if I sat too close to the television during *H.R. Pufnstuf.*

My father folded to the floor as though a candlepin bowling ball had taken out both of his ankles. He cried out "Oh, no! Not Jacky! Not *Jacky*!" and began to sob. At the same time, my mother fainted, but with all of us crowded into the tiny kitchen, she fell right at my brother Jimmy instead of cracking her skull on the stove. I guess you could call that a saving grace, though with both of my parents collapsed in a heap and not one of us knowing how to comfort them, it didn't feel like there was any grace to this moment.

In my whole life, I'd never seen my dad just let himself cry. If it had happened during Patty's extended cancer ordeal, it hadn't happened in front of me. With Jacky, the news was so shocking and swift, my father didn't have time to throw up his usual walls. Plus, the irony of this moment was how much more open my dad had become in the aftermath of his eldest son's life-altering head injury.

At the time of Jacky's accident, Jocko was a man uncomfortable in his recent retirement from HUD, a man who'd discovered there's only so much puttering one can do in an itty-bitty home shared by just two people and convinced that he would never again have purpose. Then, without warning, one of his adult offspring reverted to the intellectual level of a child, and that child needed him. So, he threw himself back into parenthood, and this time he even allowed himself to enjoy it, unencumbered by the responsibilities of being the breadwinner and disciplinarian.

Seeing him rejuvenated was more than an upside. It was a revelation.

For all the detachment and disappointment brought on by my adolescence, I'd never once questioned that my dad loved each of his children deeply. In fact, that faith was at the root of my heartbreak. So, it was a gift to be able to watch him forge a new kind of bond with his eldest son, and to imagine what remained in that jar for the rest of us to try to extract, now that the lid was half off.

Not anymore. You could almost hear the jar shatter as my father fell to the floor alongside his wife.

I saw it happen from a distance, even though I was practically standing on top of them. I wanted to throw up; instead, I threw up my own protective walls in real time, knowing that I couldn't possibly make any of this make sense. Jocko and Yolanda had made it through the death of a daughter. Now, three short years later, they were being asked to cope with the loss of their firstborn son at the exact same age, thirty-four. It wasn't fair. It wasn't even *un*fair. It was heinous.

But was it an actual curse, as my mother had posited in her darkest moments? I'd always dismissed that idea. Now, I was beginning to think it had some merit.

"Cào wǒ zǔzōng shíbā dài" (操我祖宗十八代), I remarked bitterly when recounting the scene to James a few hours later. Fuck *my* ancestors to the eighteenth generation.

"Don't say that," he said sternly. "That is very bad."

I'm not actually suggesting that my words had any real power. The very notion of curses springs from a feeling of powerlessness. However, since humans are generally far more inclined to place blame than we are to accept that most of what happens to us is blameless, I accept my share of responsibility for what happened next.

Two months after Jacky died, my father was diagnosed with esophageal cancer at age sixty-seven. Six months later, despite the recommended chemotherapy and radiation, he was deceased. Officially, it was the cancer that killed him, but it really doesn't matter what the record says or how corny this sounds or that I'm the umpteen-billionth person not even counting the country music industry to traffic in this cliché: His family knows that he died of a broken heart.

Looking back, I think I always undersold that part of him.

In my college years, when I was really feeling myself, I'd often baited my dad to demonstrate his love for me. I pushed because he was finally at an age where I figured he could be shamed. Not enough to purchase Mickey Mouse pads, but thankfully we were well past the stage where I needed him for that.

One Christmas, I guilted him into buying a real tree instead of dragging the fake one up from the basement. It wasn't that I cared that much—in some ways the faux evergreen was more interesting, with its worn and misshapen color-coded branches that no longer matched their designated holes; putting it together was a challenge that caused as many laughs as arguments. I liked the smell of a freshly cut tree but, really, I just liked testing my father's tolerance for indulging me.

The semester I spent studying in London, I complained to my mother that he'd never written me a card or a letter—not just that year, but in my life. I knew she'd nag him about it; I didn't honestly think it would matter. But one morning when I went to my mailbox, there was an envelope with a two-page, handwritten letter inside, from my dad.

"Dear Janice," it began. "Forgive me. I haven't written a letter in many years, since I was in the Navy. I don't really know how to anymore. But your mother says you told her I should write, so I'll try."

In four paragraphs total, he went on to talk about the weather back home (cold), the state of the lawn (brown), and the latest squad of Patriots (losers). He also promised to send me a tie clip in the shape of a submarine, which he'd gotten from his old place of employment, the Fore River Shipyard, because I'd mentioned that Neville, my House of Commons boss, had a thing for military ships and was impressed that I had a relative who built them. My father never once said he missed me, though he did sign it "Love, Dad."

Every word seemed forced, as though squeezed from battleship steel. I treasured it.

At Jocko Page's solemn funeral, a bagpiper in a kilt played all the Scottish hymns that had anchored the Shaving Songs Master Collection. I wrote and delivered my third eulogy in as many years. We dressed in black and rode in a limousine, again. Our motorcade passed by Chick's Barber Shop on its way to the cemetery. The sorrow was overwhelming.

Even for me, there was too much here to unpack, too many bittersweet memories, too much life set to minor chords. I can't say for sure, but I think I began plotting my exit strategy that very afternoon.

By now I was working at the *Providence Journal*, walking through every door that opened, regardless of whether I met even the bro-endorsed 60 percent threshold of knowing what the hell I was doing. Anorexia simultaneously promotes self-doubt and invincibility—you think you're successfully transforming into your leanest, most unstoppable iteration—and many of the disorder's perspectives and behaviors never leave you, even when you've resumed consuming enough calories to sustain a healthy baseline. Like my mother, I'd pushed past the loss of so many loved ones by not dwelling, by keeping it moving, by pretending, I suppose, but not because those losses didn't hurt—rather, in spite of how much they hurt. As anyone rooted in the Northeast will tell you, resilient vegetation can range from the sturdiest oak to the thinnest, most pliable beach grass. Botanists aside, no one questions why that is, or how that is, or whether it can continue. We learn to respect the things that endure and flourish.

I rose from copy editor to lifestyles and arts & entertainment editor (wheelhouse: movies and television). It took a few years, but eventually my dream opportunity came calling in 1990: a job with the *Los Angeles Times*, editing a new entertainment section in the burgeoning Orange County bureau. Taking the position meant leaving behind all the tragedy of recent years, but it also meant leaving my family and leaving James, whose professional life was in Boston.

Every life meets a multitude of crossroads; I'm better at the going than I am at the staying. Going makes it harder to fail, I think, as counterintuitive as that may seem. At the very least, you're taking a risk by going. If it doesn't pan out, you pat yourself on the back for trying. But if you stay, suddenly everything you do is measured against an imaginary bar—what might have been—and no one ever imagines that they might have been a failure.

But then there's the abandonment aspect of going: You're always leaving something, usually including a few someones, behind. How do you reconcile the selfishness that takes, even when you're doing it for all the right reasons? I don't think you do. And I bet that most people who even attempt to reconcile it are women, because the going has always been easier for men.

James had left Taiwan seeking opportunities he wouldn't have had if he'd stayed. He was evolved enough in his life to want the same for me, so we talked it through and fully agreed: I should go. Solo. Maybe, down the road, he could think about moving west also, if I was really loving L.A. and he was inclined to try opening a restaurant there. Right now, though, I needed a fresh start, and I needed to take that on alone.

Plus, as he knew and I knew, I was already gone.

CHAPTER 6

Long Beach

If the sitcoms of my youth taught me anything, it is that all roads lead to California.

The Bradys and the Partridges lived there. Laverne and Shirley moved there, not to mention Lucy and Ethel. Even the Fonze ("Ayyyyyyy!") made his way there from Milwaukee in 1977 to jump the shark.

When I arrived on the West Coast shortly after turning twenty-nine in 1990, I wasn't sure if it would be permanent. I just knew that I needed a change of scenery. I rented an adorable apartment in a three-family, adobe-style house two blocks from the ocean in the idyllic Belmont Shore section of Long Beach. I joined a women's soccer league and sang in a garage band that rehearsed in an actual garage, with the doors open, year-round. I ran on the beach every single day in just shorts and a sports bra. None of it sucked.

Which might be why I lost track of my mother for the next half a dozen years or so. Not full-on "Cat's in the Cradle" neglect—I still called her periodically and visited with her just enough—but I was happy to take a mostly no-news-is-good-news approach to her well-being while living my best life in a different time zone.

She was fine. She understood. I was making her proud. All the partial truths we tell ourselves when rationalizing selfishness.

It's a "baby of the family" specialty, selfishness, and I admit to leaning into it during my California sojourn, content to let my older, geographically closer siblings tend to our mother's needs, which at that time seemed relatively rational. Yolanda (herself the youngest of six DiMartinis children) always did better when she had no one relying on her, an odd upside to her husband's death when the two were empty nesters. She even seemed to make peace with her antidepressants in those moments, though inevitably she'd overcorrect at some point, dialing in her childlike tendencies and pretending to be potted firmly in the now, safely removed from "the troubles." I didn't miss being absent for these highs any more than I wanted to be around whenever they'd eventually give way again to the lows, usually precipitated by ditching her meds—she'd outgrown them, they were making her worse, none of your business—amid some kind of crisis or burden that even her most nimble inner child couldn't dodge.

But I did miss James, and he only made it harder by being so patient with me.

It takes a secure man to give a woman space and permission to graze, trusting that he will benefit from any comparisons. Even though I dated a bit, none of it progressed much beyond a goodnight kiss, probably because I never met anyone who seemed like an upgrade. I understood what I had in James—a bright, good-humored man who adored me—however much I was trying to keep my options open. Selfishly (that word again), I didn't want to lose him for no good reason.

That's why we tried to never be apart for more than a few consecutive months, even though he was regularly working twelve-hour days, on a path to rock star chef skills and owning his own restaurant in the Boston area. He would forgo days off to stockpile time, then travel west to be with me for a stretch. I would also fly to Boston whenever I could, which wasn't that much. Occasionally, we would meet somewhere in the middle. The result was carefully curated quality time with very little arguing. We couldn't wait to see each other. Romance felt like a manageable limited priority.

One night in early 1994, I arrived home from work and James surprised me by opening the front door of my Long Beach apartment as I was fumbling with my keys. He was wearing a typically natty suit—inky-blue Valentino Garavani, I think—and an expertly knotted, floral-print tie. As I stepped inside, I noticed that the floors of my living room were strewn with crimson rose petals. There were more of them all over my glass-topped dining table, along with candles and an open bottle of Sonoma Valley pinot noir. Whatever was on the stove and in the oven smelled amazing.

"What are you doing here?" I asked him. But it was just the kind of thing you say to keep your mouth busy when your brain is caught off guard. I knew the answer before I formed the question. It had been a nerve-racking couple of weeks in Southern California.

On January 17 at four thirty in the morning, I felt my whole bedroom shake, and then I heard car alarms begin to go off by the dozens. It was still dark out, so why were my windows lit up like a Fourth of July fireworks finale? I got up and looked out to see sparks coming from the transformers that topped telephone poles up and down my street. The room was still twitching and rolling, and I couldn't be sure that this wasn't a dream, so I stood there wondering if I should stay put or get the hell out, and by the time I could make any sense of what was happening, it was over. That's the nature of earthquakes, in my limited experience: There's never enough time to react, but it's okay because having more time wouldn't make you any less fucked.

The Northridge earthquake, as this event came to be known, clocked in at magnitude 6.7—then the strongest ever recorded in an urban swath of North America. It shook the ground all the way out to Las Vegas, and it claimed the lives of fifty-seven people, with nearly another nine thousand injured. The stuccoed, two-story house where I rented a two-bedroom unit on the ground floor sustained cracks that would leak like a sieve in future rains, but it was a minor player in damages that reportedly totaled around $40 billion. Most unnerving: There were strong aftershocks that continued for days.

James had lived through many earthquakes in his thirty-four years, a condition of growing up in Taiwan. He understood when I would call him in the middle of the night, too afraid to sleep.

"Do I get up and stand in a doorway if I feel a tremor?" I wondered aloud.

"Why a doorway?" he asked.

"Um, I don't actually know. It's what they say here, maybe something about structural integrity of the frame? You've never been told that?"

"Never," he said. "After an earthquake, when you see it on the news, do you see rubble, rubble, rubble, doorway, rubble? Does that make sense to you? I don't get it."

"Now that you say that . . . I guess I never really thought about it."

"In my country, they tell us to move away from large windows. We sometimes pile into a bathroom. Maybe you want to do that? You can lie down in your bathtub for protection; you can put blankets and pillows in there."

"You want me to sleep in the bathtub?"

"Some people do."

"That seems extreme."

"And standing in a doorway all night is normal?"

"Fair."

"Some people also say to find a pocket. Like at the end of your bed, you can sleep on the floor between the bed and the bureau. Then if pieces of the ceiling fall, they maybe hit the furniture and make a pocket underneath."

"If the *ceiling falls*?" I said.

But we both knew I'd considered that exact scenario, having seen far too many pictures of high-rise apartment buildings pancaked in the wake of an earthquake. James understood I was terrified of a catastrophic collapse, and instead of trying to talk me out of that fear—never a good strategy when negotiating with a Catholic—he was urging me to focus on the holes that might plausibly exist, even in my debris-filled worst-case scenario. I couldn't tell whether he was just humoring me, but he sounded serious and earnest (his English had improved so much, there was now very little that he couldn't get across without parlor-style guessing games; plus, I'd gotten so familiar with his syntax, the grammatical imperfections hardly even registered anymore). It was an idea, at least. I could try it, or I could lie awake all night.

"So, what you're saying is, I could put some pillows and blankets on the floor and sleep down there between the bed and the bureau and that's not a crazy thing to do? I'm not being a total baby?"

"It's not crazy, and you're not being a baby," he said.

"Well, then, I'm moving my blankets to the floor. Right now."

He advised me to have a flashlight, extra batteries, and some water within reach. I added a Tupperware container full of pretzel rods and peanut M&Ms, which made it feel more like a pajama party—albeit a paranoid, sad pajama party for one. I slept there for more than a week, while thousands of aftershocks rattled the region.

The gap between the edge of my bureau and the end of my platform bed was about two and a half feet. Both pieces of furniture were fashioned from solid pine, so lying between them really did feel like being in a coffin, awaiting a lid. I thought about how far I'd traveled to put some distance between myself and death, and now here I was in a confined, stressful space that made me think about it again, nightly.

I admit that I don't know if I believe in heaven. I want to, desperately, because I'd have a lot of friends there, and I'd be quite content to spend eternity listening to them throw shade at all the silly things happening on earth (I pray that they've seen *Vanderpump Rules*, for example). I just don't trust the men who brought us the pearly gates concept in the first place, the same way that my mother didn't trust them when they laid down rules about how she should confess her sins. I think it's possible, and maybe even probable, that all we have is this one life.

No afterlife.

No reunions with lost loved ones who might restore us to something resembling whole.

No do-overs.

Lying awake on my bedroom floor night after night, looking straight up at the leaky ceiling that might cave in on me at any moment, I worried that I hadn't done enough to justify my existence. I was thirty-two. Patty and Jacky only lived to thirty-four, roughly the same age as Jesus, depending on which historian you believe.

“That’s pressure,” I told James by phone. And that’s why I couldn’t have been surprised when, a week later, he showed up at my apartment to cook me dinner in a suit.

While he stirred things in sauce pots and poured me a glass of wine, I changed into a short black dress and high heels. I even put on eyeliner because, at least to me, eyeliner is foreplay, especially in your own living room. We ate roasted duck with black plum sauce, charred bok choy, and sticky rice. Lingering at the table for hours, we talked about everything *but* natural disasters.

“I’ve been thinking about what it might be like to adopt a child,” I began at some point after we’d run through the day’s news headlines, sports standings, and personal and professional gossip. “Not now, obviously, but I mean someday.”

James and I had talked around the edges of this many times before. We were both the youngest of our respective families. Neither of us felt a personal need or genealogical responsibility to procreate. We agreed on the merits of giving love and shelter to a child in need—one who already existed rather than one who began as a wish in our own image.

“It’s a good thing to do,” James replied. “I’ve always thought that. So many kids need a home.”

“Maybe I’m just feeling my own mortality,” I said. “I’d like to know that I made a difference. You know, whenever my time is up.”

He smiled and took my hand. We got up from the table and danced to Van Morrison’s *Tupelo Honey* album.

You can take all the tea in China
Put it in a big brown bag for me . . .

In that moment, I was convinced that even the imperfections of this bicoastal relationship were oddly perfect for us.

But that was about to change.

James and I were in bed.

We were naked. And not even just regular naked but postcoital naked, which is pretty much the last place I'd pick to set a story that I might someday be asked to tell my grandchildren.

I don't have a memory for sex. Every theme song of every late twentieth-century television show, sure, but please don't ask me to recount the details of any single episode of shagging, because to me it's all tapioca. I love tapioca, mind you; I would be sad if tapioca didn't exist. It's my favorite of all the puddings. But there's only so much a layperson can do to make tapioca much different from what it innately is. (Whipped cream? Meh.)

James, on the other hand, would remember about the sex. He'd probably also be able to tell you what we had that day for lunch, what book he'd read that afternoon, and the exact hue of the bougainvillea blooming outside my Belmont Shore apartment. James is a details guy. If you're ever the victim of a crime, you want him as your eyewitness. That's why I found it so odd that he'd misread all the signs. Marriage? Now? Who was asking for that? Not me.

I mean, sure, it was a reasonable request on paper. We'd been dating for nearly eight years—much of it transcontinental, with him based in Boston and me in Southern California—and I was thirty-two. So, probably, if we'd been reading the manual, it was time. But in the winter of 1994 I wasn't anywhere near ready to be engaged, and James was far too perceptive not to have known that.

The ring said otherwise, though. He was holding it between thumb and index finger, in the traditional manner of a suitor confident enough to liberate the gold-enrobed diamond from its open box while the question still hangs in the air.

"I love you so much," he said. "Marry me?"

"Oh," I answered.

Just . . . *Oh.*

I'd never been one of those girls who dreams of her wedding day and spends time auditioning names for her someday children. In fact, I was pretty sure I wanted one child at most, possibly not even from my own womb, and single parenthood wasn't out of the question.

I don't idealize marriage like my sister Carol. As a young girl, she wrote in loopy cursive on the back of my parents' unframed wedding portrait: "I hope I am as happy as my mother and father were on their wedding day. They are the best people in the hole [*sic*] world, and I hope I have children as good as we are now."

I'm a realist. Marriage is about compromise. Marriage derails careers—women's careers disproportionately. Marriage is for people like my Greatest Generation parents, who weren't given much of a choice. They were a couple brought together by convenience—and, sure, I guess, a kind of love—who had kids because they were supposed to and tolerated everything that came after. You see those compromises close up and you say to yourself, "Not me, sister. I'm too smart for that. When I get married, it will be for all the right reasons. It will be on my terms, or it won't be at all." You don't expect your boyfriend to propose marriage just because he purchased airplane tickets.

Okay, that's not fair. But it is kind of true.

James had been feeling the pull of home when he arranged for us to travel that spring to the small, homogeneous village where he'd grown up in southern Taiwan. He hadn't been back there since moving to the United States in the mid-1980s, the better part of a decade ago. Now thirty-four, he was eager for his mother and three brothers to meet the white American girlfriend whose command of Mandarin was about as precise as a Jackson Pollock knockoff painting. Oddly, the only thing that worried him was the girlfriend part.

A man of his age was expected to have a plan, and that plan was expected to include marriage. James reckoned that if he could present me as his fiancé, no one would needle him about whether we were a serious couple. Plus—and here's where even a critic had to admire the simplicity of his prioritizing—we'd be able to share a bedroom in his mother's house.

Usually, I was the one who thrived on order and logic. Here, it was James feeling the need to be practical.

But he hadn't mentioned any of this as we were preparing for the trip, and I foolishly thought I'd cleared the last travel hurdle when I finished my malaria shots. After years of seeing how he fit into my native world, I was ready to see that equation flipped. More than ready; I was excited.

"Why?" I asked him, unable to hide my disappointment over his complete misreading of the moment. "Why like this?"

It wasn't just that I didn't want a commitment of such magnitude to be dictated by convenience or propriety. It was that a marriage proposal after sex is, at best, overtipping.

James didn't see it that way, of course.

"I wanted . . . I thought . . . I mean . . . *naked*. Like nothing between us, you know? Only you and me and this ring. I mean . . . Everything I have, I give to you."

For a guy with a limited English vocabulary, James really knew how to turn a phrase. He often amazed me with the poetry of his words, so much so that I was intimidated by the exactitude of his expression. *Imagine how his thoughts would read in his native language*, I marveled. Maybe I was overthinking this marriage proposal. Maybe I'd been a little too well trained to see an imbalance of power, if not a nefarious plot. With my parents, every interaction was a dance, another opportunity to confirm or deny the established order of their relationship. Ironically, it seemed that James viewed his proposition as just the opposite: a stripping away of pretense and, more than that, a symbolic attempt at underscoring our status as equals.

I appreciated the gesture. Still, though, my answer was the opposite of poetic. It was the opposite of romantic. It was a gentle but emphatic, stunningly ineloquent no.

"I'm sorry," I said. "I can't. It's just . . . Ugh."

"That's okay," he replied softly, returning the ring to its velvet box. "Really."

An awkward silence followed. Then—so much worse—awkward hugging. All the while I stared at my clothes on the floor, trying to calculate a reasonable path to retrieving them quickly, as though they were knitted with aeronautical superpowers. But even if I'd owned a cape bedazzled with an *S*, the truth is, it wouldn't have mattered. Because that's the thing about a naked marriage proposal: When it bombs, there's absolutely nowhere to hide.

"Really, Janice, it's okay," James was insisting.

I didn't believe him.

Even with the diamond back in its box now, a safe distance from the living room, where we'd settled into watching whatever was on TV, I was sure that the damage of the naked proposal would linger for a very long time.

"You know it's not that I don't love you, right?" I said.

"I know," he nodded.

"Maybe we could . . . Maybe there's something we could do to show our commitment to each other, without actually getting engaged," I offered. "Like, what about a promise ring?"

"What's that?" he said.

"You know, some kind of ring—*not* a diamond—that we each wear as a symbol of our bond. It's like saying, 'Hey, everyone, just to let you know: We're together and we might even get married but we're not quite there yet.' Do they have that in your country? Is that a thing?"

"Matching rings, you mean? Yes. We have that. Some people do it."

"Would *you* want to do it? Would it help? I mean, I know it's not the same as a diamond, but if we wore those to Taiwan so your family could see . . ." (I was already assuming we'd make the trip anyway; whatever awkwardness lingered between us, we knew we would at least be pampered and well fed there. Right now, I wanted him to know that I understood the significance of meeting his mom for the first time, and why it was important for him to show her that he wasn't just messing around.)

"Yes. Sure. We could do that."

"And it would be fun to shop for rings together, right? I think that would be cool. Want to do that? Let's do that."

"Good idea. Let's do it."

Even if he didn't mean it, I felt better.

James was so easy. It almost wasn't fair how easy I had it. Even though I'd just nixed everything he had planned for this day and then some, he wasn't taking the opportunity to sulk or mope, as I undoubtedly would have. I was sure he was hurt and embarrassed. I would have been. Instead, he was agreeing to go ring shopping. Again.

Someone should one hundred percent marry this guy, I thought to myself. I just wasn't sure if it would ever be me. I was still too broken to feel I could commit to anyone. Knowing what you want is hard enough; how often does that happen in synch with each other?

The next morning, we drove over to Little Saigon, a mostly Vietnamese section of Orange County where strip malls offered dozens of jewelry stalls that we thought might yield the perfect pair of promise rings. We were right. A few hours in, we found his-and-hers bands—24-karat gold, etched with vaguely Asian symbols reminiscent of the double happiness characters familiar to Chinese couples everywhere—that were stylish and just ambiguous enough to work. They looked like a Far East version of Claddagh rings; maybe to some people they resembled wedding bands, but not to us. Anyway, we would wear them on our pinky fingers. Who could read too much into that?

James seemed content-ish. Now all I had to do was persuade the good people of Taiwan to accept me, and to understand why I couldn't commit to a gainfully employed man of extraordinary character and intelligence, who was regularly commuting 5,200 miles just to court me.

That seemed like a big job for a little ring.

Taiwan is a small island with a large chip on its shoulder. At least, that's how I saw it.

Much like Boston, which struggles with an inferiority complex rooted in mostly made-up, overstated, self-inflicted comparisons to New York,

Taiwan has trouble seeing past the shadow of its often-hostile big brother, mainland China. And not without good reason. It doesn't help that many citizens of Taiwan descend from refugees of China's wars and political unrest (who maintained ownership of the island by suppressing thousands of indigenous peoples, just to be clear). It is a love-hate relationship between the two lands; they are one in spirit, if not in ideology.

The capital of Taiwan is Taipei, which is where most tourists go when they come here. But James grew up in the south, closer to the port city of Kaohsiung, so that's the airport where we touched down in the spring of 1994 and were met by two of his brothers. It wasn't the greeting that I was expecting.

Though James hadn't seen most of his family in a decade, the reception seemed more like he'd just ducked out for a gallon of milk. It was warm, but extremely nonchalant by Western standards. No hugging or kissing, no loud declarations of cheer. The vibe was "Good to see you. Glad you're back. Let's eat." But that was only my impression of it, filtered through the definition of repression bequeathed to me by my emotionally unavailable father. While it's possible that James's brothers didn't feel comfortable displaying their emotions in the public arena that is baggage claim, it's just as possible their internal dialogue made such displays unnecessary, if not unseemly. *Check your cultural biases,* I reminded myself, *and do it before you get to his mother's house in Pingtung.*

The area where James is from, about a half-hour drive east of the airport, looked like no suburbia I'd ever seen. Its croplands were masterful grids of rice, pineapple, sugar cane, and other essential things; its small towns crowded the road with modest, low-slung brick and cement dwellings from where the residents spilled out onto the sidewalks to work and eat and play mahjong. James's dad had been in the military, so the government continued to provide housing for his mother long after she was widowed. We entered her house through a large iron gate set into a high brick wall that ran the length of a narrow alley; the gate opened into a small courtyard filled with tropical plants and single-gear bicycles. As we approached the dwelling, I heard splashing and saw water gushing out of the open front door. James's mother was cleaning the tile floors, not with a broom but with a bucket.

It was a one-story home, just like the ranch that I'd grown up in except that it was even less spacious. The bedrooms were singles pretending to be quads. The cramped kitchen—not even big enough for a café table—was piled high with cooking vessels and produce; with no cabinets to tuck them into, every utensil and foodstuff was out in full view. Just off the kitchen there was a rudimentary bathroom that made the one in my parents' house seem palatial. It was the size of a shower stall, though it didn't actually have a shower. It did have a small bathtub, and a pail for washing your hair. It also had a rusty porcelain toilet that I knew to be grateful for. Any bathroom that featured more than a ground-level hole or a trench was a luxury for private residences in this part of the world.

James's mother, the individual I would come to know on her own terms as Yù Yīng (玉英, pronounced *yoo-ying*), was a sturdy bonsai of a woman, compact and steadfast, even in her seventies. She met us outside. Again, no hugs and kisses, even for her newly returned son. James did put his arm around her as he introduced us; I went in for a hug anyway, and to my surprise, she hugged back—unconvincingly, but still.

I'd practiced what I would say to her. *"Nǐ hǎo"* (你好, *hello*). *"Hěn gāo xìng jiàn dào nǐ"* (很高兴见到你, *nice to meet you*). "*Wǒ ài nǐ*, Mama" (我爱你, *I love you*). That last one felt super weird. I was only just meeting her, why would I claim to love her like a second mother? But James had asked me to say it as a show of respect and promise—just like our rings, he argued craftily—so I complied.

"Hi," she said back, thereby exhausting her English vocabulary. I knew that the rest of my three-week visit to Taiwan would require a lot of smiling, nodding, and pointing, but we seemed to be off to a decent start. Next up: extended family and friends; there would be a lot of them.

As prepared as I thought I was, I'd underestimated the waves of well-wishers about to descend on the Tseng family home. In the weeks before our trip, James had bought boxes and boxes of brand-name American toiletries, medicines, vitamins, and candies. He loaded an entire large suitcase with the items, threw in two pairs of shorts, two T-shirts, six boxer-briefs, and a pair of flip-flops and announced that he was done packing.

"Is that really all the clothes you're bringing?" I asked.

"That's it," he answered. "I can borrow more from my brother."

"Okay. But why would you do that?"

"You'll see," he said. And I did, not long after we arrived in Pingtung.

We'd just finished our first home-cooked lunch and were sitting in Yù Yīng's living room when about a dozen neighbors came knocking. They were there to welcome James home, of course, but also to get a look at the *nǚ péng yǒu* (女朋友, *girlfriend*). The most advanced in age squeezed onto a small couch, two armchairs, and the four folding chairs pushed up to a low square mahjong table in the living room. The rest sat on the floor or stood around the fringes of the room. I was in the center, sharing a chair with James, feeling on display the way one does at a bridal shower brunch, and without so much as a mimosa or peach Bellini to take the edge off.

Between the local accent and the speed of its delivery, it was impossible for me to make much sense of the conversation filling the room. Every few minutes I heard my name leap out randomly, sometimes followed by *"piào liang"* (漂亮, *pretty*), which made me laugh. *Kě ài* (可爱, *cute*) I could maybe buy. *Tǐ jiàn* (體健, *fit*), sure. But *pretty* was quite a stretch, even in a foreign country where people were making every effort to be nice. Plus, the people saying this were clutching fistfuls of the gifts James had brought—a Snickers or a Milky Way in one hand, Right Guard deodorant and a bottle of Excedrin in the other—so it was hard to take them seriously. A few declarations of *"piào liang"* probably seemed appropriate in return for all this American loot.

Days upon days of similar drop-in sessions ensued, to the point where I began to worry whether James had packed enough of the very items I'd questioned him about bringing at all. And every hour that I sat receiving guests in the living room, I had to find ways to look as though I were fully engaged in conversations that I had no hope of understanding. So, I focused on the lizard.

He—I've decided it was a he, based on his cheekiness—was the color of unpolished pewter, about six inches long, and very quick. He first appeared on the wall behind the sofa, where there was a brass-rimmed clock, about the size of a dinner plate, that I imagined was the door to his lair. He would emerge from behind the clock every afternoon at 3:30 P.M., which was generally right in the middle of visiting hours, just as I was fighting to keep from nodding off.

I'm pretty sure this lizard was a gecko. They're very common throughout Asia. They're also considered very lucky, since their name, *bì hǔ* (壁虎), is similar to another word, *bì hù* (庇护), which means "shelter"—as in "protection," as in "avoid disaster." For this reason, you'll find gecko stickers plastered on millions of cars in China, and you won't find exterminators getting many calls to deal with the live version.

No one but me paid any attention to the gecko in James's mother's house. It would dart all over the walls and ceiling while people socialized within inches of it. I once was sure that I saw it burrow into some lady's bouffant up-do, but she didn't react, and a few minutes later it emerged on the opposite side of the sofa, so probably that was just an optical illusion.

What I don't think I misjudged is the lizard's ability to write.

I would watch its every move, from the time it emerged from behind the clock until it retreated there at the end of the afternoon. In the beginning, its movements appeared to be random, but then the more I watched it, the more I saw a pattern. At some point in its daily journey it would always embark on a route that seemed deliberate, a collection of ascending and descending lefts and rights that I struggled to make sense of until I started imagining them as letters or numbers or—of course!—Chinese characters. I studied the gecko day after day, all the while pretending to be deep in thought about the conversation swirling around me in Mandarin. Since I couldn't write down anything in the moment without seeming rudely disengaged, I had to remember the strokes in increments, then record them one small section at a time when I was able to put pen to paper in our room each night. (It turned out that James's mother was cool with us sleeping together, even without an engagement ring. He'd underestimated her, not for the first or last time.)

Piecing together the gecko's moves over more than a week, I concluded that the pattern revealed to me was this: 宁静. Whatever the heck this was.

"Looks like the symbol for *níng jìng*," James said when I showed him my scribbles. "It means 'serenity.'"

He asked where I'd seen it and why I wanted to know.

"Just something I saw on a wall," I replied. He wouldn't understand. And anyway, this was between me and my little reptilian friend.

I considered what the gecko might be trying to tell me: Perhaps its message was in keeping with its reputation for good fortune. Perhaps it was making the point that, to avoid disaster, you sometimes must accept misfortune. Perhaps acceptance is the only way to neutralize the universe's power. I could certainly buy that logic, given the many crises of faith I'd been through recently.

Still, I thought, what an odd thing for a lizard to say.

CHAPTER 7

Pingtung

Acceptance tends to be narrowly defined when you grow up privileged in America.

You don't even need to be completely self-involved to think it's about things like learning to like your body just the way it is, or coming to grips with other people's shortcomings, or reconciling your many minor failures with your need to be perfect, and perfectly in control. Any of that can seem like enough to sort through in an era of living in the moment, without the benefit of things like viewer-recorded television, when fitting in depends on staying awake to watch all of *Saturday Night Live* over the weekend, so you get what's cracking up your homeroom every Monday morning. Yes, your world is that small. But eventually you need to know that the Serenity Prayer tacked to the wall of your mother's tiny kitchen should be about something more, something subterranean and expansive, something it might take several trips to Taiwan, listening to another woman describe her own path from culpability to contentment, to even begin to recognize and process.

Too many hours spent hanging out on the fringes of conversations I didn't understand in the Pingtung of 1994 was akin to watching films in an unfamiliar language without any subtitles; it made me crave a narrative to grab on to. I think that's why I gave myself over to the lizard so quickly, conjuring an entertaining reason for its daily appearances, despite not being much of a fan of magical realism in any medium. It's probably also why I started asking questions whenever I was around James's mother, Yù Yīng, even if he wasn't there to interpret, leaving me to rely on extended family and neighbors, the youngest of whom always jumped at the chance to practice their English. I was respectful in my querying, but I didn't hide my interest in her story—my notebooks and tape recorders would have outed me anyway—and I always asked permission before recording a conversation. I'm prone to nosiness, which handily passes for professional curiosity when you're a journalist. I suppose I also thought I should get better acquainted with this woman, who might or might not be my someday mother-in-law.

So, I asked. And so, she answered. Which seems so much less remarkable than it is.

I was a stranger. And even though the basic facts of Yù Yīng's life were well known around the village, they weren't the kind of thing most of its residents wanted to talk about. They were relayed to me casually, over multiple visits and years, as unremarkable occurrences. Just about everyone here had a story that involved conflict, struggle, sacrifice, reckoning. Eventually I learned that in her twenties, Yù Yīng, a proud descendant of the Wang family (which I hoped was at least spiritually related to the Wang Lung I knew as protagonist of *The Good Earth*), had fled her native home in the south of China to escape war and political persecution, and in so doing, she'd unknowingly relinquished something precious that could never be fully regained. It was the most common kind of Taiwanese story and yet, like most Americans, I'd never heard anything like it.

Or *seen* anything like it, more specifically, because that's how I heard her words most of the time: as the voice-over of a movie that was playing out in my head. The addiction to cinema that had started in my youth—not just at those multiplex marathon Saturdays but also at home, where our rabbit-eared, tinfoil-topped TV served up everything from must-see classics to beach party blowouts and creature double features—had become my professional responsibility. As an arts editor and sometimes critic at the *L.A. Times*, I was partly getting paid to sit in the dark and consume an abnormal number of movies and shows, which is my personal version of the American Dream. So, it only makes sense that when Yù Yīng began telling me about her teenage years, full of nights working as a "cigarette girl" in her father's open-air casino, where she brushed off every drunken proposition of the men who gambled there, I pictured Anna May Wong in *Piccadilly*. That extraordinary 1929 silent film casts the celebrated Chinese American actress as a dishwasher turned dancer in a London club, where, even in black-and-white, Wong is the kind of gorgeous that burns right through a camera lens, the kind of mesmerizing that seems without effort or end. She demands your full attention, denying any impulse to look away because the movie is trafficking in the same sad stereotypes as so many others in that era's cinematic canon.

Piccadilly was another of the extremely flawed reference points I was still clinging to in 1994, when my latest overdue course correction arrived in the form of Yù Yīng's illuminating responses to my inquiries. She had so much to tell me, all I really had to do was listen—and see.

EXT. OUTDOOR CASINO—EVENING

A small, rural village in the Guangxi region of southern China, late 1930s. The casino, owned by Yù Yīng's father, has several gaming tables surrounded by low chairs and tree stumps, where men sit playing *pai gow*, dice, and other games of chance. Yù Yīng, a young teenager, is wearing a form-fitting silk dress; the cart she pushes for work, loaded with cigarettes and fruit, is perched nearby as she sits with her father at a table in the back. On the table is a stack of books that includes several volumes of Chinese poetry and a weathered copy of *Grimm's Fairy Tales*.

YÙ YĪNG

I will not belong to any of these men, Father.

YÙ YĪNG'S FATHER

Some are not so bad, when sober.

YÙ YĪNG

Your eyes are old.

YÙ YĪNG'S FATHER

Your sight is young.

YÙ YĪNG

Perhaps it's because my father encouraged me to read fairy tales. I want that ever-after happiness.

YÙ YĪNG'S FATHER

(chuckling)

And where do you expect to find that, dear child? This is China. Where there is no struggle, there is no life.

The first men who tried to be Yù Yīng's husband were gangsters.

As she tells it, her father's casino drew a mix of suckers, shysters, and thugs. Most were harmless, more delusional than anything else, because when average people gamble, they dress themselves in hope. It doesn't matter if luck has eluded them their whole lives; today might be the day that everything changes. And when you work in a place such as this, Yù Yīng informs me as she tops off my still-steaming glass of tea, you see that hope rewarded sometimes, but more often you see its folly. A man who is up can always come down; the reverse doesn't typically hold true.

The gangsters didn't care. To them, gambling was about power, not hope. In any casino, they carried weight, even when they lost at the tables—in fact, especially when they lost, because it proved they could afford to, and because it reinforced the business they were in: the look-tough business.

Yù Yīng remembers wearing her best dresses to work at the family casino from about the age of twelve. Her mother made them out of creamy silks that they were able to buy whenever the house won more than the gamblers, which was most of the time. She liked to dress in rich, dark hues that flattered her curves and shimmered in the moonlight like the blue flagstone roads of her modest village in a part of southernmost China, where the Luoqing and Liujiang Rivers divaricated into countless lesser streams still capable of irrigating life in what was then known as Liujiang County.

As a cigarette girl, she sold snacks as well as tobacco. "Pears were the most popular item in my cart," she remembers. "They were round—more like the apples you get in America—and always perfectly crisp and juicy." When someone would order one, Yù Yīng would use a small carving knife to remove its golden skin, beginning at the top, near the stem. Her father had taught her to carefully move the blade in a precise circular pattern so the entire peel—sliced no thicker than a strand of vermicelli—came off every time without breaking, resulting in a delicate coil mounded to resemble a striking cobra. It was a slow, seductive ritual that earned her many customers and liberal tips, along with more than a few marriage proposals.

I gathered that the casino was a dissonant place for a woman of such refined tastes. Yù Yīng recalls dice and *pai gow* tiles in constant motion, bumping up against each other with increasing frequency as the games and players got more aggressive and more liquored up. The stacked and shuffled tiles produced a clickity-clackity concerto that she was grateful for, as it muted the specifics of the men's conversations.

Yù Yīng says she tried not to listen to them talk about her parts—her wide eyes and rosy lips; her flat nose and long ears that strangers likened, admiringly, to sugar pea pods; her still developing breasts. Their jokes were never funny. Some boasted about how they would have her for their wife one day, and that took on a scary immediacy if they were having a good night at the tables. It became about how they might *win* her—possibly with the next bet, or the bet after that. "I tried to just focus on my pears," she recalls, uncomfortably.

Nevertheless, they persisted, because as long as women have been around, men have failed to take a hint.

I thought back to my first job as a waitress, at the mall by the Braintree cinema, where I hustled to deliver hot fries and pies à la mode and never broke stride when an unwelcome remark or look or touch came my way. There were booths to wipe, ketchup bottles to "marry," and nothing we waitresses did or didn't do would discourage the offenders; it would only get us fired. Listening to Yù Yīng recall a similar dance done decades before mine at a much younger age, in a whole other service industry catering to a whole other part of the world, I was struck by how little had changed.

Yù Yīng cut to the chase, as she always seemed to in our conversations: She didn't greenlight any of the gangsters who came on to her as a teenager. In time, however, she would concede to an arranged marriage that wasn't charted in her private fairy tale, and she would make the best of the struggle-filled, happy-enough-ever-after that resulted, in keeping with her father's prophecy. I had neither the words nor the standing to tell her then that I understood her initial instinct to hold out for something more, if not exactly the romantic perfection we both coveted. It also definitely wasn't the right time to disclose her son's marriage proposal, which I'd rejected only weeks before this first microburst of conversations in her living room.

I already knew that I wanted more time with Yù Yīng because I was already intrigued, and intrigue is the journalistic equivalent of dopamine. Most people would say the word *intriguing* is largely positive by definition—"arousing one's curiosity or interest; fascinating"—but in journalism, it's also code for enigmatic, aberrant, inscrutable, hard to crack; in other words, a challenge.

Yù Yīng would be a challenge to get to know. I mean that as a compliment, but I also intend the pejorative. I mean that I anticipated she'd be as frustrating as she was wonderful, as confounding as she was wise. And I mean that because she presented a puzzle, because I couldn't manage her story as adroitly as writers and editors think they ought to be able to do, I had a feeling I would learn as much or more about myself from our interactions as I would learn about her.

❧

The Pingtung that James and I encountered in the spring of 1994 was not at all the same place he'd left behind a decade earlier.

Everywhere we went, he commented on the altered landscape—more development, more pollution, less of the farmland and open spaces that had played host to his childhood adventures. When we weren't entertaining guests in Yù Yīng's home, James and I motored all around his modest hometown on a borrowed, well-used moped. A tour of personal landmarks included the schools he attended and ditched, Buddhist temples that had occasionally coaxed him to pray, and the shipyard where he worked for a time, building sweet wooden fishing boats that had little in common with the mammoth submarines and battleships my dad had helped construct. We took in neglected baseball fields where the kids of his generation had made games out of whatever and whomever was around, using a rock or a coconut for a ball, a bamboo stick as a bat, folded newspapers as gloves. We picnicked in the bamboo groves where he often went to catch snakes ("All gone now," he assured me when I recoiled at their mention. "Too many pots, not enough snakes."), and we visited what was left of traditional neighborhoods where he once walked girls home and ran with juvenile gangs.

"You were in a gang?" I asked, unable to conceal my astonishment.

He pointed to a gaggle of small, circular scars dotting the outside of his right wrist—the ones that I'd never worked up the courage to ask about—and confessed that they were cigarette burns acquired during initiation rituals.

"Not real gangs," he said. "Just kids fooling around, acting cool. You know, stupid stuff."

"Illegal stuff?" I asked. "Did anyone get hurt?"

I could tell he didn't know how to answer. My idea of what constituted harmless delinquent behavior probably was not going to match up with what his culture and circumstance found acceptable. But James is generally incapable of pulling punches.

"Sometimes," he said. "There was fighting and blood. And broken bones. Hardly anyone ever died, though."

I couldn't fathom him instigating a fistfight. It seemed completely at odds with the tolerant, happy-go-lucky man I knew. Plus, he was so little; how did he not get his ass kicked?

"I'm too smart for them," he said. "I pick up a rock and hold it inside my hand. I hit before they expect it. That's how I win."

This James, the one who would add weight to his fist and make a point of striking the first blow, surprised me, but he shouldn't have shocked me. He was actually just one of the new/old personalities that revealed itself during our trip to Taiwan. Another was James the Chauvinist. Or maybe I should say James the Chauvinist Apologist, since he was less of a perpetrator and more of an accessory to the crime.

The offenses were many, but the one that rattled me most happened on a quiet weeknight just after dinner, when James and his brothers were sitting around, picking their teeth and watching television. One brother was telling a story that had the attention of the room. His toddler son walked past with a cookie, part of which broke off and dropped on the floor. Instead of picking it up himself, the dad continued telling his story while vigorously snapping his fingers and pointing to the fallen dessert. I looked to my left, where the snaps were being directed, and saw his wife swooping in from the kitchen. It wasn't bad enough that she'd been summoned and directed like a border collie; now her husband also saw an opportunity to add to the evening's entertainment. As she bent low to pick up the cookie bits, he cocked his shin and (carefully, it must be said) launched an abbreviated kick that just missed her backside with the ball of his bare foot. Then he laughed as she felt the leg pull up short and swatted it away without flinching.

The whole room laughed, actually. Even the wife laughed, albeit with an exasperated shake of her head. I did not laugh. I just looked over at James, who looked back at me uncomfortably but said nothing.

We talked about it later, of course. He said that he understood how it looked, and why it bothered me. He didn't try to defend it, but he also had no intention of challenging it. I might have judged that cowardly, except for what happened a few days later, when I had to make my own decision about whether to protest the status quo.

James came into our bedroom after breakfast. He had something to tell me, and he was clearly nervous about it.

"We're going to the cemetery today," he said. "My father's cemetery."

I knew that James had lost his forty-eight-year-old dad in 1971. I'd been told that the cause was a stroke. James was just twelve at the time, so his memory of the man was limited, but his reverence was undiminished.

"Okay," I responded. "Are we going now?"

"Yes. Now," he said. "I'm going, with my brothers." Long pause. "You can't come. I'm sorry."

"Oh, I see." Another pause. "You mean, I'm not allowed?"

"Right."

"Can I ask why? Is it only for family?"

"Not exactly."

"Is it because I'm a woman?"

"Kind of. It's just a thing here, with my brothers. I can't explain it."

"That's fine," I said, "but you mean to tell me your mother has never been to your father's grave?"

"Right."

"What?"

"She hasn't been there. She didn't even go to the funeral."

"Wow. Seriously? That's harsh."

"I know it seems that way. I'm really sorry."

"No, don't be sorry. It's not your fault. And I don't actually care, for myself. I guess I'm just offended on her behalf. It seems . . . ridiculous, and kind of sad."

"I know. I could tell you they were only trying to protect her, from the sad things—after so much hard times, she deserves to be protected—but that doesn't make it better. I can't explain; it's just the way it is in my family. She's never been to the cemetery, so you can't go, too."

I was curious about the scope and definition of those hard times, beyond losing her husband at such a young age, but that seemed like a topic for another day.

James left the room.

I shook my head and let the exasperated air escape through my lips. I reminded myself that this wasn't my culture; I shouldn't pass judgment. Still . . . A group of overprotective men deciding that a grown woman shouldn't be allowed to visit her husband's grave? Every molecule in my body objected.

Five minutes later, James was back.

"Never mind. Let's go," he said.

"Where are we going?"

"To the cemetery."

"I don't get it."

"My brothers want you to come."

"I thought you said I wasn't allowed."

"They said it's okay."

"Um. Okay . . . Is your mother going?"

"No."

"But I can go?"

"Yes."

"Because I'm not Chinese. Is that it?"

"Yeah."

Now I was *really* offended.

What do I do here, I thought? My mind raced through a list of possible responses.

Option 1: Tell them I'm not going? Make an all-or-nothing stand on behalf of his mother and unnecessarily coddled women everywhere? Would the decision-makers care? Would they even get it?

Option 2: Make an excuse to get *out* of going? But what would that accomplish, other than embarrassing James, who would then have to keep up the lie that they'd undoubtedly see through immediately?

Option 3: Go. Because at least it's a small evolutionary step in their sexism, and the reporter in me really does want to see this "forbidden" place?

I was torn, but I was too jet-lagged and intrigued to be militant.

Oh, hell, I thought. *Just go.*

When his father died, James wore a black armband and stayed home from school for forty-nine days. Also, he wasn't allowed to cut his hair. They didn't always follow Buddhist traditions in his semi-Christian family, which left room for incorporating the traditions of other faiths as desired, but this time they took no chances. If observing a few rituals meant that your loved one might have a better eternity, that's what you did. So, a week after expiring, his father was buried in a heavy wooden casket made in the traditional style, with three humps on the lid for good luck. It took twenty men to carry the coffin from the hospital, where he died, to the cemetery, a couple of miles away.

James described the funeral scene to me as we rode to the cemetery with his three brothers. I don't know why I'd never asked about it before, other than that whenever we'd talked about his dad it was clear that the memories were more respectful than fond. His father was a career soldier who'd been a strict disciplinarian at home, routinely issuing beatings with a vine dried stiff enough to be woven into a chair. The one time that James could remember connecting with him on a more positive and intimate level was in 1969, when Taiwan was vying for its first Little League World Series championship in Williamsport, Pennsylvania, and his dad woke him up in the middle of the night to watch the final game on a small black-and-white television that drew dozens of neighbors to his living room. I'd probably watched that momentous Taiwanese victory with my own father, never imagining I'd someday meet a man who regarded it as one of his greatest days.

When we arrived at the cemetery, after about thirty minutes of driving, I was fully fixated on James's ancestry. All my indignation had left me. I just felt grateful for the opportunity to glimpse another part of his past.

We were in the countryside, in an area with few structures, where most of the acreage was given to grass and trees and crops and dirt paths. We parked at the edge of someone's farmland and walked through the fields until we arrived at a patch of hillside that was dotted with bumps in the earth—similar to a ski run of moguls, except they weren't covered in snow and they had cement bunkers built into them. The bunkers were tombs. Each had a little archway with a stone tablet for a door. There were Chinese characters written on the tablets and sometimes on the archways as well. A few displayed pictures of the deceased.

Visiting your ancestors is no passive task in Asia. You're expected to do things. As we approached the family gravesite and the brothers began unloading bag after bag that they'd schlepped all the way from the car in the hot sun, I understood what was ahead. The first order of business was to sweep.

With brooms made of bundled twigs, they cleared the dirt and brush that had collected in front of their father's tomb. Then they set out the food they'd brought to honor him and nourish his spirit in the afterlife—steamed chicken, seasonal fruits, bowls of rice, brewed tea. They lit candles and burned little piles of joss paper. They waved bunches of incense, the smoke swirling around their heads as they each bowed three times and kneeled in prayer. I stayed silent and off to the side, fascinated.

When it seemed okay to speak, I asked James to translate what was inscribed on his father's tomb.

"Well, the right side is east, so that's where they put the date and time and place of birth," James explained. "It says my father was born in Guilin, China, on October 10, 1922, at 2 P.M."

"East is for birth because the sun rises in the east?" I asked.

"Maybe. I think so. It would make sense, since this section on the left (west) has the date and time of death: February 2, 1971, at 4 P.M."

"And in the center?"

"Well, over the top here, on the arch, it says what province or region he was born in. That's Guangxi."

"I see. So, Guilin is in Guangxi?"

"Right."

"And this main panel is like the headstone? It has the largest writing, so I assume it's supposed to be read first."

"Right. That's where they put the name, in the center."

"Family name first?"

"Yes. This part says Tseng—same like Zeng [the way it would be spelled in China]—and next to it is my father's given name," James said, running his fingers over the characters carved deep into the slab of cement: 曾桥生.

"Qiáo, like 'bridge.' And Shēng, like 'born,' or . . . 'life.' Tsēng Qiáo Shēng," he said, stringing together the full name as it would have been pronounced in his father's homeland. (I heard it as *tzen-chow-shuhng.*)

He stopped there, but I wanted to know what else was written on the stone.

"What do these other characters mean?" I asked James, pointing to a section of text beside what he'd just read.

"More names," he said. "Other family members."

"His parents?"

"More like his legacy."

"Oh. You mean his wife and children?" I wondered.

"Well, his sons," James answered. "And his grandsons."

I must have looked quizzical.

"What?" James asked me, getting ahead of what was bound to come anyway.

"So . . . not your mother," I said. "Or your sister, or your nieces. Only the male members of his family."

"Right," James confirmed, looking away—maybe hoping for a freak monsoon to swoop in and end this latest interrogation.

But I was done.

Though this wasn't an official *L.A. Times* reporting assignment, it registered as a moment to step back and question my objectivity. I may have moved to California under the influence of silly sitcom stars, but my heroes once I got there were real people in humble service to the stories of other real people. In the words of my longtime friend and former editor Marty Baron (Liev Schreiber played him in the Oscar-winning *Spotlight*), the moral core of journalism begins with valuing the truth and giving voice to the voiceless. It also demands that we "avoid self-appointment as moral authorities."

It wasn't right of me to expect answers from James that came imbued with sufficient outrage to satisfy my naïve Western agenda. As always, the truth should speak for itself.

And if Yù Yīng had no official place here, in this tabernacle of intransigent thinking and partisan power structures, I knew that there were other arenas in which she could—and should—have a voice.

CHAPTER 8

The Bump

No matter where or how many years you've lived, the day you realize that most of our world is run by men is the day you start strategizing on a global level. If you're male, you're looking to get ahead. If you're not male, you need a strategy just to not get run over.

For some women, even those inclined toward tacit upholding of the status quo, there are opportunities to rock the boat from the inside, the way my mom did when she hijacked a regular old weekend in 1966 and turned it into a monumental mother-daughter day on the lam. Yù Yīng's refusal to yield to the most aggressive and possessive gamblers in her family's casino told me she was probably cut from the same cloth as Yolanda DiMartinis Page, never mind that one wore handstitched silks in her youth while the other was raised on store-bought cotton.

If you ask James to tell you a story about his mother, he'll quickly dial up a memory from when he was a teenager, still trying on his coolest self and running with two-bit neighborhood gangs. The story he tells is vivid, even though he wasn't there to witness it unfold.

"My mother was at one of the street markets in our village," he begins. "She was probably picking out vegetables—you know, checking how fresh, talking price—when a neighbor—he lives across the street—comes up to her.

"He starts waving his hands in her face and talking very loud—shouting, I think: 'Your son should not date my daughter!' 'He's no good!' 'He's so terrible!' This kind of things.

"My mother, who knows this man and his family for many years, from when we were children and my father was alive, does not even look at him. She buys the vegetables. Then she turns around and moves very close to his face. 'You think who you are?' she says to him. "You think my son is not good enough? My son is handsome. My son is kind. Your daughter is ugly, but we don't say anything. Your daughter comes to my house to be with my son; we welcome her and share our rice. She feels so lucky. You should feel lucky, too.'"

"What did the man say?" I wonder aloud.

"Nothing. He just looks scared, and walks away," James answers.

"Did the man forbid his daughter from seeing you?"

"No. But a few months later I got another girlfriend. And then I went to the army. So, we forgot about this guy, pretty much."

"Your mother told you this?"

"Yes. She told me when she came home from the market that day."

"And how did it make you feel?" I ask. "Were you embarrassed? Proud? Both?"

"Just proud," he says. And I nod, because it's not hard to draw a line between that story and the type of woman he seems unembarrassed to prefer: the sharp-tongued, independent-minded, fierce and fiercely loyal "softer sex" that other men might deem a lot to handle.

Girls sometimes marry their fathers. Boys sometimes marry their moms. Did this mean, if I ever did take James up on his proposal, we were destined to be Jocko and Yù Yīng? It sounded like a bad idea for a sitcom, let alone a fruitful union, but it made me curious to hear more of her story. Most immediately I wanted to dig into the details of how a girl growing up in rural China in the early 1900s finds the courage to challenge the patriarchy, even in small, impermanent ways. But Yù Yīng looked confused when I asked her for examples of how she'd stood up for herself as a child.

"Every day," she answered, flatly.

Oh, right, I reminded myself. *It's all a struggle.*

As we continued to talk, though, specifics emerged. This time, we were gathered for lunch in the urban Kaohsiung apartment of James's second eldest brother, Cháo Fēng (潮豐, pronounced *chow-fung*, which for me always comes out sounding like the familiar Cantonese rice noodle, chow fun), about midway through my three-week introduction to the family in 1994. While Cháo Fēng's yappy white shih tzu ran in circles around anything and anyone with legs, Yù Yīng somehow shut out the incessant barking and summoned a flood of youthful memories. She recalled how her parents had initially rejected her pleas for a formal education, because girls had other skills to master and anyway what did she need to know that couldn't be gleaned from the piles of books her father had accumulated when unwise scholars gambled more than they had in cash?

Pushback? At nine years old, Yù Yīng took it all the way to a hunger strike, refusing to eat or drink for three days before her parents caved and enrolled her in one of Liujiang County's best private schools. When I asked her why those classes mattered so much, she said it was because they represented expansion rather than contraction, doors opening instead of closing. I let her know that I was impressed by her shrewd assessment, and by the resolve she'd shown at such a young age. That's probably why she told me next about the bully.

In a cavernous classroom that had once been a temple, where carvings of gods and mythical beasts stared out from the rafters like sentinels sent from heaven to help keep young souls in line, Yù Yīng's early twentieth-century education came infused with the aromas of incense and faith. She learned to write with a brush, on paper made of grass or rice, at long wooden tables that served as communal desks. Girls sat with girls, boys sat with boys, on different sides of the room; the two never mixed or even spoke to each other without permission.

"She was already a bully when I arrived," Yù Yīng remembers. "Her name was Zhāng."

The way Yù Yīng tells it, Zhāng (张, pronounced *zhahng*)—always allotted just the one name in these recollections—targeted her on that first day in 1933 because it was immediately clear that Yù Yīng wasn't easily scared and wouldn't be likely to surrender her lunch or any pocket change to this bigger-than-most girl who was shaking down half the class. It took a few months, but eventually Zhāng made the move she'd long been plotting: She told their teacher that Yù Yīng was the one who'd been extorting money and food from their classmates, as well as stealing their textbooks, and that a quick check of the thief's personal belongings would prove her allegations justified.

In class the next day, the teacher called Yù Yīng to the front, and when he examined her satchel, it contained the calligraphy book of a student named Hé (何, like *huh*). Zhāng had made the switch during morning calisthenics. She'd also given up some of the twenty yuan she'd collected from each student's breakfast money to make it look as though Yù Yīng had a pile of cash that could only have come from a covert exaction.

"Hold out your hand," the teacher demanded, making no room for a syllable of defense. Yù Yīng complied, choosing the left to preserve her use of the right.

Thwackkk!

His bamboo rod cracked down on her knuckles.

Thwackkk!

No weapon had ever seemed as loud, or as contemptuous.

Thwackkk!

At least three more times he repeated it. The skin split and bled. Then he instructed her to turn her hand over, and he went to work on her palm.

We all have our ways of coping with pain. Yù Yīng's was to pretend that this was nothing more than a manufactured melodrama happening between the covers of a book. "None of it felt real to me," she explained, casting herself as a character in a fictional scene. The rod was not actually tearing at her flesh, so it demanded no tears in response. "I could create that distance, and it would allow me to withstand."

Of course, another useful thing about distance is that it lets you observe.

During some of the most trying moments of my life, I've felt a clarity that can only come with stepping outside of yourself, looking down on your circumstance as though you're a filmmaker evaluating a boom shot. You notice things that weren't in your field of vision previously. Assumptions get recalibrated.

Hearing that Yù Yīng shared this coping mechanism made me curious about all the other places where our worldviews might intersect—all the things we might have in common beyond our shared love for James. I hadn't expected us to bond over a penchant for detachment, but it made sense. Across cultures, oceans, and generations, we were just two of the millions of women who'd conceived what they needed to survive.

While Yù Yīng absorbed her punishment, most of her classmates struggled to process the surprising fall of someone they saw as a model student. Their mouths hung open like the hinges of a lion dancer's mask; their eyes expressed fear and concern. But there was some smugness in the room as well; Yù Yīng could feel it. And she knew instantly, even before she caught Zhāng smiling just a little from the back of the class, what had happened.

She decided that she wouldn't get upset. Not in public. Not that day, anyway. She'd let the bully have her moment of false triumph. Then, when it suited her and the perfect opportunity presented itself, Yù Yīng would simply get even.

❧

I'm a big fan of revenge fantasies.

This might have started as a takeaway from my mother's elaborate plot to have the last word with my father on my greatest day, but it hit a whole other gear when I was exposed to literature and films (and literature turned into films, seldom for the better) that gave my id permission to wander. The list is all over the place: *Carrie*, *The Princess Bride*, *Hamlet*, *The Count of Monte Cristo*, *9 to 5*, *Thelma & Louise*, *Lady Snowblood*, *Fried Green Tomatoes* . . . I remained a squeamish kid nestled inside a squeamish adult, but I loved imagining all manner of not-too-gory comeuppances because they reinforced a fundamental belief that the world could be made to be fair. Not always, but sometimes.

When Yù Yīng began telling me about her encounter with the bully and about how she plotted to get even, I listened without embellishing. It was only later, when I sat down with the full transcription of that interview, that I started embroidering—not to co-opt her experience but to share in it, letting it be the creative inspiration for yet another movie shooting only in my head. This one began with her explaining how she'd come up with a plan, step one of which was befriending the bully. "Does anyone really think the Italians invented 'keep your friends close, and your enemies closer?'" she would ask rhetorically, in voice-over. "Whether or not Sun Tzu said it before Machiavelli, I guarantee you the Chinese thought of it first."

Then, she would lay out the rest of her plot: how she'd offered Zhāng an olive branch in the form of drawing lessons, because she'd gotten close enough to observe her nemesis doodling things in the margins of books that weren't hers to deface. "My kindness caught Zhāng off-guard," she would say, "which was the only way it could have seemed genuine."

Even imaginary screenplays should adhere to Chekhov's Law, whichever translation of it you prefer: *One must never place a loaded rifle on the stage if no one is thinking of firing it.* Among the stack of books in Yù Yīng's father's casino, noted back when she'd first told me about fending off handsy gamblers and their propositions, was a volume of *Grimms' Fairy Tales.* It was a detail that informed how I thought of Yù Yīng and Zhāng spending their afternoons together, on the fringes of a nearby meadow, illustrating the blackbirds that nested in trees. Yù Yīng would confide in her new friend that she'd always regarded these creatures as beautiful and intelligent looking, despite or maybe because of their sinister quality. "Most people think of them as bad luck," she'd say. "To me, though, they seem like warriors—menacing, but you want them on your side."

Eventually, it would become clear that Yù Yīng only said that because her plan for the bully depended on those blackbirds, along with a full bag of rice. But first, we'd have to understand about the trees.

When you're engaging in mental moviemaking, you can go down as many rabbit holes as you like. You can start researching the Liujiang County landscape (once you realize it's a name eclipsed by history in Guangxi Province, having been redrawn and demoted to a district after a 1950s merger formed the county of Luzhai) and find yourself thrilled to discover that pine was prevalent in the hills and mountains of Yù Yīng's native region. You're thrilled because where there are pine trees there is rosin, and you're pretty sure the sticky liquid is used in everything from construction of homes to the making of musical instruments, even in this part of the world. If rosin could be easily found in Yù Yīng's village, it's reasonable to assume that it wouldn't be such a big deal if a little of it were to go missing. That's convenient for where your revenge fantasy is headed.

Now you need some form of poison. Preferably one that's even easier to procure. Belladonna, while not native to Yù Yīng's region of China, has long been cultivated for its medicinal properties and usefulness, sometimes combined with opium, as a general anesthetic. If there's one thing a girl learns, growing up in the country, it's how to forage. So, Yù Yīng would have known where to find *Atropa belladonna*, because it's credible that her well-read father would have pointed it out while they were walking through a forest, perhaps to impart a lesson in Greek mythology along with an important bit of botany.

(One could argue for animating this portion of the exposition, to make it more entertaining. *Atropa belladonna*, a leafy green plant with shiny black berries, is named after Atropos, one of the three Greek fates who wove the threads of life and death. Atropos was the one who cut the threads, extinguishing life, and this plant was capable of doing the same. Yù Yīng's father would have imparted that warning to his daughter. But he also would have noted that, if one could control its poisons, the result of ingesting belladonna might only be temporary paralysis and loss of consciousness, which had proved useful in both surgery and tactical warfare. The key, he'd have added, was to show reverence and care in handling the plant.)

And then there's the matter of procuring enough rice, by far the hardest element of the dastardly plan I was constructing on behalf of Yù Yīng.

I knew from *The Good Earth*, as well as from Yù Yīng's stories, that average families in this era valued rice the way misers value gold, whether the hallowed starch was intended for eating or for planting. If she didn't want to get caught or cause anyone to starve, Yù Yīng would have to take the rice little by little from every kitchen she was invited into, siphoning a few grains at a time until she'd collected a bag the size of a fat baby. If she could do all of that—and in my imagining, it was completely possible—all she'd need to do next was lure Zhāng to the exact spot she'd picked out for them to come to rest in that meadow, to draw the birds.

EXT. GRASSY VALLEY—AFTERNOON

Liujiang County, China, 1933. Yù Yīng and Zhāng approach from different directions and meet in a meadow surrounded by rocky outcroppings known as karst hills, famously rendered in the landscapes of so many Chinese artworks. When their paths intersect, the two girls stop and talk.

ZHĀNG

Did you bring the brushes?

YÙ YĪNG

Of course. And the ink. I also brought a few dumplings leftover from lunch. My mother must have lost count this morning.

ZHĀNG

I ate too many lunches already today, at school. But I do love your mother's dumplings.

YÙ YĪNG

(hooking her arm inside Zhāng's as they walk)

Let's sit over there, by the trees. Your appetite will be better in the shade.

ZHĀNG

And there are more birds there.

YÙ YĪNG

Yes (looking pleased). There are.

YÙ YĪNG

(voice-over)

I think that many of you will be ahead of me now. You will have guessed that the dumplings were laced with the belladonna. Not too much; just enough to render her unconscious. And yes, I applied the rosin all over—on clothing and bare skin alike—once she was knocked out and prostrate in the grass. I had hidden a full bucket of the stuff under a bush, along with the bag of rice; now, all I needed to do was layer the grain generously over the rosin until her body was so completely covered that she looked like a crispy rice cake.

(beat)

I will admit that I did contemplate sparing her face—the eyes, if nothing else. But I hate revisionist fairy tales, and Zhāng was as evil as any conniving stepsister. I reminded myself of her victims and her lack of remorse. It pushed me to continue.

YÙ YĪNG

(disgusted, as she coats Zhāng's body in rosin and rice)

She said she ate too many lunches today. *Too many lunches!*

YÙ YĪNG

(resuming voice-over)

I kept working until the rice ran out. Then, I packed up whatever looked like evidence, moved off to the other side of the meadow, and waited for the birds to do their part.

That's the type of revenge story I hoped to hear from Yù Yīng when she first introduced the idea of a school bully, the one I wanted her to tell me because I was programmed to anticipate a shocking, dramatically crescendoed denouement in a tale where the protagonist—a woman who'd devoured all her father's books, but most voraciously the Brothers Grimm volume that contained *Cinderella*—has a score to settle with an unrepentant ogre. I wanted her to regale me with something powerful, complex, and unsettling; the more outrageous, the better.

But Yù Yīng didn't think in screenplays. That was me.

Her revenge story—the real one, not the one I concocted in my fertile counternarrative—was considerably less theatrical and far more believable, if still plenty unsettling in its own way. It was also no less satisfying to the woman who lived it.

Finishing the last bites of her lunch in Cháo Fēng's apartment, still oblivious to the small, shrill canine circling our feet, Yù Yīng told me the simple truth. Several weeks after she was reprimanded in the classroom, when the cuts on her hands had healed into mostly emotional scars, she led an ambush of Zhāng along a secluded path that many students used to get home from school. With their classmates gathered round, Yù Yīng accused Zhāng of lying to the teacher about who'd been extorting lunch money and stealing textbooks.

"I gave her a chance to apologize and pledge to change her ways," Yù Yīng recalled. Zhāng refused. "So, we beat her until the blood ran out of her nose and mouth."

Yù Yīng offered no additional details and expressed no regret for the pummeling. She couldn't condone her use of the same violent tactics as her nemesis, but she could admit that she felt proud when all her schoolmates, save the extortionist herself, said that she was heroic and brave. Zhāng had been stripped of her power, and she never dared attempt to reclaim it.

"People in my village still talk about the day we stood up to the bully," Yù Yīng concluded. "That was a great day."

❧

Much like *intriguing*, the word *great* is open to interpretation.

My greatest day back in 1966 wasn't rooted in the kind of violence that had enabled Yù Yīng's triumph over her dishonorable classmate, though it did involve retribution, at least for my parents. Also, Yù Yīng and I had both benefited from someone else's misery: The loser in her story was clearly Zhāng, while my win came less overtly at the expense of a fearful father humbled by temporary powerlessness and a seemingly free-spirited mother masking a mental health crisis. Even if our definitions of *great* appeared very different, the joy I carried forth from my greatest day wasn't any purer or more legitimate than Yù Yīng's. And the same goes for our definitions of "winning."

In many of our talks, Yù Yīng expressed a notion of victory that didn't seem bothered by compromises and didn't always actually seem like triumph, at least to her naïve American interviewer. For example, how does a young woman who stands up to gangsters and bullies submit to an arranged marriage in the end—and how is that a win? Ever since my visit to the cemetery with James and his brothers, I'd wanted to know more about their dad, Qiáo Shēng, the man Yù Yīng had followed out of China to land in this place. I wanted to know what she'd thought he offered her that other suitors didn't, whether and how they'd been deemed a promising match, if she'd been in love. Which is why I started down that path one afternoon, a few days before the end of my first visit to Pingtung.

INT. YÙ YĪNG'S LIVING ROOM—MIDDAY

Yù Yīng, 70, is dressed in everyday pants and a short-sleeved blouse, matching the home's prosaic decor. She sits straight-backed but not stiff, her thighs pinched together perfunctorily at a slight angle, her hands stacked comfortably at the place where her knees meet. She looks like someone who's been trained to "sit like a lady" but long ago decided how to interpret and sustain that posture. On a small table nearby, dried watermelon seeds, foil-wrapped candies, and the obligatory steaming cups of tea are laid out to sustain her guests.

JANICE

Tell me about your marriage. How did you meet your husband? Because I've been told that a matchmaker was involved, and that surprises me.

JAMES

(in Mandarin, interpreting Janice's question for his mother)

She's surprised about the matchmaker.

YÙ YĪNG

(in Mandarin, to James)

Why?

JAMES

(in Mandarin)

She just wants to know about how you met.

YÙ YĪNG

(in Mandarin)

No, why is she surprised?

JAMES

(in Mandarin)

Oh. I think it's because you told her about refusing to marry the gangsters. In the casino.

JANICE

(to James)

What is she saying?

JAMES

(to Janice)

Hang on.

YÙ YĪNG

(in Mandarin)

Does she *know* any matchmakers?

JAMES

(to Janice)

Do you know any matchmakers?

JANICE

I don't think so? I mean, not that I'm aware of. Oh, wait; there was a woman I met at this party one time, in L.A. She was some kind of psychic-slash-matchmaker. She told me I had a fiery aura that was giving her not-ready-to-be-in-a-committed-relationship vibes. She also looked at my palm and said one of the lines indicated that I should be careful, because otherwise I might end up pregnant when I didn't want to be.

(pause)

Also—now I remember—she was super adamant that I shouldn't have more than two children. She said that if I did have two children, I should have my tubes tied immediately. She said it like, multiple times. I have no idea why. It was wild.

JAMES

(unfazed, to his mom in Mandarin)

No.

YÙ YĪNG

(in Mandarin)

Tell her I will explain. But she really should know some matchmakers.

JAMES

(to Janice)

She's going to tell you the story.

In romantic comedies, which I happen to adore, there's a well-known, near-essential device called the meet-cute. It's the scene where potential lovebirds have their first encounter, often awkward, always life-altering. I find that meet-cutes aren't exclusive to romance, but they do always have that unexpected, written-in-the-stars quality that forever bathes them in the most magical light.

My meet-cutes have unfolded in the typical places: classrooms, offices, restaurants, Europe. Yù Yīng's one meet-cute seems to have happened right outside her front door, during a moment in her youth when everything seemed orderly, until a mysterious boy came along and gave their tidy world a shove.

It was just after dinner on one of those sticky summer days when sensible people find a reason to stay inside until sundown. Except for the destitute, the streets of Yù Yīng's village were nearly empty. But she and her friends didn't care about the heat. She was thirteen; the hours after dinner were about playing and hanging out, and fewer people meant the chance to socialize without the scrutiny of an entire town.

On this undistinctive evening, she was standing in front of her house—a three-story dwelling made of timber and stone—chatting with a schoolmate she called Ā Mèi (阿妹, pronounced *ah-may*, meaning "little sister"), a common term of endearment among besties. Yù Yīng didn't have a lot of friends; she'd singled out this girl because she found in her the compassion and open-mindedness that was so often lacking in others their age. Ā Mèi was Muslim, which already made her an outlier, and she had bound feet, many years after that practice had stopped being fashionable in this part of the world.

Imagine thinking it stylish to curl a child's toes until the bones break and the flesh stretches to wrap under the arch, eventually contracting and melding into bowed, half-moon nubs that barely support the weight of her body. The practice was barbaric when it began, somewhere around the tenth century, and no less barbaric when it finally fell out of favor, for the most part, in the early 1900s.

Ā Mèi was in constant pain, her blackened, swollen limbs throbbing so intensely that she begged Yù Yīng to loosen the bandages before the start of every school day. Yù Yīng would then rewrap them in the afternoons, before their slow shuffle home.

"The smell was awful," Yù Yīng told me, repeating her foul assessment—"*chòu, chòu, chòu . . .*" (臭臭臭)—as she fanned the air beneath her wrinkled nose. Ā Mèi's toes were dead, along with a significant chunk of her self-esteem. She couldn't dance or run like the other children; it was an effort just to move. And so, she got fat, which made her the target of additional jokes and taunts. The capstone indignity came every evening when Ā Mèi had to wash and care for the mummified hooves of her grandmother, whose own toes were long ago bound tight enough for her feet to squeeze into three-inch lotus shoes. It was a ghastly reminder of the repulsive, unavoidable endpoint to all this wrapping.

Yù Yīng felt sorry for Ā Mèi, but that wasn't why they were friends. Ā Mèi was gifted. She saw people fully and intelligibly, including the things they kept hidden, even from themselves. She had great instincts about character and personality. It made her a keen observer of relationships, which brought depth to the gossip that so often passes the time in small towns. Ā Mèi was insightful. Yù Yīng didn't find that quality in any of her other classmates, or really at all, outside of her books.

The two girls were standing in the deserted street, probably chatting about nothing of consequence, when Yù Yīng spotted a boy she didn't recognize—roughly her age, maybe a year or two older—walking toward them on the opposite side of the road. He was handsome—not that she allowed her gaze to linger.

He crossed the street.

Yù Yīng turned her back to him, pretending to give her full attention to her friend. The unknown boy was directly behind her now—she didn't know how far, but she could feel his oncoming presence over the next minute or two as she conversed and waited for him to pass. Perhaps another glimpse, closer up, would provide some clarity. She was merely curious, she told herself; who was this stranger, and what business did he have being in her neighborhood?

Suddenly, she felt a bump. It was little more than the brush of two shoulders, and yet it was an earthquake. In the China of Yù Yīng's childhood, girls and boys who were not siblings did not engage in physical contact. The boy who bumped into Yù Yīng could not have done so accidentally because that kind of accident simply didn't happen here.

"I was so surprised," Yù Yīng admitted when she described the moment to me, decades later. "I thought to myself, 'There was enough room for you to walk. Why touch me?' Isn't it funny? How innocent I was."

The boy certainly thought it was funny. Yù Yīng noted that he turned his head, just a little, to reveal a sly smile as he proceeded toward the West Gate, where brides would always pass as they left the village for distant lives with husbands they'd probably never met.

Then he was gone, and life in her slice of Liujiang didn't pause for a girl to contemplate the motives or significance of a careless, unknown boy passing through town on his way to who knows where.

Yù Yīng had stopped talking and seemed done for the day.

I looked at James. "Is that it?" I asked. "Is she saying that the boy was Qiáo Shēng?"

He shrugged.

"And what about the matchmaker? Is that Ā Mèi?" I continued. "Does Ā Mèi somehow arrange their marriage? And is Yù Yīng in on the plan? Is that why she agreed?"

He shrugged again.

"I don't know this story," he said. "My mother is tired. She needs to rest now. Maybe we can talk more later."

"Okay. Of course," I said. "I don't want to push her."

"Right."

"But I'm curious, even if you don't know the story: Do you think this boy was your father? Why would he do that—go out of his way to bump into her, in broad daylight, and then just keep on walking?"

James just looked at me and, once again, lifted his shoulders into a shrug and answered my question with a question of his own.

"You ask me, who I gonna ask?"

CHAPTER 9

THE CHEESE TRAIL

My first trip to Taiwan with James had been many things, but it was one thing above all else: exhausting.

It seemed like I'd been everywhere, met everyone, and eaten everything that might be important to developing a deeper understanding of this man who'd already been in my life for nearly a decade, and who might still be carrying around the ring that campaigned to make it a lifetime. Because I had no idea whether the diamond that was last seen in my Long Beach bedroom had been returned to its point of purchase, I had to assume that it could pop out again at any moment, whether we happened to be in a public place or in flagrante delicto.

There's nothing more tiring than feeling constantly off-balance.

I'd seen a side of James in Taiwan that I wasn't so in love with—the one who pretended not to notice things, even though he knew that I knew: He sees *everything*. I wasn't sure how to reconcile this foreign, seemingly apathetic James with the highly principled man I'd boarded a plane with three weeks ago in America. That's what made it so remarkable when, just as our return flight lifted off the tarmac at Kaohsiung International Airport, my traveling companion leaned over and extended his right arm in a formal handshake.

"Hi. My name is James," he said. "Nice to meeting you."

His smile was wide and winking.

I smiled back, relieved, delighted, completely disarmed.

"Well, hello, stranger," I said. "Where've you been?"

The handshake evolved into a full mea culpa. With his left hand layered over the top of mine, he leaned in and murmured contritely, "What can I say? It's my country. I can't explain what happens to me here. I'm sorry."

"I know you are," I said. "Thank you for that."

"Of course," he replied.

Context is such an important ingredient in romantic relationships. Now that I'd seen where James was from, I had a more complete log list of his dualities—he didn't just speak in multiple languages; he straddled multiple worlds. They tugged at him, sometimes simultaneously, demanding full fealty and mindfulness. Also, now that I'd met his family, it would be impossible not to see and hear his mother when he would shake his head, accompanied by a self-admonishing *"tch-tch-tch,"* or mutter *"Āi yā!"* (哎呀, the all-purpose verbal exclamation point for errors and exasperations) as he exhaled. Each time I'd seen and heard Yù Yīng speak, it amplified her connection to James. They shared a way of communicating that was at once straightforward and layered, deeply seductive and artfully, maddeningly simplistic. Like James, Yù Yīng talked in sentences that frequently did not match her expression; the more heightened her reminiscences got, the more her face seemed to flatten.

James does this thing with his mouth after making certain points: He smashes his lips together in a visual grunt, like a toddler clearing his bowels. Then he dips his chin quickly, completing a silent tagline that says "Fact."

"What can I say? It's my country. I can't explain what happens to me here," he'd just said, deploying his signature move to underscore the sincerity of his apology. And now I knew where he'd learned that move, because I'd seen Yù Yīng do it, too.

We'd been in Taiwan for the better part of a month. I'd had time to question and absorb, if not nearly enough time to compile a satisfactory sketch of her life. In fact, she'd left me hanging at the point where her thirteen-year-old self had just been knocked off balance by a strange boy passing through her neighborhood. Part of me wondered if that was intentional for James—if he'd purposefully filled the rest of our time in Pingtung with so many group dinners and family obligations that if I wanted to hear the rest of his mother's story, he'd have to facilitate those conversations over time. Maybe over a lifetime. The diamond ring from my bedroom was probably still out there, lurking, after all.

Anyway, my interest in hearing whatever Yù Yīng wanted to tell me was always transparent, given that I'd started recording our conversations almost immediately. Slim reporter's notebooks and wonky tape recorders followed me everywhere in the 1990s. It was clear even before I met Yù Yīng, just from the bits of family history James had shared, that her life had the conflict and heft to become a powerful written narrative. Once we started talking, it was also clear that she would only be able to provide the basic plot points of that life; I would need to engineer and implant what journalists call the "connective tissue." By the end of my first visit to Taiwan, I knew about her casino days, her hunger strike to demand an education, the bully, the boy, the bump, and so much more. I didn't know how much those stories would fill in and change over the decades to come, by her hand and by mine, but I understood their value even as seedlings.

Something else I realized, maybe as I was sitting on that plane just getting airborne, was how much Yù Yīng had already challenged and brought out in me, including the most obvious of things: patience. I would need a lot of it, as would James, if our multicultural relationship were to go the distance. Like his mother, he could be hard for me to understand—literally, of course, but beyond that, confusing and confounding and all the other things they'd be right to say about me, too.

"You're an interesting guy, Mr. Bond," I said when we'd reached cruising altitude. "Something tells me there are many more layers to be revealed."

James nodded, even if he didn't have a clue what that meant.

"But, just to be clear," I added so sweetly that I might have actually batted my eyelashes, "if you ever snap your fingers at me, unless it's during a tango lesson . . ."

"I know," he said. Neither of us needed to complete the thought. We both understood that if James were to disrespect any woman the way his brother had in my company, no one would be laughing it off. In relationship terms, to borrow a line from *The Alamo*'s Davy Crockett, he'd be "dead as a beaver hat."

Thank you, again, John Wayne. And thank God we were on our way home.

In Southern California, as in New England, newspapers aren't an easy career choice. You're either passionate about being an ink-stained wretch or you should find something less aggravating and more lucrative, like swallowing knives on stage for a living. I loved journalism from the minute I first sat atop my dad's shoulders on our living room couch, armed with a whirring eggbeater, a fertile imagination, and an intense curiosity about almost everything contained in the pages he was reading.

I wrote a lot when I was a kid—stories and poems, badly drawn comic books, flowery cards and letters, and super-dramatic journal entries. I thought I'd grow up to be John-Boy Walton, the earnest wannabe writer at the center of TV's *The Waltons*. But then I saw *All the President's Men* and decided I would rather be Woodward or Bernstein, whichever was the shorter, darker, shaggier one played by Dustin Hoffman. I had no clue how hard it was to report breaking news and investigations every day. Not just the physical demands of the job, but also the mental constitution one needs to constantly press for answers, or at least quotable nonanswers. The closest I came to being that brand of journalist was in January 1986.

I was twenty-four, working at the *Old Colony Memorial* (again, weekly newspaper, not funeral home) when I got a tip that three local families were planning a road trip from Plymouth, Massachusetts, to Cape Canaveral, Florida, to see a close relative rocket into outer space as part of the space shuttle program. I drove over to one of their houses, where a large motorhome was parked in the driveway. The kids were frantic with excitement, and the adults were practically whistling as they loaded up the vehicle and told me their story. They were just regular folks with regular hopes and dreams, they said. They couldn't believe this was happening to one of their own.

They would spend the next several days making their way down the East Coast, with a brief stop in Disney World, so they could personally cheer on the cousin-in-law who had won a contest to be the first teacher in space. I watched them drive off in the direction of the interstate and then went back to the paper to write the story, which we ran on our Living Now cover with multiple photos of the clan standing in front of their RV.

Now I was proud, too. And emotionally invested. It was a classic rookie mistake.

If you're old enough, you remember where you were when the space shuttle *Challenger* fell out of the sky. I was watching it live on a newsroom TV. I saw the boosters ignite, and I felt the thrill and pride of a region and a nation as the massive craft slowly lifted itself off the ground, ascending into the gorgeous blue beyond.

It was several more seconds before the first puffs of white-gray smoke appeared in the camera frame. Even then, no one in our group of journalists had the background to know that this wasn't normal. I know now that we remained euphoric long after we should have, long after the folks at NASA had deduced a catastrophic mechanical failure and switched over to crisis mode in their control rooms. When we did find out that the shuttle had combusted, I felt a familiar nausea. How could this have happened? How could New Hampshire high school teacher Christa McAuliffe and all six of her crewmates have perished just seventy-three seconds into their mission? How could I reconcile that devastating news with the giddy, wide-eyed family of dreamers I'd seen headed in the direction of the Most Magical Place on Earth just days before?

And then I felt my stomach drop another level with this realization: I would have to call them.

That poor, unsuspecting family, who were right now probably sitting in some sterile holding room at the Kennedy Space Center, hustled there by authorities eager to get them away from the media, would eventually be released to their hotel rooms the same way I'd returned home in an emotional fog after every death scene I'd hoped to somehow cheat. The shock of any life ending, but especially a young life, defies verbalizing. It leaves a family winded and dazed, and the last thing you want to do in that state is talk to some dutiful stranger looking to document your pain, however compassionately.

In this plan-ahead age before cell phones, I had asked where McAuliffe's relatives would be staying, just in case I needed to fact-check something before my story ran. Now, I would have to use that information to press for a comment about the tragic events of this morning.

Gross.

I delayed reaching out for as long as I could, which was far more doable at a weekly publication in the pre-internet era. That publishing tempo gave me a day or two to sit on the story—just enough time for their grief to metastasize into anger, which had its plusses and minuses. By the time I reached them, some were already back home in Massachusetts. At first, they didn't want to say anything. Then, they said too much. They admitted to feeling let down by NASA for going forward with a launch in record cold temperatures for such an activity, and they questioned whether safety inspectors had been vigilant enough. Perhaps the whole program had gotten too "cocky," one cousin speculated, her voice sounding brittle and still in shock. "I don't think they really did their jobs," she said flatly. "I was all excited about [the space program] beforehand; now, I couldn't care less. I think it was a horrible waste of human life."

I mostly listened and apologized for invading what I knew was a sensitive time. They were raw, and they were communicating some harsh things that I thought they might regret. I wrote a lot of pointed comments into my draft, but if I put everything they told me in print, they would never be able to take it back. Even in the moment, I knew that I was projecting. I didn't want to add to their hurt any more than I would want someone to magnify my own family's wounds for the sake of a story. I have enormous respect for hardcore journalists with unshakable purpose and spines of steel, who love exercising their inner pit bulls in the field. They're the righteous, riveting heroes I came of age worshipping, in newsrooms and on-screen. I just wasn't one of them.

Consequently, while Los Angeles in the 1990s saw headline coverage of earthquakes, videotaped police brutality, widespread race riots, and a former football superstar accused of a gruesome double murder, I was more likely to be at my desk in the *Times*'s Orange County bureau editing a Hootie & the Blowfish review, or idling on a Hollywood red carpet for my chance to ask some flavor-of-the-moment movie star, "Who are you wearing?" Not that "soft news" is a piece of cake. It can take as much skill to get an honest answer out of a celebrity as out of a politician, or a prisoner. But the former was a challenge I relished, and a conversation I was good at, with people who should be able to handle hard questions that come with being in the public eye and raking in obscene amounts of money.

Right after Patty and Jan died, I'd sought out one of their nurses at New England Medical Center—a seemingly unflappable young woman who was only a few months into the job—to thank her for the extreme kindness she'd shown, not just to them but to every traumatized loved one in their obit. She appreciated my words but confessed that the experience had wrecked her. Critical care was not her thing, she'd concluded; perhaps the maternity ward was more her thing. I could relate, then and now.

While the *Challenger* disaster is an outsized event without comparison, it cut so close to home for me that I decided I wanted no part of interviewing grieving families on a hard news deadline. Instead, I would volunteer to be the person interviewing famously prickly stars like Vanessa Redgrave or Tommy Lee Jones. That was my idea of a challenging assignment. And sometimes it was also my dream assignment, like the time in the mid-1990s when thirty-four-year-old me was dispatched to Beverly Hills, tasked with listening to the irrepressible Lauren Bacall opine on acting and, among other things, her legendary romance with Humphrey Bogart. At some point in our conversation, I asked if the sultry siren was aware that, in swanky Laguna Beach, a top hotel advertised something called the Bogart Suite, which capitalized on claims that the actor had slept there with his then mistress, Bacall. She calmly told me that this hotel was full of shit.

"I didn't even know there *was* a Hotel Laguna," she said emphatically. "I went to Laguna once, before we were married; never stayed there. Listen, people make things up all the time."

Then she recounted how, when she accompanied Bogie on his sailing trips up and down the coast of Southern California, the moneyed Republican residents of Orange County would invite them in, but always with a measure of contempt.

"[They] used to say to Bogie, 'You know, you're a great guy—*for an actor.*' Well, thank you—*for nothing.*"

Before moving on to her next interview of the day, the actress who grew up in New York as Betty Joan Perske asked me where I was from.

"Originally? Boston," I told her.

In her famously direct, magnificently smoky-voiced way, she commanded me to immediately quit California and move "back home."

"Real people live there," she said.

The funny thing was, James had been telling me the exact same thing.

By now there were numerous forces pulling me back East.

Besides James, who had designs on owning a restaurant with Chin Chin, the delightful and perceptive sister who'd introduced us when she and I were coworkers at Mandarin Garden, there was my family to consider. My mother had been advised to give up smoking because of a heart condition known as mitral valve prolapse. Despite her fickle relationships with pharmaceuticals and therapists, she hadn't had a significant depressive episode in years. But nicotine withdrawal was threatening to lead her in that direction again.

"I feel like I've lost my best friend," she'd whine whenever the subject of cigarettes and doctor's orders came up.

"Don't worry, Ma," one of her kids would say helpfully. "If you really want a best friend who's out to kill you, we can draw straws."

It wasn't that we lacked empathy. It was just the way we moved through the world now—covering fear and exasperation with droll comebacks. My sister Nancy was that way about the hard-to-pinpoint health issues that had recently sprouted as she attempted to navigate the backside of menopause. She scoffed at feeling foggy and run-down all the time; what woman in her fifties didn't feel that way? Isn't that why the double espresso was invented?

In early October 1995, knowing that autumn presents New England at its most seductive, James suggested I fly to Boston for an impromptu visit.

"You can see your mom," he offered. "Then we can drive to Vermont . . . to peep."

"Peep?" I said, wondering what similar word he might have intended. "Oh, you mean leaf peep?"

"Right. Peep the leafs," he confirmed.

I grinned through the phone.

Vermont is a beautiful, eccentric state with an official Cheese Trail and many wonderful places to stay, none of them more fabled than the Trapp Family Lodge. If you're a serious fan of *The Sound of Music*, your bucket list probably includes visiting this inn, where Maria von Trapp put down roots after she escaped Nazi-occupied Austria with the Captain and their yodel-ay-hee-hooing brood. James knew I was a fan, and instead of judging me for it, he'd made a reservation for two nights in one of several private chalets that sat apart from the Tyrolean main lodge, overlooking the majestic mountains and quaint village of Stowe—a spectacular place for peeping leafs, or leaves.

Our first night there, we were at dinner in the lodge's formal dining room, just starting to tuck into our dessert course, when I sensed something was up. I sensed it because James literally said, "Can I ask you something?" Then he took a large swig of Rémy Martin and reached into the pocket of his Hugo Boss sport coat. He placed the small box on the table, near his cocktail glass. It was again black velvet—unopened this time but unmistakably containing the same question that had confronted me in Long Beach a year ago.

"Would you . . ."

"Whoa, wait. Are you really doing this . . . Here?" I asked.

He froze.

I froze.

Maybe in the Hollywood musical version of this moment a spotlight illuminates just our table, so the rest of the room falls away before I have to speak my answer. But in a crowded restaurant in real-life Vermont, where waitresses hover in kitschy Fräulein Maria dresses, you don't feel isolated and in tune. You feel conspicuous and cornered. You feel taken for granted. You feel . . . naked.

I didn't want to let James down. Not again. I didn't want to embarrass him, or myself. I just wanted the box to go away, quickly, before any more von Trappist voyeurs had the chance to see it. On that point, at least, James and I were finally speaking the same language in our brains. Without a word, he slid his hand across the tablecloth and back into his jacket, removing the small black jewelry coffin from view as though it had never been more than a David Copperfield illusion.

We picked at our shared dessert and paid the check, trying not to look anyone in the eye as we left. I told myself that at least those who witnessed our discomfort would have a good story to tell their friends—the one about the weird, aborted marriage proposal in which the ring didn't even make it out of the box.

"What do you think was going on there?" they would ask each other.

"I don't know," someone would say. "But whatever it was, she clearly doesn't deserve him."

And that someone would be right.

Only, here's the funny thing: I actually *was* ready to make a commitment to this man.

In the months leading up to this moment, after our trip to Taiwan had shown me the Complete James Bond Tseng and no fatal flaws had followed us home, I was convinced that we'd be together for a very long time. I knew that another marriage proposal would surface eventually; maybe I even sensed that it would happen here, at this shrine to maple syrupy romance. That didn't bother me. The public proposal was what bothered me—just as much as the bedroom version, for different reasons.

When it comes to real-life romance, unlike the stuff that feeds my guilty pleasures on-screen, I don't like being put on the spot in front of an audience; I don't understand how that's considerate or respectful or even smart. And because I can't let go when I'm bothered, because I have to overthink and try to corral the bothersome thing, I frequently ignore Voltaire's wise adage about the best being the enemy of the good.

"Can I ask *you* something?" I said to James as we walked back in the dark, across the wide, sloping lawn that led to our chalet.

"Sure," he said, bracing.

"Did you really think I'd respond well to that? I mean, do I seem like the kind of girl who wants to be proposed to in the middle of a dining room filled with edelweiss and cheeseheads?"

He stopped walking, and not to quiz me about the word "cheeseheads."

"It wasn't what I planned," he said. "I . . . panicked."

"What do you mean?"

"The ring. It was like fire on me. What's that expression?"

"It was burning a hole in your pocket?"

"Right. That's it. Burning my pocket."

"So, you thought it was a good idea to just plunk it down on the table?"

"Like I said . . . My brain was *yǒu jīng shén bìng* [有精神病, *insane*]. I panicked. I'm sorry, okay?"

He was now two for two on marriage proposals ending in apologies. And I was one stone-cold bitch.

This wasn't what I wanted, to be wasting a formerly promising night in the Green Mountains editing his talent for proposing clumsily. It seemed shallow and off-topic, even if it was honest and mattered more than I wanted to admit.

I guess on some level I felt set up. This was the same man who had tended to my earthquake-battered psyche with roasted duck and Van Morrison. The same man who once sent me sixty long-stemmed roses, with a handwritten card that read: "Sixty seconds in a minute. Sixty minutes in an hour. Every second of every minute of every hour, I think about you." Seriously. I wasn't endorsing style over substance. I wanted both. I wanted it all, the way Lucinda Williams writes about so perceptively in her chart-crossing hit, "Passionate Kisses." (*"Is it too much to demand, I want a full house and a rock and roll band?"*) I wanted to be sure James knew *that* was the girl he'd be marrying.

"Come here," he said then, pulling me close. Standing behind me with his arms wrapped around my waist, he lifted his gaze toward the treetops. "Do you see?"

"What?" I said. "Where?"

"See how many stars there are? So shining. So bright."

"They're fantastic," I said, taking in the brilliant carpet of constellations that twinkled all around us. "The sky is so clear up here."

"Right," he said. "So beautiful to look at. Only, let me tell you, you can't hold them in your hand."

Fearless, he again removed the box from his jacket.

"But I do have this one star, from my pocket"—the box was open now—"for you."

I don't truly know why it mattered so much how and where James proposed to me. (As he would say, "You ask me, who I gonna ask?") I guess I'm just one of those people who needs everything to click into place, the way it does in movies when the good guys hit upon the correct combination to disarm a briefcase full of deadly plutonium. James had finally cracked the code; third time's the charm, as they say. Before I could think about reining anything in, the answer was out of my mouth.

"Dùi" (对), I said in my pidgin Mandarin, misusing the word, which James again pretended not to notice. *Dùi* means "correct." What I meant to say, he knew without question this time, was "*shì*" (是).

Yes.

❧

In hindsight, it seems clear that I was in commitment-worthy love long before we set foot on the Cheese Trail. I'm sure I'd melted a bit more each time James drove an hour south in his not-yet-repossessed Porsche just to drag me away from my old job at the *Providence Journal* for a proper lunch, and whenever he'd sent me a carefully selected card or poem or flower, and absolutely when he'd met my SoCal earthquake anxieties with tenderness and strategy, not judgment.

Excepting reality-TV-level narcissists, there's nothing wrong with adoring being adored. James taught me that. And, while I may not have known for a ridiculously long time when I might be ready for any kind of next step, I knew I *was* ready the moment he said the thing about corralling the stars, because it was the impossible made possible—grand vision leavened with dependable pragmatism. It was both how I saw my best self and exactly what I needed in a life partner.

All through the four-hour drive back to Massachusetts, where James would secure my mother's eternal adoration by asking for her official blessing on our engagement, I ignored the leafy landscape in favor of staring down at the newly acquired bauble on my left hand. It wasn't the diamond he'd used to propose the first time, in Long Beach. ("No good," he said of that one; "unlucky," I think he meant.) This model seemed like an upgrade.

"Not for nothing, but the stone does seem to get a bit bigger and sparklier every time," I joked. "Maybe I should have kept saying no?"

"Yeah, you think so," he joked back. (At least, I think it was a joke.) "This ring is store credit only. If I return it, maybe I just buy one Rolex for myself."

The sturdy gold band he'd purchased needed no adjustments. It was perfectly sized, just like every other wearable item James had ever bought me.

"I don't know how *you* do it," I'd say whenever I opened a gift box to find another expertly tailored top or bottom, or the ideal accessory I didn't know I needed. "It fits me like a glove."

"Of course," he'd reply. "I'm holding you every night. I don't know your size? Come on, man."

You learn a lot about a person during ten years of dating—even ten years of bicoastal, clumsily bilingual dating. After all that buildup, at thirty-four and thirty-six years old, the two of you shouldn't need much runway to get from the engagement to the altar. So, we quickly settled on a long weekend that coming May because even though I hadn't fantasized my dream wedding ever, I did know that if I was going to do this at all, I was going to do it in spring. "(I'll Be with You) In Apple Blossom Time" was one of my favorite titles in the Shaving Songs Master Collection. If my dad couldn't be there to walk me down the aisle, he would at least be the melody inside my head.

I wish I could say I was as sure about everything else that happened during the next seven months. Planning a wedding isn't ever easy, but it gets very complicated when you find out you're pregnant and you don't want to be.

That news arrived in April. We'd been careless on just one recent occasion that I could recall—a celebratory night in March when the classic combination of too much alcohol and too little common sense had taken over, seducing us into having the unprotected sex of the invincible. Despite everything our mothers tell us, most women know that oftentimes we get away with our bad decisions. Until we don't. And then we realize we're not really smarter than the odds. Too late, though.

When I confirmed the pregnancy, first by peeing on a stick in the stall of an *L.A. Times* restroom and then with a blood test at the kind of upscale Orange County clinic where the doctor just assumed it would come as welcome news to any woman fast approaching thirty-five, James was back in Boston preparing for our Memorial Day weekend nuptials. I had to break it to him over the telephone—not as a giddy expectant mom but as a pro-choice pragmatist who was already leaning toward termination.

"We don't even live on the same coast," I pointed out, as though he wasn't aware of the geography. "I don't think I can do this right now, with everything so up in the air; I think we need to settle a ton of other things—who's moving, for starters—before we decide if we want a kid. We're not ready to be parents. Right? I mean, *I'm* not ready to be a parent. I drive a two-door convertible with cowhide-print seat covers, for God's sake. I don't think I want this, Kao Shun. Are you okay with that?"

He didn't hesitate.

"Not my decision," he said. "Not my body."

"I know, but . . ." I pressed him. "Listen, I get that that's the thing you're supposed to say. And I know you'd never try to tell me what to do. But how do you really feel?"

That was a trap, and James knew it.

"Not my decision," he repeated. But then he added, "I mean, of course, if you ask me, I will say I would like to . . . I will say I am *happy* to . . . You know. But more important is you. Do *you* want this?"

What a question.

My mother didn't "want" me in any sense that could be considered purposeful. We know that I was a mistake of insufficient willpower or laziness or lack of a calendar or whatever. But she had me anyway, because she wasn't really given a choice, and that turned out fine, I think.

My generation—the girls who could have it all—were supposed to have more choices. We were supposed to be bold, and maybe a little bit selfish, because what was the point of having options if you couldn't exercise them to have the life you wanted instead of the life that just happened to you? I believed in the power of my convictions. I believed in the rallying cries: my womb, my vagina, my rules. But it's easy to believe in the abstract. When it really was my womb and my prerogative, it felt like a test.

Most Catholics, even the long-lapsed ones, bear the foundational scars of being taught to fear their choices. My mother wouldn't confess her sins to a priest, but she did confess to her children that she stayed faithful to her religion primarily because she thought she'd be "struck down by lightning" if she strayed too far from its tenets. I was young and impressionable when, one random afternoon, my television served up a 1961 movie called *Hand in Hand*.

It's the story of a seven-year-old Jewish girl and a Catholic boy who's maybe nine. They live in small-town England, surrounded by genial and proper bigots. The kids forge a naïve friendship, trespassing to explore an abandoned house and pin-pricking their fingers to become "blood brothers." Then, as intolerance invades their collective consciousness, they tempt fate by sampling each other's church services, to see if God will either bless their innocent union or smite them.

To their relief, nothing bad happens, and thus emboldened they set out on a boat to discover the wider world, only to find that their comeuppance is due. The tiny vessel capsizes. The girl washes up on a riverbank, limp and unresponsive. The boy believes he's killed her.

While not exactly the lightning bolt that my mother imagined would come for her the way it came for Patty McCormack at the end of *The Bad Seed*, the passive-aggressive denouement of *Hand in Hand* struck me as divine retribution just as scary. It didn't matter that the girl ultimately survives and the boy is absolved. Or that his priest and her rabbi come together on a serene-looking street to convey to the viewer that God is not prejudice or punishment: God is mercy; God is love. I didn't even remember that upbeat ending until I rewatched the movie many years later. My main takeaway as a child was the same as what my mother had internalized from her strict religious upbringing: Rein it in, little lady, and watch your step. You're not the boss of you. *He's* the boss of you.

Fear is not a good reason to decide to have a child, and neither is defiance a good reason to decide against it. I hope I didn't acquiesce to either, but I know that I felt both as I picked through my feelings and wondered whether I was truly free to make this decision on my own.

It wasn't just the moral toggling. My "you can have it all" generation was also waking up to the fact that our eggs hadn't read any of the feminism manuals. I had to consider that getting pregnant after age thirty-five could pose problems, regardless of whether I felt more inclined to do it then. Was I willing to pass up what might be my only shot at bearing a child, simply because it wasn't exactly what I wanted right now? In the end, after much internal debate and several soul-searching conversations with James, I made the choice that seemed the most honest and authentic in that moment.

I aborted the pregnancy.

James offered to fly out for the procedure, but I told him no. If there was anything to the threat of God's wrath as handed down in highly cinematic stories, he should not be implicated. This was on me, whatever the hell that meant.

A compassionate and sturdy friend drove me to the clinic, where protesters shouted their case from a barely legal distance. It was over so quickly, I don't remember much, beyond waking up feeling a bit unsteady. My friend seemed concerned about my mental state. I wasn't sad, though; I was relieved.

I admit that I sometimes think now about what might have been, as I assume most women do even when they know they did their best with a difficult decision in real time. But my Tao of Three Wishes makes no room for revising this event because I don't regret it, and I definitely wouldn't change the path it put me on, or the child who would one day come into my life as a result.

CHAPTER 10

The Yangtze

Bacall (and Dorothy) had it right. There's no place like home.

It took me many years to figure that out, and many irrefutable signs before I was convinced that I couldn't ask James to uproot his professional life in Boston if everything that mattered most to us both was back East.

Dedication to a dream had made him a successful restaurateur within a decade of arriving in the US. In 1994, he and Chin Chin at last opened a restaurant in Norwell, a quietly affluent South Shore town known for being the final resting place of the "Chekhov of the suburbs," John Cheever, and the stamping ground of Aerosmith's aging "Toxic Twins," Steven Tyler and Joe Perry, who co-owned a popular upscale tavern there. The space that the Tseng siblings leased had been a patio furniture store about five times the size of Mandarin Garden. They decided to name it Beijing House, which caused a smartass music critic I knew to wonder aloud if Beijing had a restaurant called Norwell House.

We made good use of the 'Jing, as my family insisted on calling it, when we held our wedding reception there in 1996, plugging my *L.A. Times* garage band into a corner of the dining room and letting the party rage on for nearly seven hours. My friend and former *Providence Journal* columnist

M. J. Andersen once wrote that planning a wedding is "like staging *Aida*, without the elephants." She was right, though elephants can be easier to wrangle than a herd of in-laws arriving from Taiwan.

For them, and for our friends in the restaurant business, we had a separate, late-night wedding banquet in Chinatown, to which I wore a red silk dress known as a *qí páo* (旗袍). I hoped that Yù Yīng would see it as an homage, rather than a clumsy appropriation, but I knew that this was a line I would walk often in my marriage to James. I am not, and never want to play at being, Chinese.

There is a saying—because there is always a saying—that goes *"Liáng tǐ cái yī"* (量体裁衣): *Measure the body, then tailor the suit*. James would sum it up as "Adapt to your circumstances." If you're the bride at a Chinese wedding banquet, it's okay to wear a *qí páo*, he assured me. The adage also seemed like sound marital advice, along the lines of "Do not open a shop unless you like to smile."

I could think of many proverbs—authentic and not—that applied to my new relationship status, with my husband and I still living on separate coasts. I told inquisitive family and friends that we were debating the optimum cross-country move: Would it be east or west? In truth, I wasn't in any hurry to make big changes, and they knew it. James knew it, too.

"Talk does not cook rice," he might have said. But he didn't. Instead, he told me he was in this for the long haul and a few more months apart meant nothing in the context of a healthy marriage. It helped that he was from a place where it wasn't uncommon for couples to live separately for the sake of a job. So, following our honeymoon in Italy, I returned to Long Beach and my husband went back to Boston. We would work it out. That's what we promised each other every night when we talked by phone.

Unfortunately for James, I wasn't leaning east, because my career at the *Times* was also on the rise, in the most modest sense of that phrase. I'd done well enough in Orange County to be summoned by the mother ship in downtown Los Angeles, where I'd try on the mantle of a fashion editor, despite not owning a single pair of Jimmy Choo stilettos. But then in 1997, just as I was starting to let myself think that we could make it work out

West—that perhaps James could entrust the 'Jing to Chin Chin and entertain the idea of opening a second restaurant in Long Beach—I received a devastating phone call from home. It turned out that Nancy's fatigue wasn't curable by caffeine, or even sleep therapy. It was stage 3 ovarian cancer. Exploratory surgery had revealed a malignancy that extended into the nodes of her abdomen. She was fifty-four.

I remember asking Carol if she thought that Nancy would die. "Not right now" was all she said. Not. Right. Now. This is what passed for comfort in our Cancer Family. We could reasonably bet that Nancy would survive initial treatment, and we could choose not to look past that, for the moment. But when and how the disease would resurface—as it did in Patty, and in Jan, and in my father—was likely just a matter of time. Carol was telling me that the end was deferable. It was also inevitable, probably sooner than we wanted to admit.

My mother, still battling heart issues, was already conjuring the cloud that typically engulfed her when the road ahead looked menacing. My oldest sister was about to undergo aggressive chemo and radiation treatments. My only choice was not even a choice in that moment; it was a spiritual directive, endorsed by no less than a Hollywood legend.

Move back home. To Boston. Where real people live. And die.

James and I were in bed. On the Right Coast this time. We'd moved into a small condominium in the town of Brookline, just over the Boston line, which made it an easy commute to my new job as managing producer at *BostonSidewalk.com*, a digital city guide launched by Microsoft to compete with newspapers like *The Boston Globe*. It was 1997, the era of eager funding for half-baked media business ideas barely sketched out on a cocktail napkin. At thirty-six years old, I was happy to observe its many lessons from inside the cushy MSN bubble.

On this otherwise unnoteworthy autumn night, James was feeling chatty and wandered into a comment about desiring to visit China one day. For some reason, my memory laces his part of this conversation with more halting grammar than some other talks we've had. It's funny how you hear people differently when they're saying things that don't comport with expectation.

"I've always wanted to walk the Great Wall," I said, enthusiastically. "Imagine how awesome that must be."

"So many tourists there," he scoffed. "I will like to visit Guilin, in the south. So beautiful, that place, like a painting. Also, I have a sister living there."

There was a pause while I processed the record scratch. Then I started the long, slow, familiar job of trying to extract the facts behind this extraordinary news.

"Uh, hmm, well," I said, "maybe we could visit both places. And, also . . . *You have a sister in China?*"

He didn't flinch at my astonishment. This wasn't an abnormal exchange, to him. It was just a minor fact that he'd somehow forgotten to mention in more than a dozen years of conversations between us. Long-lost relatives are as common to families in Taiwan as nasty divorces are in America.

"Oh, yeah," he said. "My Old Sister is there. Probably she is, I think, around fifty-something now. I never saw her before."

"You mean you've never *met* her?" I said. "Seriously? How is that possible?"

"Okay, let me tell you," he began.

For a smart man, James could be astonishingly inept at storytelling. Even with fundamentally uncomplicated narratives, he had a habit of jumping around in time, confusing key facts, contradicting himself, and skipping over wide swaths of what an outsider required to establish a toehold, never mind keep up. When we first met, this was funny. Now it was more often annoying and occasionally infuriating, like so many things in a supposedly evolving relationship. I didn't want to talk in circles; I just wanted the throughline to make me understand: How could he have a sibling he didn't know?

In James's defense, but not really, I'd stopped asking much about his family because I was saving my questions for his mother. Yù Yīng, who'd talked mostly about her childhood and teenage years in our first conversations in 1994, left off with a cliffhanger about the sly, mysterious boy who'd bumped into her in the streets of her Liujiang village. We hadn't had time to pick up that thread during her visit to Boston for our wedding in 1996, but I did already know, from the sketch that James had provided when we first met, that his father (the brash boy behind the bump?) had been in the military and died in his forties, leaving his mother and siblings to raise James, the youngest, from adolescence. He'd told me that his parents had fled the mainland because his dad was aligned with the Kuomintang—the nationalist party led by Chiang Kai-shek, which was pushed out by Mao Tse-tung's communism. I understood that this was a standard origin story in today's Taiwan, where a significant percentage of the immigrant population derived from China's civil war, which I'd started learning about back at Mandarin Garden when Benny Wu used to impart history lessons between games of Battleship. But it never dawned on me that James's parents might have left more than just their ancestral roots in China. Even as James was explaining it now—in his usual circuitous, confounding fashion—I couldn't fathom how they'd left a child there.

"And they really couldn't go back for her?" I asked when he was finally finished, despite anticipating the answer. "No one could have found a way to get her out?"

"Impossible," James confirmed. "You know, communists—they shut down everything. No one can come in until Nixon goes there to open the gate in 1972."

Once I'd shaken off the additional shock of Richard Nixon's name popping up in our bedroom—nearly as unsettling as the surprise appearance of a diamond ring—I asked what happened when China reopened to tourism and James's family embarked on a search for his Old Sister. His version of the story was short on details: They'd enlisted the help of an investigator to locate her; his mother and siblings flew to the mainland for the reunion in 1987; many tears were shed, of course, but life went on.

"It must have been so hard for you, though," I remarked, "after your sister was found, and they all went to China to meet her. Were you disappointed that you couldn't go?"

"Oh, well," he replied. "At that time, I'm still not a US citizen. Also, I'm just a few years out of the Taiwan army. How can I go to China?"

"I get it," I said, having been told about his country's then-mandatory conscription policy requiring two to three years of military service from most of its young men. "But you *have* to be curious. You *must* want to see her in person, right?"

I was projecting again. I'd parted with too many loved ones to feign indifference to the reverse—a blood relation found instead of lost. What a concept. The story of Tǔ Xiù (土秀)—the nickname (pronounced *tōō-shō*) he said his sister had acquired, for reasons he'd never even asked about—grabbed hold of my heart from the very beginning, despite how little James really knew of it. What I discovered in my husband's pillow talk that night was enough to convince me he needed to meet his oldest sister. *We* needed to meet her, in part because if she was anything like the sister I did know—Chin Chin, whose astute intuition had matched me with James in the first place—not making an effort to close this loop would surely be our loss. I didn't need to be reminded that life is too short to put off what is already long overdue.

❧

My mother never got sick. Not with a cold or a flu or anything of the sort—at least, not that any of her children can recall.

When we were kids, we were as prone to contagion as to flatulence, and she often scurried from room to room with cold facecloths and hot water bottles, tending to multiple sick children with snot and phlegm flying out of their hacking, sneezing faces. No matter how many of us were ill, no matter how many germs infested our tiny house, no matter that the man she slept next to would invariably be the sickest and whiniest of her infected babies, she never ever caught what we had. Never.

It was an unsanctioned miracle.

Not only was she sturdiest whenever the rest of us deserved to be quarantined, but she was also at her most compassionate and nurturing. It made you want to be sick a lot because you got a dollop of pampering. You got tea and toast and flat ginger ale if your tummy was unsettled. You got to stay in bed and watch reruns of *The Dick Van Dyke Show* and *I Love Lucy.* If you had a fever, your sheets were changed at least once a day, so that when you crawled back under the covers, the linens were stretched tight across the mattress, pressing cool against your skin, and filling your nostrils with the faux fresh aromas of Lysol and laundry detergent.

I was aware that my mom had contracted rheumatic fever when she was young, and that her heart had developed a murmur because of it. But, other than that and her bipolar meltdowns, she appeared to be the picture of health—if the picture of health smoked Kents.

When the smoking and the murmur finally caught up with each other in the late 1990s, Yolanda summoned her deepest Italian stubbornness to dodge death numerous times. After one hospital stay to treat congestive heart failure, she returned home as frail and defeated as I'd ever seen her. I flew in from California and showed up at her door unannounced. She whimpered like a whipped puppy as she let me in, clinging to our hug much longer than I could remember ever experiencing.

"I'm sorry," she said after pulling away, as though there'd been a clock on the embrace, and she'd embarrassed both of us by exceeding its limit. I told her not to apologize. What I didn't tell her, because I didn't know it then, was that I'd still be feeling the imprint of that hug decades later.

My mother wasn't big on hugs. She preferred to hook your arm and cozy up the way girlfriends do in high school hallways. I suppose she was more comfortable with being a girlfriend than she was with being a mom. Obligation wasn't her thing. Fun was her thing.

I didn't just know this from the epic adventure that was my greatest day. I knew it by how seldom she'd ask about the mundane parts of my life as a child, from homework to the status of my underwear supply. After my father died, my mother began traveling to all the bucket-list places he wouldn't, which was pretty much everywhere not named Quincy. She got her first taste of Italy, tracing her ancestral roots in Sulmona and Rome. Then she hopped on a bus bound for Branson, Missouri, where she saw shows every night and went backstage at the invitation of one of my favorite repeat interview subjects—Brenda Lee, with whom I'd stayed in touch over the years.

"That gal," she said admiringly of the four-foot-nine-inch pop singer nicknamed Little Miss Dynamite. "Hair done up bigger than she is!"

Once unleashed, my mom's wanderlust simply wouldn't be contained, which sometimes made it hard to keep up with her. Midway through a 1990s vacation in Miami with Carol and Nancy, seventy-something Yolanda walked off to seek out a restroom while her adult daughters lounged at the beach. When she'd been gone long enough that worry seemed reasonable, they decided to go looking, eventually finding her a few blocks down in an outdoor bar, sipping a large gin and tonic with a cheerfully lubricated group of newfound friends.

I loved this about my mother.

She was so fiercely independent and committed to the doctrine of joie de vivre that she once told me, "If the day ever comes when I can't drive, you won't have to take away my keys. I'll just lie down in the street and let the car roll over me." Well, that day did come, finally—minus the runaway car—in 1999 after three years of pretending it wouldn't.

First Yolanda's mitral valve gave out, then her kidneys, then her stubbornness. Shortly after that, with the seventy-seven-year-old in a coma and her doctors forecasting at best a few weeks more of life in this compromised condition, we surprised them by refusing to subject her to dialysis. *They* were conditioned to keep her alive. *We*, on the other hand, were conditioned to question the quality of the life they were sustaining.

My siblings and I took turns sleeping in her hospital room, just as we had with Patty, Jan, and Jocko. During my shifts, I sometimes read aloud from the growing stack of *People* magazines in her room, convinced that my mother would not have wanted to miss out on the latest movie star rehab or Kennedy annulment. Other times I chain-surfed the cable channels, desperately searching for reruns of *I Love Lucy* and *Dick Van Dyke*. But mostly I just sat quietly by her side, letting the memories wander in as they pleased.

I was pretty young, maybe seven or eight, when my mother first told me about the only time her mother slapped her. She recalled that the blow came out of nowhere, interrupting a cheery morning when, at roughly my age, she'd made the mistake of saying, "Mama, I think I have a cancer on my lip."

WHAPPP!

The palm of her mother's hand hit the left side of her cheek and continued across the bridge of the nose, hard enough to leave a mark. Though no one had ever advised the children of this, because no one was allowed to utter it, the *c*-word—cancer—was *vietato* (forbidden) in the DiMartinis household.

"My mother thought it was a curse," Yolanda explained. "She was afraid that even speaking the word would bring it into our house, into our family."

The slap sustained its might throughout my mother's life. She remembered the sound and the sting of it. She also knew the lesson she took from it: that words have power and some are too dangerous to even utter, which may or may not have been what her mother had intended to impart.

Curse—the *other c*-word—that's the one that scared my mother the most.

After Patty had died, and then Jan and Jacky and my dad, and with Nancy's long-term prognosis uncertain, my mom asked me at some point if I thought our family was "cursed." She wasn't saying it in the half-joking way that people do when they've exhausted all rational explanations. She was completely serious.

I wasn't sure I believed in curses, but it didn't matter in the moment. I was intrigued by the question and what it said about her state of mind. When you hang the Serenity Prayer on your kitchen wall for motivational reasons that have nothing to do with Alcoholics Anonymous, it's generally a sign that you struggle with reconciling darkness. You're looking for reassurance—not that life will be trouble-free, but that you will be able to cope when the trouble inevitably comes. In this way, faith in curses is no different from faith in God. The idea is that if you give yourself over to the forces beyond your control, you will find peace just in knowing that someone or something greater than you is dictating the outcome.

But where a benevolent God might absolve you, or at least forgive you, a curse suggests that you're being punished for some wrongdoing either current or inherited. It suggests blame, and the need for atonement. This is the Serenity Prayer gone very dark. That my mother was even considering it signaled that she carried some imaginary guilt over what had happened to her family.

"What did I ever do in my life?" she asked, agonizingly and I think rhetorically, but even if I'd affirmed her general good character, she wouldn't have been convinced.

Maybe she hadn't been a model Christian. Maybe she'd unintentionally hurt someone or, heaven forbid, had sex that wasn't for purposes of procreation. Maybe she'd even enjoyed it. A lot.

Of course, that's the paradox of the Serenity Prayer plaque. You don't hang it on your wall unless you think you need to be reminded of its tenets every day. You do this when you can't internalize the prayer, perhaps because it's never going to be an affirmation you can convince yourself to accept.

The afternoon that my mother finally took her last labored breath, disconnected from the intricate web of tubes and beeping stuff that had been keeping her alive, my siblings and I were among a large group of family assembled in her hospital room. Yolanda would have approved of that gathering. She would have positioned herself right in the middle of it, within earshot of every conversation, and under different circumstances she would have laughed heartily. Probably she would have gone on about how she'd "set her mouth" in anticipation of being served some delicious bite of food, ideally involving chocolate.

In my experience, death scenes are part of an incomparable, alternate universe, and they're never as they're portrayed in the movies, especially when it's the culmination of a long illness. Sometimes, the dying is loud, preceded by protracted writhing and convulsing that tests whatever shred of faith you still have in the wisdom and decency of medical care. Sometimes, as with my mom, you sit around for days, weeks, maybe even months watching for clear signs that the curtain has dropped.

"Shhh. I think . . ."

Silence.

"What? Did she stop breathing?" someone asks.

"Maybe."

More silence.

"Wait. No. I just saw her chest move."

"Oh, yeah, she's still going."

Robust discussion resumes. And . . . scene.

In the end, it's all very anticlimactic. There are no dramatic confessions or wise last words, there's only the comatose patient slipping without fanfare into whatever it is that comes next for us. Fade to black.

And then you're left with just the nothingness and the exhaustion, all melting into something between grief and relief.

It took me many weeks to process surviving after my mother died. I would get up in the morning and find myself still sitting in the same spot on my couch hours later, unable to think through how I should move. Putting one foot in front of the other suddenly seemed like a skill I had to relearn. I felt as though I'd lost my center, my compass for navigating the world. Eventually, you set new coordinates. But moving forward is not the same as moving on, and moving on is not the same as burying.

The song we'd sung at my mother's funeral kept running through my head. It was Frank Sinatra's "Young at Heart," which was woven into my eulogy and belted from every pew by a chorus of doo-bee-doo-bee-dutiful mourners.

You can go to extremes with impossible schemes
You can laugh when your dreams fall apart at the seams

That lyrical snippet would often lead me to recall my greatest day, which I grew to understand as a collision of duty, defiance, amusement, and abandon.

I know now that my greatest day is my greatest day mainly because innocence appreciates with time. It reanimates the five-year-old in the back seat of that dependable, seaweed-green Chevy Nova, about to embark on a once-in-a-lifetime, exceptionally wild ride with her ma. That little girl doesn't have the vantage point to see anything that lies ahead. She only knows this day is special. *She* is special.

In the weeks and months after my mother's death, I'd sometimes struggle to push aside the sadness and trauma of accumulated loss just long enough to revel in the memory of our impromptu adventure as it was—as it felt then. I still make that effort today, as a kind of daily affirmation of my own. What I see in those moments is a luminous summer day that stretches on forever.

The sand is hot under my feet.

The salt crusts my freckled skin.

The air smells like sugar and grease.

And watermelon sherbet.

To anyone who doesn't already know this firsthand, I can confirm that New England winters blow. They look magical on film, but really they're not so much fluffy and white as they are frigid and gray. The sky is gray. The snow is gray within thirty-six hours of falling, at least wherever there are plows and commuters. The dominant flesh tone is gray, as is most of what you eat and wear and dream.

Both of my parents had died in winter months, my father in December and my mother in January. Each time, I sank into the bleak landscape and was grateful for the low expectations it cultivated. I was an orphan now, at thirty-seven. That hardly made me Oliver Twist, but it did create a void, even with the surrogate guidance of three older siblings and one very close maternal cousin, all of whom had had a strong hand in raising me.

By spring of 1999, James was convinced that I needed a dramatic change of venue to chase away the funk. We'd talked increasingly about visiting China to meet his long-lost Old Sister. We'd also talked about climbing Beijing's Great Wall—well, I did, anyway—and taking a cruise down the Yangtze River before its waters were allowed to swallow up several ancient towns and landmarks that stood in the way of the government's Three Gorges Dam project. I don't think I could have planned a trip to save my life just then, but Asia is the one place on earth where James is fully at the wheel and I'm mostly comfortable riding shotgun. He surprised me with airplane tickets and a three-week itinerary; in May, we flew from Boston to Beijing by way of Detroit and Tokyo.

China doesn't let you visit it casually. It insists on your full attention and very quickly establishes who's boss. *You* have lived your whole life in a place with a few hundred years of recorded history. *It* measures time in dynasties and movements that stretch back thousands of years.

As you explore Beijing's outsized historical footprints, including what's left of its walls and fortresses—no more impenetrable over time than other manmade monuments to delusion—your tour guide peppers her remarks with phrases like "my government" and "after our liberation." You feel small and coddled.

Three days in Beijing isn't nearly enough. I could have spent a week just absorbing the Forbidden City, but James couldn't wait to move on. During our three-hour flight south, he confessed that he was most excited not for the scenic beauty or the nautical miles that would move us closer to his family reunion, but for the spicy hot pot cuisine that awaited us in the port city of Chongqing, where we'd embark on our three-night Yangtze River cruise. He wanted the kind of heat that Billie Jean and Martina only played at ordering up from the temperamental Mandarin Garden chefs. If my new husband wasn't dripping sweat into his dinner napkin, his face the color of my mother's all-day-simmering marinara, he wasn't happy.

Chongqing was James's culinary Mecca. For our one evening meal there, before an early-morning cruise departure, we settled on a place that looked out over the harbor. I'd eaten from many a hot pot by this point, but I'd never eaten from a hot pot that bubbled as fiery red and slick with oil as the cauldrons occupying every table of this dining room. Vegetables, meats, and offal fished out of that Sichuan broth were a more insane color than my hypothetical Crispy Shrimp Lip Gloss, and their peppery aromas infused my lungs with a familiar Mandarin Garden kitchen burn. Soaked with perspiration, James swooned. Dinner for two, including beer, cost us less than the equivalent of $10—a bargain, notwithstanding that it nearly burned a hole in my colon.

I take after my dad in a few problematic ways, one of them being that I'm not a fan of boats. Besides the high potential for seasickness, being on the water for prolonged periods of time is unnatural, and far too confining for my taste. Unless, of course, it's the only way to see a part of the world that's fascinating and endangered. Then, you simply pop a few Dramamines, suck it up, and go.

Our cruise along the Yangtze was all those things.

The three-story riverboat was small and dated, and not in a quaint, Mark Twain kind of way. But the accommodations were more than adequate given that we spent most of our time on deck watching the spectacular scenery float by. As our little boat drifted downstream toward Shanghai and the East China Sea, we threaded mountain ranges where temples clung to the cliffs and villages still teemed with life, despite their impending relocation. Sites along the way had names like Three Travelers' Cavern, the Fragrant Stream, and the Gorge of the Ox's Liver and the Horse's Lung.

In places where the river narrowed and the mountains towered high enough to block the sun, I thought our vessel might bump against the sides, the way my mother and I had on the Paragon Park Congo Cruise. There were no crocodiles breaching the water or cannibals threatening from the shore. But there was, at one point, a half-naked brigade of sinewy men who emerged from nowhere to pull us—in smaller wooden rowboats we'd boarded for this side excursion—through a shallow channel that required the use of bamboo tow ropes looped around their waists and chests. They clambered over the slippery rocks in handwoven straw flip-flops, heaving in unison and shouting rallying cries, sometimes even singing them, as they went. Those melodic, antiphonal river songs, known as *hào zi* (号子), were mesmerizing—a kind of vocal drumbeat that was at once lilting and dirge-like. You could call them folk songs, maybe even spirituals of a sort; they reminded me of Native American ceremonial songs, but also the chant of the guardsman ("O-ee-yah! Eoh-ah!") at the witch's castle in

The Wizard of Oz. The *hào zi* seemed to propel the tow men through the trickiest sections of rushing water, their backs hunched like perturbed cats when the current required more straining.

I felt like Katharine Hepburn's prim and proper Rose aboard the *African Queen*: utterly useless. My existence in this place served no purpose but to exhaust and possibly endanger the lives of other people acting in servitude. Honestly, I had never felt whiter.

While our cruise ship wasn't Disney-level, it endeavored to provide passengers with activities to help pass the time. There were painting and calligraphy lessons, card games and variety shows. One morning, James and I decided to join a group that had assembled on deck for a demonstration of qi gong, the traditional art of marshaling energy through breathing, meditation, and movement.

The qi gong master ran us through a series of dancelike exercises—familiar stuff that I'd seen elderly ladies practicing in parks, both here and back home. Then he asked for volunteers, but he didn't wait for anyone to raise a hand. Instead, he grabbed my arm and led me to the front, along with three or four others plucked from the crowd.

James had the grin of someone expecting to be entertained.

The master instructed his "volunteers" to stand in a horizontal line, legs hip-width apart, arms dangling by our sides, eyes closed. We could hear him behind us, speaking in an unfamiliar Chinese dialect from what seemed like a distance of at least several feet. Then he stopped talking and about half a minute passed in silence. I felt a push, like the full force of a firm hand against my back, leaning into the hollow between my shoulder blades. I was propelled forward, and as I stepped, I instinctively opened my eyes. The crowd was wide-eyed and gasping, then clapping. I had no idea what had happened.

Then he did it again, to the next person in line.

This time, I watched as the qi gong master summoned his strength in silence, raised his right hand, and held his body in a kind of martial arts strike pose. Slowly and smoothly, he thrust his flattened palm forward in the direction of a tall German tourist I'll call Rolf. The man lurched a full step, just as I had, only this time I saw what had made the crowd gasp. The master's hand never got within six inches of Rolf's back. Whatever force had propelled us, it wasn't flesh meeting flesh. It was unseeable, unknowable, and, one had to assume, all powerful.

I'd spent a lot of time thinking about spiritual energy after my mom died. By this point, I wasn't what anyone would call "religious," but I remained open to the concept of a higher power that wasn't vengeful. The psychic push of the qi gong master made me consider whether my mother's hand could still be guiding me, not just in the realm of memory but in ways more tangible and present.

Why was I even here? Because of her. Because James had wanted it to be a respite from the constant reminders that she was gone. Neither of us had imagined that it might be something more therapeutic—a chance to grieve more deeply, by proxy, through experiencing this place that was also slipping away.

James and I had come to see history that was about to be forever altered. Once fully operational in 2012, the Three Gorges Dam would help control floods along the Yangtze, but it would also raise the reservoir waters to 574 feet above sea level. Thirteen cities, 140 towns, and 1,350 villages would be obliterated by the project, causing upward of a million people to be displaced and introducing a host of ecological issues, including increased landslides. More ships, carrying more tourists, would be part of the perceived net gain.

And then there was the fact that downriver lay the next chapter in our journey—the one that would take us to James's ancestral birthplace and the full reunification of his family.

I felt driven to understand my place in this country and this story, because something told me I wasn't just here to observe. That force seemed more pull than push. I can't say for sure if it was my mother's adventurous spirit tugging at me. But it was insistent, firm, and very, very real.

CHAPTER 11

Guilin

I hate telephones.

This might have started in my teenage years, when the only phone in our little tan ranch was a rotary-dial landline (also tan) that sat atop a just-big-enough table in the living room. To get any privacy, you had to pull the entire phone into the kitchen, stretching its distressed, slender, six-foot cord tight around the corner so you could squat by the wheezing refrigerator and mumble low into the receiver. It was as annoying as it was humiliating, which is just what you need more of in your adolescence.

My mother also hated talking on telephones, so it's possible I could have inherited her aversion long before hormones and attitude got involved. I never asked for her reasons, because it doesn't really matter what our mutual antipathy stemmed from; it's just a fact that neither of us spent much time on the phone, even when I lived in California and would call Boston to check in on her. "Alright. I'll let you go, then," she'd say after no more than a few minutes of small talk, and most times I'd just take the easy out. But then a curious thing happened when she died: I had the overwhelming urge to call her *all the time*. Like, I'd wake up in the middle of the night thinking I should ring her. Or I'd lose my train of thought at work because . . . *call your mother.* It was unrelenting.

Eventually, of course, the blaring became more of a background noise. Then I might only think of her when I had good/bad news, or there was an occasion, or I would see or hear or smell something and think, *I should call Ma.* Sometimes I might even move to pick up the phone. But then I would remember, *Oh. Nope. Can't call her. She's dead.*

The artist-designer Itaru Sasaki built a "wind phone" in his garden so his neighbors in Japan could use the unwired telephone booth as a conduit for conversations with the deceased, carried on the wind. You can call that too on-the-nose and more than a little delusional. I call it genius.

Everyone knows that one of the hardest and harshest things in the grieving process is accepting the death of communication, and yet it still clobbers us when the realization settles in. There will be no further exchanges—no questions, no statements, no time. And suddenly, whether you took full advantage of your ability to converse or foolishly squandered too many of those opportunities for no good reason (my failure to return my brother Jacky's call before tragedy struck in 1986, just for example), you miss it as though it were your lifeblood. Which is exactly where I was, emotionally and psychologically, when I arrived in Guilin, the intoxicating southern China city James and I made our way to immediately after disembarking from our Yangtze River cruise.

I couldn't talk to my mother now. She was gone. But I could talk to James's mother. She was here. I could ask Yù Yīng all the things I hadn't bothered to question about my own mother's life—such as how and why her story unfolded as it did, whom she'd loved, what she'd sacrificed, whether she'd found any measure of peace. I could ask for those details by way of James, who'd be learning along with me, and maybe that would spare him a few regrets whenever it was his mom's time to go. Plus, I was still deeply curious about Yù Yīng's life, as a story and as family history, including for any potential future offspring who might one day call this woman Nǎi Nai, the term for paternal grandmother.

The last time I'd seen her was at our Chinatown wedding banquet in 1996, when she'd sanctioned my wearing of the *qí páo*. That might have been the perfect occasion to hear more about her own courtship and marriage, except that I barely had the minutes and mental capacity to write my wedding vows, let alone get through another challenging interview with this person who was no longer just my hypothetical mother-in-law. Now, three years later, I was beyond eager to resume the talks we'd begun in 1994, during my first visit to Taiwan with James.

I knew the mission would require doubling back to restart her memories, which was fine. This time, I was prepared for all the revising and embellishing, something I secretly appreciated as that was my own instinct, too. My previous sessions with Yù Yīng had encouraged me to be less assiduously analytical; her loose, fragmented recollections imparted the permission I thought I needed to just go with the creative flow.

James was never more relaxed than when he was in his homeland, leaving the restaurant in Chin Chin's capable hands while he attended to the infinitely more rewarding business of family. He'd arranged it so we wouldn't be meeting his oldest sister for a couple of days, giving us time to settle in and enjoy the local attractions with Yù Yīng and two of his three brothers—Yǒng Míng (永明) and Cháo Fēng—who'd traveled with their mother from Taiwan, just as they'd done in 1987, when they and the eldest brother, Sān Guāng (三光), first set eyes on their newfound sibling. We ran into them in the lobby of the hotel as we were checking in; same as last time, the welcome was warm and genuine and miles from effusive. When Yù Yīng smiled in my direction, that was enough. She hadn't aged much, though she did appear shorter. Or maybe it was just the difference between wedding-appropriate footwear in Massachusetts and the flat, tropi-casual attire she had on for this occasion. I went in for a hug, as she'd come to expect. She said something about me being too skinny (*tài shòu*, 太瘦), as I'd come to expect.

Hours later, when we'd all gathered in Yù Yīng's room for tea—the kind you drink and the kind you spill—I was reminded of the surprisingly deep connections we'd already unearthed in our limited conversations, perhaps because there's a difference between interviewing and chatting. I recalled her great satisfaction in taking down the school bully, which had summoned my own greatest day with my mother—an event whose darker hues only revealed themselves to me in later life. Then there were Yù Yīng's rebellions against unwanted suitors and autocratic decisions that had rankled me on her behalf, but also on my own behalf, as a woman who'd more than once felt hemmed in by manmade rules and expectations.

I'd never been much of a rebel, which made me that much more of a fangirl when I encountered fearless women in the wild. I was the girl who blushed when embarrassing things happened to *other* people. Like the time in junior high school when a classmate was doing the fifty-yard dash during gym class outdoors, and her disposable Mickey Mouse pad shot right out of her track shorts, whirring through the air like a helicopter blade before coming to rest—blood side up—atop a tuft of grass. (Our unflappable gym teacher, Miss Toohey, calmly picked up an orange plastic traffic cone she'd used to mark the finish line, walked across the field and dropped it over the maxi pad, abolishing our nervous giggles with her shrill metal whistle before resuming class.) Yù Yīng didn't seem embarrassed by anything. Not her wins, known to involve rule-breaking and revenge, and certainly not her losses.

I'd met James in the wake of what felt like a personal nadir, the deaths of my beloved sister and brother-in-law within months of each other, so I knew what it felt like to go from a loss to a win. Yù Yīng knew this feeling also, and she wasn't too proud to tell me how her counterculture convictions had once or twice been tempered by pragmatism, in a good way.

Again, there is always a saying. The best way to sum up Yù Yīng's entertaining tale of betrothal, told to me as we sipped our aromatic tea from tiny ceramic cups in her Guilin hotel room, is a quote from Sun Tzu's *The Art of War*: "There is no instance of a nation benefiting from prolonged warfare."

In the spring of 1941, most of southern China was consumed with news that the Japanese military was advancing in their direction. It had been nearly four years since Japan invaded, causing the Chinese government to shift its capital from Nanjing to Chongqing ahead of a brutal beating known as the Rape of Nanjing, in which hundreds of thousands of Chinese were assaulted, tortured, and massacred. Yù Yīng's home province of Guangxi hadn't yet fallen into enemy hands, but no one could feel secure with so many refugees spilling over the borders. Unmarried females had the added risk of being swept up and enslaved, often forced into marriages with invading soldiers, all of which is to say that while it wasn't a good time for much, it was quite a lucrative time to be a matchmaker.

The job of putting lives together isn't quite as godlike as it sounds. Through some combination of data and deduction, observation and hearsay, a very human assessment is made. It's not always correct, but it can be quite astute, and it can work in ways that make free will and serendipity seem highly overrated. Now seventeen, Ā Mèi was an excellent matchmaker, which I'd pretty much assumed from the moment Yù Yīng told her meet-cute anecdote. It came as no surprise, then, to hear Yù Yīng put her friend at the center of everything that came after the bump.

Ā Mèi didn't orchestrate their initial collision, mind you. That was entirely the boy's doing—the one who'd traveled all the way from Zhongdu, a town about nineteen miles west of her village that belonged to a chunk of Liujiang County known as Zhaisha, just to jostle Yù Yīng in the street. Why? As Ā Mèi later explained it to Yù Yīng, "For the fun of it, mostly." His father, a tailor and fabric merchant when he wasn't restoring hotels, had spotted Yù Yīng months earlier, as she was being paraded around the village for winning a local beauty pageant. The son was soon dispatched to get a closer look, in case he fancied her for a wife, and that's when he took it upon himself to not just look but also touch.

I didn't love the implications of that explanation. Suddenly, their beguiling brush seemed less coyly romantic and more disrespectful, not to mention immature. Unless it was just clumsy—a playful way to stand out? Perhaps the boy knew it would be years before anything might come of their encounter, and this was his attempt at being memorable. He was seeking to leave a mark. Which he did—not just on Yù Yīng, but more importantly on Ā Mèi.

As a budding matchmaker, Ā Mèi was the agent who could give Yù Yīng a modicum of agency, or what passed for it in these times. Ā Mèi could be the voice of reason when her friend's parents demanded that their daughter finally give up on her quest for storybook romance; she could persuade them to let her find the right husband for Yù Yīng. And when Ā Mèi located the boy who'd rocked both their worlds that day in the street—the boy whom Yù Yīng had more than once confessed she still wondered about—it would be easy to convince both sets of parents to accept the union. His father had already approved the attractive bride; her father was desperate. The hard thing would be convincing Yù Yīng.

"I was so angry." She nearly spat as she told me her reaction to the plan. "I said no."

But Yù Yīng's ire was mainly about powerlessness, and Ā Mèi knew it. Hearing the defiance that still coated her voice all these years later, I wished James wasn't in the room, so I could speak candidly about rejecting his first two marriage proposals. I think she would have understood how off-balance they'd made me feel—how unseen, in a way, even though that had been the opposite of his intention. It seemed fair to conclude that she and I shared an aversion, not to relationships but to being cornered. I was again startled by how much I identified with this woman, despite the enormous gulf in our circumstances.

As Yù Yīng continued to fume over her parents' autocratic decision about her marital status, there was also no mistaking the delight she took in responding to it. First, she said, Ā Mèi stepped in to offer an idea: What if they let the boy, whose name was indeed Qiáo Shēng (James's dad; nailed it), pay a visit to Yù Yīng's home? Yes, it would go against tradition, but these two had already met, and since that introduction didn't follow convention either, what Ā Mèi proposed was really a reintroduction. In private, the matchmaker persuaded her client and friend that she'd at least get more than a glimpse of the boy's adorable backside as he walked away this time, and he'd get to see that she was more than just an object to be jostled.

Yù Yīng did like the idea of that.

A visit was arranged, and it began as expected, because in meetings such as this, small details carry a great deal of weight. Did you greet your guest with tea and watermelon seeds and other welcoming snacks? Did you behave "like a lady"—that is, did you sit in the proper position and take care not to talk too loudly or show your teeth when you smiled? Yù Yīng's plan was to play the gracious hostess on the surface but also let Qiáo Shēng discern the formidable woman inside the dutiful girl he was proposing to marry.

Yù Yīng says she was already coming to terms with the idea that he'd be her husband; none of this was about thinking she could continue to defy her parents indefinitely (a seasoned observer of gambling always knows when to fold), or about Qiáo Shēng's worthiness—she didn't know anything about him, beyond the impressive sturdiness of the one shoulder that had grazed her. She'd learn that he was descended from hardy, hardworking stock who'd lived for centuries in the Fengcheng County village of Shuidong, in the southeastern province of Jiangxi. His parents had moved as newlyweds to Guilin before settling in Zhongdu, where they now ran an inn, and Qiáo Shēng taught himself to repair clocks, hoping that might be his vocation. Only, lately he'd been thinking more about becoming a soldier, because clocks weren't going to stop the Japanese from overrunning China.

Though she didn't show it, Yù Yīng was pleased to hear such selfless initiative coming from a man she'd previously only seen as presumptuous and brash. Character is exponentially attractive in a potential mate, and nearly irresistible when combined with spark. So, Yù Yīng continued to listen as Qiáo Shēng talked on, and on, and when the pronouncements and promises finally ended, she simply rose, bowed, and made her exit. She claims she didn't say a word, but she did turn back to look briefly in Qiáo Shēng's direction as she left the room. I imagine the profile of her cocked head, artfully framed by the doorway, made her look even more beautiful than she had the day he first approached her. Yù Yīng is sure of one important thing: This time, he was the one who noted *her* sly smile, which lingered just long enough for her to part her wetted lips and flash a glorious mouthful of teeth.

Whatever Yù Yīng saw in Qiáo Shēng, and vice versa, their reintroduction was, as Ā Mèi wisely predicted, enough to convince them to move forward with the marriage. Yù Yīng had let her suitor know what and whom he was courting, and he hadn't shrunk in the face of it. If I'd thought it would translate, I'd have congratulated her on cracking the code to their briefcase of plutonium *(click)*. Instead, I just asked, "What do you remember about your wedding?"

I had in mind the period films that had dazzled me—Zhang Yimou's *Red Sorghum* and *Raise the Red Lantern* among them—wherein a bride dressed all in red is transported in a sturdy wooden sedan chair, known as a *jiao zi* (轿子), across miles of rugged country just to get to her groom. Yù Yīng confirmed that she had, in fact, been carried this way by her four brothers for the entire nine or so hours it took to get from her village to the home of awaiting in-laws in Zhongdu, after her parents had said their goodbyes and marked her departure by throwing a pot of water onto the ground outside their front door. (They do this because discarded water, like a daughter betrothed, cannot be returned to you. It is forever gone.)

"It was a very old *jiao zi*, very heavy," Yù Yīng recalled. "The ride made me dizzy, but I dared not open the curtain even just to get my bearings and a breath of fresh air. I stayed inside the whole time."

I naïvely asked if she'd donned a *fèng guān* (凤冠, *phoenix crown*) and a special silk robe for the ride—again, the kind of cinematic flourish I'd been trained to expect. "Not at all. Who can afford those?" she said. "We were so poor. A phoenix crown is just the stuff of operas. I wore a chiffon hair flower, a simple red dress, red shoes—all hand-sewn."

The groom was also dressed head to toe in red. His embroidered vest alone took several months to make, and that was only manageable because his father was so proficient with a tailor's needle and thread. In more abundant times, when cash and optimism weren't as scarce, a bride might have several outfits to change into at various stages of her wedding celebration. Yù Yīng reported having just one, and feeling fortunate that it was of decent quality.

Fortune. It plays a huge role in Chinese weddings, even in the shadow of war. You start with an auspicious date (theirs was in October 1941, the Year of the Snake) and offerings that court goodwill for all involved. Qiáo Shēng's parents pledged one *yuán dà tóu* (袁大頭)—a large silver dollar, highly prized—for the purchase of their future daughter-in-law. They also presented impressive betrothal gifts: half a pig—the head *and* the shoulders, two full legs (not just the trotters), luscious pork belly meat—and two live chickens. It must have been enough to please the right deities because good things started to happen almost immediately: The groom's family, who'd never had a drop of luck raising pigs, suddenly had six fat hogs in their barn as the nuptials approached, allowing them to sell half and butcher the other three for an unexpectedly sumptuous wedding banquet. But the best news was yet to come: Just three months into the marriage, Yù Yīng discovered she was pregnant. It was an auspicious union indeed. She gave birth on October 24, 1942, at four o'clock in the afternoon. It was the Year of the Water Horse. The girl was named Xiù Líng, but she would more often be referred to by her nickname, Tǔ Xiù—no minor detail, as I would come to understand.

There's a reason for every moniker that is handed out in China. Chinese philosophy is rooted in the five elements: water, earth, fire, wood, and metal. *The Book of Changes* assigns an element to each of the twelve signs of the zodiac, forming a cycle that repeats every sixty years. Horses are known to be fiery. But a horse influenced by the element of water, as are all those born in the lunar year of 1942, is expected to be deep, wise, and diplomatic.

Water yields. It is deferential. Though this can be a positive trait in humans—without it we would have no decent mediators and even worse politicians than we do—it can also be a negative, especially for females, when strength and resolve are inevitably tested. Qiáo Shēng had insisted on the name Xiù Líng because one interpretation of *líng* (灵) is "clever." But Yù Yīng wanted her daughter to have the element of earth, for stability and grounding and to make her, above all else, nurturing. In China, naming is as good as willing an inheritance. Entire fortunes can be made and unmade by a name, which is why they would call this girl Tǔ Xiù—*tǔ* (土) meaning "earth" and *xiù* (秀) meaning "beautiful" or "excellent"—so that her character would be unimpeachable and her future would be secure.

The Excellent Earth. It was a name that even one-upped Pearl Buck, not that Yù Yīng had considered the author in choosing it.

CHAPTER 12

Limbo

"I found out many years later that Ā Mèi killed herself," Yù Yīng told me, her face as unemotional as if she were relaying the market price of Guilin's famously plump and juicy pomelos. We were still in that southern China jewel of a city, where we'd traveled to meet James's mother and siblings, including his reclaimed Old Sister, following our Yangtze River adventure. Hours had passed since Yù Yīng told me the story of her arranged marriage and the unusual matchmaking that had happened on the sly. She sometimes dropped these kinds of fragments into the dinner conversation, or the idle chatter during a car ride, or the silent spaces as we strolled city streets.

"Oh, how sad," I said, preparing to keep up with her train of thought the same way I'd gathered myself to stay in stride with Neville Trotter MP as a House of Commons intern. "What happened?"

"The pain became too much. Her bound feet had developed sepsis," Yù Yīng reported. "I heard she walked halfway up the mountain near our village before collapsing. She may have died from exposure, or perhaps an animal got to her. When the tea gatherers found her corpse, they say the mangled nubs of her bare feet were shredded down to the bone."

I shuddered as she went on.

"And do you want to know the saddest part?"

She knew I did.

"For several days after, while the mourners came and went from the home, her family still bound her body with fresh cloths every sunrise and sunset," Yù Yīng marveled, reminded of how her poor friend had literally orchestrated her own death march to slip those bonds, and her caretakers responded by rewrapping her spirit for eternity.

"A roulette wheel has more logic," she concluded, shaking her head.

I could have asked many more questions about Ā Mèi's demise. I didn't. Tragedy doesn't always need to be sifted and analyzed. At least, that's my excuse for not having a therapist: Just the thought of inching back through my own darkness to clean out the drainage ditch exhausts me. I do know that's bananas and I'm not doing myself any favors; therapy is the healthiest kind of exercise. I just don't think I have the will, or a big enough shovel. Like Yù Yīng, and my own mother, my instinct is to keep moving forward, even when my toenails fall off from all the running.

I didn't need to know more than Yù Yīng wanted to tell me about Ā Mèi. I knew that she loved her and credited her with arranging a marriage that was at least better than most. I assumed that after she took in the news of Ā Mèi's death, she processed and grieved it in her way. Then, I imagined, life went on for Yù Yīng, the way it always does, with most people unaware of the tiny hole left behind, as unrepairable as all the other holes in the universe.

I'd love to know the number of near misses (though I do wonder why it's not "near hits") experienced in an average lifetime. It must at least be in the trillions.

On a Monday in 2001, I took a United Airlines flight from Boston to Los Angeles for a business trip. Eight days later, that same flight, UA175, was hijacked by terrorists and rammed into one of New York's Twin Towers, instantly killing everyone on board and joining the annals of worst days in

American history. Do I call my near miss luck? Does that make the people who died *un*lucky? To me, it sounds judgmental, like the ones who didn't dodge disaster weren't deserving of good fortune, weren't worthy of being saved. Applied more broadly, that general premise would have to include my sister Patty, my brother Jacky, and my superhero brother-in-law, Jan. It would also extend to the losses of my father and my mother.

No.

The more stories I heard from Yù Yīng, the more sold I was on the randomness of tragedy. I'd spent so much time questioning the fairness of the cosmos, demanding to know—more than once out loud—"Who gets to live?" Then I met a woman who showed me the wisdom of answering that question with a question—either her son's patented "You ask me, who I gonna ask?" or its less cheery antecedent: "Why ask?"

Maybe my need for order could be temporarily realized in a precisely shoveled driveway or a freshly shaven chin, but there was no such order to the universe. The souls who died were neither being chosen for a higher calling nor punished for their sins; it was time to let that twisted Catholic BS go. In Yù Yīng's world, life was understood to be impermanent; its span could be determined by anything, including the trajectory of a bullet or the touch of a loving hand.

"Tǔ Xiù nearly died when she was two," Yù Yīng was saying now, not long after she'd finished telling me about the end of Ā Mèi. It's impossible to know whether the two were connected somehow in her mind, or merely came out in the same slipstream of consciousness that flowed without much prompting on this one evening in Guilin. I didn't ask her to go on; she just did.

"We were in the mountains," she explained. "It was after the Japanese came."

I knew some of this history from James, who'd told me his father made good on his intention to become a soldier, emerging from officer school in Guilin to become a top-ranking Kuomintang air force master sergeant. When Qiáo Shēng was deployed to the frontlines, his wife and daughter took refuge with her parents, who still lived in her hometown, until everything fell apart in the winter of 1945.

Yù Yīng remembers waking up to warning shouts and instantly rousing Tǔ Xiù, who was curled beside her on the mat that was their bed. The toddler knew a less frantic version of this routine: Sometimes, when her mother had to help with a harvest, they would also get up before the sun. So, she slid willingly into a baby sling known as a *bēi dài* (背带), its ruby-colored straps of cloth binding her securely to her mother's back, where she promptly summoned sleep again even as her body took flight.

In the dark, Yù Yīng's entire family spilled out of their houses and into the woods, joined there by perhaps a dozen neighbors looking for the quickest and safest ascent. They'd settled on a path and were about halfway up the peak when a baby among them started to whimper, which quickly became a wail that bounced off the trees and built. There was a sharp, whizzing sound. Then another. The bullets weren't many or well-aimed—they appeared to be coming from a considerable distance downslope—but they were enough to stop the fugitives in their tracks. Yù Yīng says she felt a rush of air around her shoulders, and then Tǔ Xiù stirred for the first time inside her sling.

"Shhhhh," Yù Yīng both consoled and admonished before the child's tiny moan could turn into anything more fully formed. *"Wǒ men yī dìng yào hěn ān jìng"* (我们一定要很安静, *we must be quiet*), she whispered.

Everyone around them ducked and crouched. The baby's father clamped a hand over his son's mouth to muffle the cries. Yù Yīng stopped and unwrapped the carrier to comfort her daughter; that's when she discovered that Tǔ Xiù had been hit.

There was blood running out of the toddler's neck, but she didn't appear distressed. She wasn't even crying. Trying not to panic, Yù Yīng probed for an opening with her fingers, struggling to pinpoint the wound in the darkness. She exhaled when she realized that the bullet had only grazed Tǔ Xiù's head, searing off about an inch of skin in a horizontal line just below the earlobe. They could not have come closer to disaster.

Luckily, a woman born in the Chinese countryside knows what to do when she's stuck on a mountain and needs to stanch a bleeding flesh wound. She grabs a clump of mud and grass and applies it to her child's neck as a poultice, thankful that the mud mixture also cools and comforts. Yù Yīng might have wished for a moment to breathe, but she knew they had to resume fleeing before the soldiers closed the gap and one thing or another gave away their position again. At least the baby wasn't crying now.

The infant's father was huddled just a few feet away from Yù Yīng, where he still had his papa bear paw over the mouth of the child cradled in the crook of his arm. His wife's head was buried in the front of his shirt, and only then did Yù Yīng see that she was pounding at his chest and weeping, without either her fists or her mouth seeming to make any sound.

The baby was unmistakably dead.

They'd learn later that he'd been suffocated by his own father's impulse to protect their party from further detection. Now, as Yù Yīng looked on in horror, the man rose and walked toward the edge of the mountainside, where the trees stopped and the earth abruptly gave way to nothing but sky. His wife moved with him, clutching at his clothes like a beetle flailing in high winds. They reached the cliff, and before anyone in their party could protest, he dropped his cradled arm parallel to his thigh, then quickly thrust it back out in front of his chest, releasing the tiny body to the black hole of the valley below.

What the fuck.

Yù Yīng had stopped talking, and I was aghast as I realized what she'd just recounted. I looked up from my notes and asked her family to repeat their rough translation, in case they'd misspoken any important details, or I'd misinterpreted them because they so closely resembled a scene from some miniseries I saw on television when I was a teenager—*Holocaust*, I think it was, with Meryl Streep and James Woods. Whether you see it dramatized on-screen or you hear about it in the hotel room of a woman who claims to have witnessed it, the smothering of a baby isn't something you process easily or move beyond quickly. Yù Yīng wasn't surprised that I was unsettled by these events; she'd just had more time with them, and she knew there was so much more tragedy waiting to be disclosed.

"We all wept for him," she told me, for the record.

She didn't say whether she meant the father or the baby.

Yù Yīng leaves a lot of things unsaid, and what she does say doesn't always add up. That's not only because she was in her seventies when we met and still telling stories at one hundred; it's because, as the proverb goes, the best memory is not so firm as faded ink.

Actually, the trickiest thing about memory is its skill at both fading and sharpening. Whatever we think we remember, we tend to think we remember exactly. As much as distance enables clarity, it also enables false clarity. I would leave every conversation with Yù Yīng knowing I'd heard the most extraordinary things, and this was well before I had transcripts to refer to—before I'd even had a chance to go back over my minimal notes. I knew they were extraordinary not because they were always outsized, verifiable, fully formed accounts, but because they were whatever had floated to the surface as she stirred the sediment of her life. It didn't matter that her memories grew more unreliable by the year—that she would give me numerous contrary accounts of the same event or be certain of "facts" that were out of sync with history or not be able to remember when or how many times she'd been pregnant. I got very used to her picking up a narrative thread wherever she'd last left off, only to reverse herself and chart a completely different, incompatible course by the time we bid goodnight. It was as comforting as it was maddening.

It was comforting because we all have selective memory, some of us more deliberately than others. Already I've chosen not to remember certain events that make me uneasy, disconsolate, insane. I hope that when I'm approaching a century on this planet, I, too, can keep only the version of history that my brain deems correct and constructive.

That's why I choose to believe Yù Yīng when she tells me their time on the mountain lasted many weeks, through much of the winter, with temperatures sometimes dropping below freezing. She says they slept outdoors among the pine and ansu trees except when they could find temporary shelter—perhaps an abandoned hut or a sympathetic farmer's barn—and they foraged for edible greenery, fruits, fungi, and potable water wherever it could be collected.

"We discovered how little it can take to sustain a life," Yù Yīng says. And that would be a valuable lesson when at last the spring weather came and their diminished enemy was in retreat. They could go home then, but to what? Yù Yīng reports that the Japanese had burned most of her birthplace to the ground. They'd poisoned the village water supply and butchered the livestock. They'd emptied the warehouse where all the communal food and supplies were stored. Anyone who elected to stay would need to start over, on land as tired as they were.

The weather gods never seem all that concerned when humans dig themselves into an unnecessary hole. Drought that follows war is just like any other drought from a meteorological standpoint, but as a pain point it's far more acute. Once the rice and seeds became prohibitively expensive, widespread starvation in what was left of her Liujiang village was inevitable.

"Do you know what it is to see people starve?" Yù Yīng asked me. She hadn't been told about my eating disorder, so she wouldn't have considered how ashamed the question made me feel. I think she just wanted to convey that whatever I thought starvation looked and behaved like, from anything I'd read or watched, the reality was far worse. So, she held out her wrist, which happened to be wrapped in an ouroboros made of white jade. It could be seen as an allegory for infinite regeneration, but Yù Yīng knew different. When the body devours itself, it leaves nothing recognizable behind.

Death is ugly. Most of us can't face that ugliness, so we make it beautiful by forging it into art, sometimes wearable. We make it a symbol. We make it eternal. Like the old rugged cross.

Yù Yīng didn't see anything redeeming in the suffering that heaved day and night in her town. She saw it as just another thing to survive. And the ouroboros was a reminder that she *had* survived, but a great many had not.

INT. YÙ YĪNG'S IN-LAWS' HOUSE IN ZHONGDU—LATE AFTERNOON

Zhongdu, China, spring 1946. Yù Yīng is in the kitchen with Qiáo Shēng's father and stepmother. She's holding a letter and appears stressed.

YÙ YĪNG'S MOTHER-IN-LAW

(flatly)

You cannot take her.

YÙ YĪNG

What are you talking about? Cannot take whom?

YÙ YĪNG'S MOTHER-IN-LAW

You know what I mean, Yù Yīng. Tǔ Xiù. You cannot take Tǔ Xiù with you.

Sitting off to the side, Yù Yīng's father-in-law doesn't contribute a word to the conversation, but with downcast eyes he looks at Yù Yīng and tilts his head toward his wife, as if to say, "What she said."

I always knew we'd get here, ever since the night that James's family history slipped into our pillow talk and revealed the existence of a sister who'd been left behind in China. We were now in Guilin primarily so James could meet her, but I also wanted to understand the fuller story and impact of her abandonment, whatever mother and daughter were willing and able to share. I was under no delusion that we would get beyond scratching the surface. "Abandonment issues" covers a lot of ground.

The day my sister Patty died in a hospital and the news was delivered to her two daughters at home, her ten-year-old had the most honest reaction

I'd ever heard: "But, who's gunna do my hair in the mornings?" That's survival. Children are built to prioritize whatever meets their needs in the moment. Eventually we grow up, and most of us realize that a lot of our needs aren't ever going to be met, so we stop looking for someone to do our hair in the mornings. But we don't stop missing it.

Maybe I wanted to know how Tǔ Xiù and Yù Yīng navigated the wrenching separation that came their way in the spring of 1946 because I was still looking for guideposts as I bumped along the walls of my own losses. Maybe if I could understand what had happened to them, I could manufacture a shovel big enough to dig into some of what had happened to me, if I could ever get over feeling selfish for asking the questions honestly.

According to the people who taught catechism classes in my Braintree church, you can't get into heaven if you're not baptized. That's even if you die as an infant or are raised by people who don't make your state of grace a priority. The best you can do in that case is purgatory, where you still have a chance, or limbo, where you're just plain stuck, eternally.

Limbo describes large swaths of the human condition. In way too many parts of the world, including China, it also describes the cycle of war that makes lasting peace unattainable. Not long after the Japanese surrendered in the fall of 1945, the Chinese civil war that had begun in 1927 resumed, which sent Qiáo Shēng off to the next front line and Yù Yīng back to Zhongdu, where she was expected to care for his parents. The political future of the country was once again up for grabs: It would either be shaped by Mao Tse-tung's Communist Party doctrine, aimed at empowering the peasants and farmers, or Chiang Kai-shek's Kuomintang, promising a return to minority rule that favored the usual power brokers. Qiáo Shēng was in service to the latter side, the losing side.

About eight months into her time in Zhongdu, the letter arrived. It wasn't preserved—nothing was, once the political persecutions ramped up—but it's thought to have been crafted as more of a directive, with an economy of words—or, in this case, characters—that rivaled a Jocko Page dispatch.

"Come to Shanghai," it began without pleasantries or fanfare. "You must leave now, before it will be too late. Use the money I sent. Be careful."

It did not address Yù Yīng specifically, from what she remembers, nor was it signed, just in case it should fall into the wrong hands (the same reason it was promptly destroyed). Yù Yīng knew her husband's handwriting and no-nonsense way of communicating. She'd pack a few things and retrieve the wad of cash from where it was hiding under a bedpan—Master Sergeant Qiáo Shēng's wages, or what the postman had delivered of them—which would need to be sewn into the folds of what she was wearing if she hoped to slip it past the scoundrels en route. When she felt ready, she'd grab Tǔ Xiù's hand and hit the road, as unceremoniously as Yolanda escaping with her girl in the seaweed-green Chevy Nova bound for Nantasket Beach.

Until her in-laws said, *not so fast*.

When Yù Yīng began sharing this portion of her story with me, in broad brushstrokes during our first trip to Guilin and as fleshed out as she could make it in subsequent tellings, I tried to imagine what it might be like to uproot your entire life in an instant just because the man you love says go. I hadn't even been able to relocate from California to Massachusetts without the additional push of my mother's heart troubles, my sister's cancer scare, and a new job beckoning.

Yù Yīng knew that their side was losing the war. She knew that her husband, now stationed in Shanghai, would not have a lot of warning whenever it was time for him to join Cheng Kai-shek's government in exile, though at this point Cheng hadn't yet laid plans for that exile to be in Taiwan. She had to trust that he knew more than she did about their optimum window for escape. But she still had difficulty blindly accepting Qiáo Shēng's decision to summon her at this exact moment in the spring of 1946, when Tǔ Xiù was three and routine felt like safety. It was an order that Yù Yīng might once have met with questions and exploratory pushback. Her husband's letter required a leap of faith that seemed extraordinary. Then came the conversation that Yù Yīng had never even considered: the one where her in-laws forbade her to bring Tǔ Xiù along.

It's probably hard for most Westerners to fathom that command. Qiáo Shēng could order his wife to leave, but this child—his father's only biological grandchild—would not be part of the bargain, they insisted. Their reasons were many, but these three were paramount:

1. If Tǔ Xiù departed, it would leave her grandparents diminished and without enough family to look after them.
2. Surely Qiáo Shēng's exile was temporary. In a few months or years, Cheng Kai-shek's revitalized army would overpower their Communist opponents and retake the mainland.
3. Traveling with a small child wasn't safe. The journey from Zhongdu to Shanghai was more than a thousand miles and would require multiple forms of transportation (trucks, buses, trains, boats) in addition to long days on foot. If they were intercepted by officials or Mao sympathizers anywhere along the way, it could mean severe punishment, even death.

That last reason was the conversation stopper. I could imagine Yù Yīng defying anything and anyone to keep Tǔ Xiù by her side. But I could also see how that impulse surrendered quickly to the argument that she could be putting her daughter in grave danger. It must have seemed that the only way to save Tǔ Xiù was to leave her. But how does a mother do that?

There's a word for a child who is abandoned but not necessarily orphaned. It's the label you use when the status of the parents, dead or alive, is unknown. That child is called a foundling. Its parents, if alive, are called deserters.

If Yù Yīng fled to Shanghai and went on to depart the country with her husband as planned, she and Qiáo Shēng would also be branded enemies of the state, as would any of their offspring. Tǔ Xiù, if left behind, would need to bury her heritage—whatever shards of it her three-year-old brain insisted on retaining—and live as a foundling until and unless China's political climate changed. Her grandparents would assume the guise of a couple who'd somehow come upon the unrelated foundling and taken her in without asking any questions. Her parents wouldn't be dead; they would just be erased.

I said before that the worst thing that can happen to any parent is to watch their child die. I still believe that's true. But having a child taken from you—even when you're the one who does the leaving—and knowing that this child will live on without being certain of your love must be its own circle of hell. This is what Yù Yīng would be signing up for if she could summon the strength to abandon Tǔ Xiù the next morning, kissing her cheek on the way out the door, hours before the sun rose over Zhongdu.

I imagine it's a decision she's thought about ever since.

CHAPTER 13

State of Grace

In a posed photograph taken just after their reunion in 1987, Yù Yīng and Tǔ Xiù appear unmoored. They're frozen in a state of in-betweenness that only tells the viewer they're overcome with emotion; it doesn't tell us which emotion(s) or whether that's a good thing. Both women have tears in their eyes.

Tǔ Xiù is squinting and holding her mouth in a grimace that could either be a forced smile or a wince. Yù Yīng just seems stunned. Her eyes are wide and uncomprehending, her lips are pursed as though on the brink of quivering. Tǔ Xiù has an arm around her long-lost, miraculously undead mother's back. Yù Yīng's upper arms hold stiff against her own sides, their bottom halves are out of the camera frame but, based on her posture and what I know of her personality, I imagine they're dangling without purpose, perhaps waiting for her to remember how to use them. If you didn't know the context of this snapshot, you could just as easily think it's two women saying goodbye as saying hello. Two women in pain, or soul sisters over the moon. You probably wouldn't be wrong in diagnosing any of those things.

I remember when the *Challenger* space shuttle blew up in 1986 how, in the hours that immediately followed the tragedy, many videos and photographs showed teacher-astronaut Christa McAuliffe's mother, Grace

Corrigan, assimilating everything happening in the sky. Early on, Corrigan's weepy, hand-to-face reaction was presented by newspapers and TV stations as a picture of anguish, seemingly timed to the moment when she started to comprehend that the mission had gone horribly sideways. But it was later revealed that those images were recorded seconds *before* disaster struck, so they mostly captured Corrigan's awe and nerves and pride as she witnessed what she thought was the successful launch of her daughter's loftiest dream.

They say a picture is worth a thousand words. What they don't say is that the story it tells is sometimes ambiguous or incomplete, which can make it misleading and prone to false interpretations. I had a lot of experience with ambiguous images—in journalism and in life—so I wanted to be careful about how I regarded the mesmerizing reunification photo of Yù Yīng and Tǔ Xiù that I first saw in 1999, when we were still in Guilin after our Yangtze riverboat cruise, especially since James and I were just about to meet her.

Tǔ Xiù had traveled about two hours north by car from her home in Luzhaizhen to our downtown hotel, and after a brief introduction in the lobby—no tears this time, even though forty-year-old James was meeting his fifty-six-year-old sister for the first time (well, *I* cried)—we gathered again in Yù Yīng's room to hear stories accompanied by salty snacks and, naturally, many pots of tea.

I don't know what I expected to see in this latest mother-daughter meeting, their third since rediscovering each other when Chin Chin had hired an investigator to search for Tǔ Xiù in 1984, more than a decade after Nixon's visit to communist China reopened the East-West channels that made such searches more possible. I'd been told that Tǔ Xiù had been found through a classified ad placed in the local newspaper, which had altered her life even more dramatically than the one I'd responded to in 1979 looking for Mandarin Garden waitstaff. I couldn't wait to hear her side of the story I'd been piecing together from my conversations with Yù Yīng. But I understood that this moment wasn't about me. It was about my husband and his family and a recurring theme in their lives. It was about reconciliation.

A few hours after Yù Yīng left Zhongdu in the spring of 1946, setting out for Shanghai before the sun came up, her daughter was forming a couple of reasonable questions.

"Where is Mama?" Tǔ Xiù asked her grandparents when the sleep had rubbed out of her eyes and she didn't see her mother beside her in bed, or anywhere in the house.

They mumbled something about Yù Yīng having to go out.

"When will she be back?" Tǔ Xiù inquired.

"Soon," they said.

Tǔ Xiù's grandparents knew that no three-year-old has a fixed expectation of *soon*, so the conversation could go on this way for weeks and months. Eventually, the girl would stop asking, until at some point she would need to be reminded of a lie that she hadn't yet been told.

"You are getting older now," her grandparents would say when she was around five. "People might ask about your family. When they do, it is important that you tell them your parents are dead."

"They are?" Tǔ Xiù asked.

"Yes," the grandparents answered. And that's where the dialogue ended, since the five-year-old had happier activities on her mind and was no longer sure whom they were even talking about. Tǔ Xiù couldn't remember having a father. No image came to mind when she tried to conjure his face. Her mother, on the other hand, could be summoned if she concentrated hard, but only as a vague outline—a feeling, really. Tǔ Xiù described it to me as a calming force, which I took to mean serenity, which made me think of my own mother, and the lizard who'd transfixed me during my first visit to Yù Yīng's house in Taiwan.

Everything loops. And loops. And loops.

When Tǔ Xiù began recounting her story a few days into our Guilin visit, one of the first things she told James and me was how hard she'd fought to attend school, just like the mother she could not remember. After her grandfather died of heart failure and her step-grandmother quickly remarried, they moved into a new house where Tǔ Xiù, then no more than seven or eight, became the resident Cinderella. She did every backbreaking household chore her large new stepfamily demanded, and in her spare time she carried much-too-heavy sacks of grain or sold bundles of firewood and homemade buttons to scrape together enough money for tuition. But they only let her go to school sporadically, because her stepmother's new husband gambled, and appropriating Tǔ Xiù's modest income ensured that the family would eat for another week.

When their debts got so bad that none of her labors made a difference, Tǔ Xiù was tossed out onto the street to fend for herself. She was taken in by a former classmate's family after a period of homelessness and grew up having to defend herself against politically motivated attacks related to her sketchy origin story—a near-constant battle during the Cultural Revolution, when the only thing that saved her from persecution by Mao's Red Guards was a lack of evidence that her parents had fled to Taiwan. It must have pained Yù Yīng to learn this difficult history decades later, but when she spoke of Tǔ Xiù's resilience, as she made a point of doing with me, her maternal pride overflowed.

"My daughter," Yù Yīng noted, "is a survivor." I didn't write it down, but I'm sure she would have followed that declaration with her and James's patented move—the mashing of lips and dipping of the chin that said "fact."

James doesn't articulate his feelings so well when he's out of sorts, as he was when we were meeting Tǔ Xiù for the first time. He's the baby of his family, just like me. They'd stopped talking about his Old Sister long before he was old enough to ingest the conversation. It was only when she was found to be alive in China that he began to process this part of his parents' history, and by then he'd done three years in the Taiwanese army, stationed on an island just six miles off the coast of China, where his unit stood in perpetual readiness to fire the cannons pointed at the mainland. Though that never happened on his watch, he wasn't yet far enough removed from the conflict to romanticize news about a sister left behind in another war waged by variations of these same political parties four decades prior.

As uncommonly sensitive and intuitive as James can be, he shuts down when he gets nervous that emotions might overwhelm him—a lot like my dad did. So, I wasn't surprised to see him gloss over the impact of meeting his sister. He embraced her, but then he undercut the hug with a joke of some sort (in Mandarin, lost on me) and the same hearty laugh he'd deployed when meeting my family. Even much later as we assessed the day's events, he was still downplaying that massive moment, using mediocre words like *happy* and *nice*. It made me kind of angry to see him be so casual about a sibling resurrected from the grave, or what felt like that to me, but that was my bias and my problem.

Instead of trying to squeeze meaningful subtext from my husband's genial interactions with his family, I focused more of my attention on Yù Yīng and Tǔ Xiù. Initially, I was struck by their differences. I guess I expected Yù Yīng's firstborn to be a carbon copy of her, the way my oldest sibling, Nancy, looked the most like my mother of all of us. Instead, Tǔ Xiù had her father's wide eyes, thin lips, and triangular nose. She also had his pronounced cheekbones and high forehead, though Yù Yīng had those as well, so that's where the DNA collaborated. When I looked at Tǔ Xiù, I saw a mixture of James, who took after his dad, and Chin Chin, who most resembled their mom. But those were just surface impressions. As I spent time with this mother and daughter who had been lost to one another and were now making up time, I began to glimpse everything they shared that had nothing to do with physical features. I saw how they regularly anticipated each other's needs without having to put them into words. At least when I was in their company, Tǔ Xiù never sat anywhere that wasn't next to her mother. At every meal, she served Yù Yīng, always making sure Mama got the first and biggest spoonfuls. And when we walked, Tǔ Xiù saw to it that Yù Yīng didn't take a step without her girl being hooked into her arm, just the way my own mother liked to travel.

Tǔ Xiù was as openly infatuated with Yù Yīng as if they'd been frozen in time at three and twenty-two years old. Now fifty-six, if she could have reasonably crawled into her seventy-five-year-old mother's lap instead of just sitting next to her, she almost certainly would have. I could still feel the imprint of my mother's unusually long hug that one time she'd forcefully embraced me toward the end of her life; I couldn't fathom how much Tǔ Xiù must have ached to reclaim the touch of the woman who'd been by her side constantly until, abruptly one day, she wasn't. For forty years, Yù Yīng may have only been a feeling to Tǔ Xiù, but our needs don't change just because we lack the vocabulary to articulate them.

Unsurprisingly, Yù Yīng's state of mind in this moment was harder for me to decode. Outwardly, she accepted Tǔ Xiù's many adorations, but she wasn't as demonstrative in kind. She seemed guarded—*detached* might be too strong, but I sensed some distance. When asked, she would always say how miraculous and wonderful it was to have regained this beloved daughter. I always believed her, but what *wasn't* she saying?

Tǔ Xiù told me how she'd "burst into tears" when she heard about the classified ad that an auntie had noticed and alerted her to, prompting them to send a letter to the address listed, in Massachusetts, wherever that was. The first big hurdle, after the shock of discovering that a sister she never knew she had was now looking for her, was getting over the idea that the sister resided in America—land of oppression and greed, according to everything Tǔ Xiù had ever been taught. Mao had once called on citizens of every nation to rise up and launch "a sustained and vigorous offensive against our common enemy, US imperialism, and its accomplices," and threatened that Americans would be "hanged by the people of the whole world." How was Tǔ Xiù going to reconcile her excitement over a sibling reaching out from such an evil place?

Putting aside her shock and unease for the moment, Tǔ Xiù checked the mail every day for more than a month, hoping for her sister's reply. When it came, she couldn't be anything but ecstatic, despite her political indoctrination. "Dear Tǔ Xiù," Chin Chin wrote. "Maybe you don't know me, but I am your sister. Your mother is alive in Taiwan, where you also have four brothers. Your father passed away in 1971. We would like to come to China to meet you."

"It was unbelievable. A miracle," Tǔ Xiù said when I asked her how it felt to read that letter. Then she added an observation that made me pause: "I had never had my mother's love. Now she was found, and so was I."

Never, she said. That was her assessment of the past; it was as if her mother had not been there at all. Her choice of words made the hairs on my arms stand to salute the chill running through me. How quickly we forget, I thought. How temporary we all are.

I often get sick when I travel outside of the US. I don't know what it is—perhaps the change in diet, or the jolt to my immune system, or the stress that goes into all the planning and navigating. Whatever triggers these things, I just know that my generally healthy self throws in the towel at some point far from home, and more than once I've found myself seeking medical assistance in a foreign language as a result.

That's what happened a few days into our Guilin visit with Yù Yīng and Tǔ Xiù, much to my dismay since it meant taking time out of my talks with them. I'd awakened that morning with my lungs on fire. James took one look at my extra-pale complexion and commanded we get to a hospital. His tone was unyielding, not that I would have challenged his directive.

The hospital was highly rated, I was told. It was where they brought Westerners—the folks assumed to have money, who might complain if they were subjected to the standards tolerated by locals who weren't given any choice. I wondered what those other places must have looked like, because this place—while clean and efficient—was straight out of a movie set in World War II. Nurses in crisp, white dresses with matching hats darted between small rooms with curtains and corridors lined with narrow beds. I was hooked up to a plastic IV bag of hydrating saline hanging from a no-frills metal pole; I spotted no monitors like the ones that had taken up so much space in all the hospital rooms I'd been in back home. I sat down on a bed the size of a cot; no one asked me to disrobe.

When the doctor arrived, he looked at my tongue for maybe five seconds before reaching for my arm. With three fingers placed on my left wrist, he felt for a pulse—lightly at first, then applying more pressure—before moving on to the right wrist. Then he got up from his chair, said a few words or sentences in Mandarin to James, who nodded in agreement (I guess) as the doctor exited the room.

"Okay, we can go now," James said.

"Oh," I said. "That's it? What did he say?"

"He says you have—let me see, in Chinese it's *zhīqìguǎnyán* (支气管炎); I think in English maybe bronk-something . . ."

"Bronchitis?" I asked.

"Yes. Bronchitis. Very bad bronchitis," James reported. "He will give you some medicine. At the counter."

I was astounded.

"He knows that without even taking my temperature?" I said. "No blood? No labs? That's really it?"

"Right," James said with a proud smile. "Chinese style."

I've since read up on what the practitioners of traditional Chinese medicine call the "tongue-and-pulse diagnosis." It has a fascinating and formidable history dating back thousands of years. There are about thirty different pulse types, with names like feeble pulse, surging pulse, floating pulse, thready pulse, wiry pulse, and slippery pulse. How perfectly poetic is it that your pulse can be slippery? I feel like that describes so many states of the human body.

In Western medicine, the heart rate gets the most attention, which is why we get our blood pressure taken so much. In the East, pulse diagnosis is seen as one-stop shopping for measuring the health of every major organ: heart, liver, kidneys, lungs, spleen . . . Again, the poetry of that idea is even more marvelous than its practicality. Through a simple, noninvasive caress of the wrist, your entire body can be accessed, divulging its deepest secrets so its every ailment might be identified and treated. If only our psyches could be diagnosed as efficiently.

With antibiotics and vitamins, my bronchitis would clear up in a few days, during which time I would sleep a lot, eat very little, and take all the time I wanted to ponder, again, why I was so invested in Yù Yīng and Tǔ Xiù's resurrected relationship. When I resumed observing them together, one on one and in groups of family assembled for lavish "welcome home" banquets, I saw their dance differently.

I decided that Tǔ Xiù wasn't just making up for lost time by sucking up all the air around her mother. She was convincing herself that this was all real, even the parts she wasn't so keen on believing. She'd confessed a few of her struggles to me—her disappointment and confusion over why her parents didn't try harder to reclaim her; the jealousy attendant in meeting siblings who grew up together, with both their birth parents and far fewer hardships; the alienation, no matter how much acceptance and love these people preached in her direction, or vice versa.

As for Yù Yīng, it no longer seemed to me that she had her guard up just because she'd been hurt in the past, or because she felt unsure about her new role in her daughter's life. I saw Yù Yīng making space for her unresolved feelings about the abandonment, because banishing them would have done a disservice to everything she and her child had been through. Letting them endure legitimized the history and the journey. I think she understood that any darkness she still carried wasn't a punishment, a curse, or a cross; it was just a by-product of life.

Being in the company of Yù Yīng and Tǔ Xiù during those weeks in Guilin was an epiphany for me; it was watching acceptance play out in real time. Here were two women who had every reason to let disappointments, in themselves and in each other, consume and define their relationship. Instead, they were rediscovering the joys of being together—each at her own pace—without denying the trauma of being torn apart.

I think that's when I first considered that the way forward might not be limited to bipolar options, like you either run from your demons or dig in and wrestle them to the ground. It seemed possible to value the dissonance. Maybe I didn't need a colossal shovel to dig out from my past. Maybe I only needed to allow myself a little more grace.

CHAPTER 14

The Gene Pool

Fate.

I've spent way too much time thinking about this one word, wondering whether it deserves to be grouped under "things I cannot change" in the Serenity Prayer approach to life. That's certainly the way my mother thought of it. But is fate really a fixed concept? Or can there be many fates in perpetual motion, constantly adjusting to the decisions we make, the actions we take?

Perhaps we should think of fate as consequence instead of as predetermined conclusion.

That's a definition I could get behind.

❧

On the first day of the year 2000, my sister Carol called me.

"Happy New Year!" I shouted too aggressively into the phone, assuming she'd reached out to wish me the same.

"I have it," she said, flatly. "Happy New Year."

It was not the perfect hangover remedy. Neither was *it* my missing purse, which I have a habit of leaving in random, unsecure places—when

I bother to bring it at all. *It* was a gene mutation, specifically a BRCA (BReast CAncer) mutation that had been the topic of much conversation in my family as the 1990s came to a close. Carol wasn't calling with good tidings for the new millennium. She was calling with a diagnosis.

The world was new to BRCA mutations then. We'd just started shorthanding the acronym (pronounced "brah-cah") and were getting used to seeing it in headlines. We'd quickly learned that everyone carries BRCA genes, which are thought to act as tumor suppressors, but a mutation in any one of them could mean substantially higher risks of breast and ovarian cancer, as well as increased predisposition to some other cancers, including prostate and colon.

At that time, of the estimated 175,000 new cases of invasive breast cancer diagnosed each year among women in the United States (it's more than 300,000 annually now), only 5 to 10 percent were thought to be hereditary. It wasn't a huge population, but the research findings loomed large for those of us at risk. Discovery of BRCA gene mutations meant that, for families with a strong history of the disease, there might finally be something scientific at the root of it, something more than tough luck to blame. It meant that I suddenly had someplace real to direct my intellectual energy, and my anger.

In the sixteen years since Patty had lost her lopsided battle with breast cancer, her legacy had narrowed and darkened. Despite the many wonderful things she was—mother, peacemaker, comedian, hair magician—what the gorgeous, green-eyed redhead had most regrettably become to us was a painful, haunting statistic. Her sisters and daughters couldn't think of her without facing the fact that we'd ceased being part of the general population. Numbers-wise, we were all at increased risk for the disease—though how much more at risk than the average Jane, the medical establishment couldn't seem to agree on. I wouldn't say that I lived in daily fear of discovering a suspicious lump. But I would say that Patty's death cast a very long shadow, and at its darkest edges was the thing I dread most: powerlessness.

The problem with sneaky reproductive cancers isn't the possibility of death; each of us lives with that possibility every day. The problem is insufficient warning. New Englanders prefer disasters they can see coming. Blizzards. Hurricanes. Epic collapses by the perpetually star-crossed home team on the brink of a world championship. Living in California had taught me that I'd take any one of those calamities over the sudden and unpredictable earthquakes, flash-flood mudslides, and wind-whipped forest fires. Or cancer, which I recognize is rarely a matter of geography. The point is, regardless of the magnitude of danger, you at least want to think you have a fighting chance.

Nancy's disease was in remission as the 1900s slipped into history. After chemo and radiation treatments, her hair had grown back into a robust pixie cut. She'd returned to working full time, as a nurse specializing in high-risk pregnancies, and she generally appeared "normal" enough that one could almost forget she was ever ill. But not really. Out of sight wasn't out of mind, or out of danger. Reports of BRCA gene mutation research weren't something our family could intelligently ignore. Anything that might arm us with information, and the necessary authorization to take advantage of tools for early detection and preventive care, had to be considered. The bigger question was as much philosophical as it was practical: Did we really want to know *all* the answers? Carol was the first to come to a decision.

Now fifty-three, she worked as an administrative assistant at the same hospital as Nancy—Tufts New England Medical Center, where there is a very fine genetics clinic staffed by world-class doctors. Carol made an appointment, considered each of the pros and cons the clinicians outlined as they counseled her, and quickly concluded that testing was in her best interest. She functioned better with fewer variables and more facts. I did, too; I just didn't anticipate that her New Year's Day announcement would decide a few important things for us all.

The official verdict was a BRCA2 mutation located on chromosome 13. Apparently chromosomes aren't as superstitious as hotels, though perhaps they should be.

As Carol's medical news spread by telephone, the requisite family meeting was swiftly convened at my brother Jimmy's house, where siblings and spouses tossed around a few of the grimmer statistics over bar pizza and internet research printouts. In 2000, these were the facts as we knew them:

- BRCA1 and BRCA2 mutations carried an 80 to 90 percent risk of developing breast cancer and a 5 to 60 percent chance of ovarian cancer over a lifetime, depending on which mutation you had and which medical source you referenced.
- Incidence of prostate, colon, laryngeal, and male breast cancers were thought to be higher in individuals with BRCA1 and BRCA2 mutations.
- Each offspring of a person with BRCA1 or BRCA2 mutations had a 50 percent chance of also carrying the mutation.

It is in our family DNA to make light of the dark. So, we began by remarking sarcastically on our obvious similarities, as Catholic-raised Italian Scottish Americans, to the Ashkenazi Jewish population, where BRCA mutations had been found to be notably prevalent. We joked about being newly inducted members of the Mutated BRCA2 Gene Pool, wondering if that came with its own cabana. Carol smiled weakly, with the playfulness of someone who's just had her identity stolen.

Her geneticist, Dr. Rosemarie Smith, had told her that the mutation revealed in her test results likely traced back to our father's side of the family. The "evidence" was circumstantial but compelling: a paternal cousin had died in her fifties of breast cancer, that cousin's sibling had been recently diagnosed at fifty with the same disease, and one of my father's brothers had prostate cancer. Further testing would be needed to confirm the doctor's suspicions, which presented every living Page in our orbit with a classic twenty-first-century dilemma. Now that we knew the gene mutation existed, did the benefits of diagnosing each potentially afflicted family member outweigh the psychological traumas of living with that diagnosis?

For Carol, who thought she knew the answer, it had been a cruel slap to find that she wasn't at all prepared. So convinced had she been of both the mutation's existence in our family and her personal immunity to it that her "positive" test resu t threw into question virtually everything she'd spent a half century believing about her body and her psyche.

I remember a conversation in the late 1980s, sometime after Jan succumbed to the ravages of melanoma and Jacky had his fatal seizure, during which Carol and I speculated on how we each thought we might die. My dad had always been outspoken about hoping for a heart attack. ("Nice and quick," he said. "No mess.") That sounded good to me, too, and just as plausible as a long illness or a freak accident. I was still in my twenties then. What did I really know about credibly scripted endings? But Carol seemed to know, the crystal-clear way you know when you're terrified of elevators or mayonnaise, that she would *not* die of cancer. Something violent, like a car crash, perhaps. But more likely old age, which offered socially acceptable crankiness as a bonus. Now, with her cancer odds dramatically increased, did Carol need to reimagine her fate, and therefore her life? At minimum, she was faced with a few new choices, some of which had to be made immediately.

She began weighing the possible benefits of cancer-prevention drugs like raloxifene and tamoxifen. She scheduled a hysterectomy and a baseline colonoscopy, which was the easy part compared with considering a prophylactic bilateral mastectomy (removal of both breasts). She also readied herself for twice annual mammograms and CA125-monitoring blood tests that could help detect cancerous activity. Mostly, like the rest of us, she wondered if anything can ever really be done to stave off your genetic destiny.

⁂

Imagine if my mother actually *had* made babies with Arnie the Milkman, as my father liked to insinuate in his clichéd cracks when we were kids. Would Arnie's DNA have been superior? Would it have spared us the inheritance of a BRCA2 mutation? Or would it only have traded one set of problems for some other—like what if Arnie's genes were predisposed toward allergies, or addiction, or cankles?

We can never know all the fates that we escape. Just as we will never know what better fates we miss out on. My father never dreamed, as he was joking about the dairy-delivering adulterer, that his genes would one day be branded defective and blamed for exposing his children to a notorious killer. Thank Christ he died when he did, before Carol's test results were in, because that revelation would almost certainly have killed him. In fact, I was oddly grateful in this moment that both of my parents were dead.

At least they didn't have to stand by while each of their descendants grappled with the implications of testing. And not having them around allowed us to move forward efficiently, without having to manage the cumulative effects of bad news. We were free to proceed at our own pace, or not at all, without having to justify our decisions to anyone. It wasn't long before Nancy served notice that she would be tested next.

None of us was surprised at her decision or voiced our legitimate questions about why a fifty-seven-year-old stage 3 cancer patient needs to be screened. Wasn't it something of a foregone conclusion that she had the mutation? And what difference would it make if she *didn't* have it? Neither result was going to change her life in any significant way. She'd already had her ovaries removed, had started taking the estrogen-modulator drug raloxifene, and was being monitored closely because of her disease and the fact that she was a nurse at one of the best hospitals in Boston. Still, we understood Nancy's need for clarity—not only for herself, but for her offspring.

If she didn't have the mutation, her children and their children could assume they carried no inherited risk. They'd be spared from having to think about screening, at least for this one scary genetic marker. Of course, it might then be considered a cruel joke that Nancy had wound up with ovarian cancer anyway, but cruel jokes are as plentiful as squirrels in the Northeast. Sometimes they get inside your walls; it's not always due to a structural failing.

Nancy made an appointment to see Dr. Smith.

She learned that her testing would be streamlined: Diagnosis for us was now a three- to four-week process rather than the six- to eight-weeks that

Carol had endured. That's because, from here on out, the laboratory would look only for the marker of our already identified family mutation. When I asked why the clinic wouldn't just go ahead and examine the whole gene string every time, just in case something else was there to be discovered, I was assured that the chances of having an additional BRCA gene mutation in the family were extremely remote. No one mentioned billable hours or insurance coverage, though I suspect that's the most honest answer. Anyway, while Nancy awaited her lab results, the rest of us mulled whether to step up and be screened as well.

Jimmy did, and eventually learned he was positive, which would demand an unwelcome conversation with his three kids when they seemed old enough to know.

Patty's daughters, who would both be examined in time, were the only definitive way to link her fatal breast cancer to the genetic cause that now seemed undeniable. If one or both had the mutation, case closed. If not, the jury would still be out—though only in the same sense that Nicole Brown Simpson's murder remains officially unsolved.

It was my turn to step into the on-deck circle.

Just shy of thirty-nine years old and still childless by choice after nearly four years of marriage, I was at a crossroads even before Carol's genetic news landed. James and I remained undecided about parenthood, but we'd become somewhat conscious of the Clock. Scores of infertile friends warned us that it was ticking. Apparently, my biological baby-making window was closing faster than a clam shack approaching Labor Day. As we again wrestled with whether to have a child, particularly at this point in our spoiled, well-rested lives, a genetic mutation mattered. Maybe not enough to drive our decision, but it mattered enough to consider. Knowing that the information was available and not attempting to at least factor it in felt irresponsible. Also, unlike Carol, I knew that I would not be surprised if I had the mutation. Two of my sisters had been diagnosed with reproductive cancers and the third now had a clinically identified predisposition to them; plus, at least one of my brothers was a carrier. I don't have nearly enough of an ego to think I'm above those odds.

As serendipity and the gods of genetic research would have it, my insurance company approved testing the same week that Nancy's results came in. Dr. Smith scheduled us back-to-back for the clinic on March 23, the morning of James's forty-first birthday. Only after our visit would I find out that my husband, according to Chinese superstition, is supposed to avoid hospitals on his birthday. People die in hospitals. Very bad luck.

My initial counseling session—equal parts background, personal history, explanation of risks and benefits, and Q&A—took about an hour. I relearned some things I already knew (at the time, roughly 9 percent of all women in the US would get breast cancer, and 2 percent would get ovarian cancer), and I discovered how much I did not know, despite many nights surfing the World Wide Web in search of the latest reports. I revisited eighth-grade biology for a tutorial on DNA architecture, likened by Dr. Smith to a room full of coiled and uncoiled extension cords where sometimes one cord is shorter or develops a kink—in other words, a mutation. (There was also something about a blueprint for the house and how the plumber doesn't care about the carpentry part and vice versa, but she lost me there.) It was explained that BRCA1 and BRCA2 mutations are dominant disorders, meaning that of the two copies of each gene that you inherit—one from Mom, one from Dad—only one needs to be dysfunctional to cause a problem. In other words, having a single perfect copy of these tumor-suppressor genes simply isn't good enough; you must be perfect across the board.

The red flags that commonly led geneticists to suspect a BRCA mutation were a family history of breast cancer, especially when it includes early onset of the disease; occurrence of other cancers in families with breast cancer history; and male breast cancer in the family. We had all but the last item covered. Dr. Smith then went over some of the pluses and minuses of testing, presenting me with a sheet of handy bullet points.

High on the benefits list was knowing what you're dealing with and getting "watched more carefully," including more frequent mammograms, clinical breast exams, CA125 tests, and transvaginal ultrasounds. (I can't say I felt great about attentiveness positioned as a benefit; shouldn't our doctors always be watching us carefully?) For men, there was the lure of prostate specific antigen tests and doctor's exams beginning at an earlier age. Also on the plus side were elective prophylactic surgeries and the knowledge-is-empowerment that results from understanding you're at 50 percent risk of passing the disorder to any biological offspring.

The full list of risks was longer, including a few items that mirrored the benefits. Its bullet points included:

- You know what you're dealing with.
- You may experience survivor's guilt.
- Your results may affect others who are close to or related to you.
- You could experience health insurance problems or job discrimination.
- You might find out something that calls a presumed biological relationship into question.
- You could get upset at the news and faint.

Seriously, fainting was on there.

And the stuff about insurance issues and job discrimination was a legitimate fear for many people, even though federal legislation and sometimes murky state guidelines were supposed to protect against it.

Reading through these pros and cons was a lot to take in on the spot. But I asked every question I could think of in the moment, fully aware that the road I was about to go down had no answers for many of my biggest concerns. Such as, if I were to find out that I had the mutation, would I let that stop me from having a child—biological or otherwise? And what about the inverse of that result? If I didn't have the mutation, who was I? Just one of the general population, at no more risk for reproductive cancers than the woman with no family history? Impossible.

Even Dr. Smith had candidly acknowledged that "genetics is a lot about fate."

"It's just the flip of a coin," she said. "You could flip a coin ten times and you could get ten heads. It stinks [if heads are mutations], but it could happen."

As the session wrapped up, I pictured a giant quarter, frozen mid-flip in the air above my head. I walked down the hall to the blood lab and sent the coin spinning on its way.

Nancy's test results, revealed to her just as I was submitting my blood for analysis, surprised no one. She had the same BRCA2 mutation that researchers had found in Carol, the same mutation that almost certainly would have been found in Patty.

This meant that my parents, in their first three of six successful attempts to make a baby, had apparently hit with remarkable consistency: three girls, three mutations. Dr. Smith had guessed right. And yes, "stinks" was certainly one way to describe that trifecta.

I expected Nancy to be emotional over the news. I thought it might sadden and scare her, as well as piss her off, to share an official link with what had happened to Patty. As feisty as she was, Nancy was also prone to negativity. She would need her supportive little sister to help her see things rationally, I assumed.

Wrong. Nancy didn't need my help. By the time I reached her back in the clinic waiting room, she'd already moved on.

We sat next to each other in stupidly uncomfortable chairs—the kind that seem designed for anything but waiting—and the whole time, Nancy didn't even shift in her seat as she told me about her counseling session. She wasn't weepy or defiant. She was oddly calm and philosophical, which wasn't at all like her. Nancy, who was giving, compassionate, responsible, funny, vibrant, and many other lovely adjectives, was not by nature accepting. In fact, the last word I'd use to describe her is *zen*.

"I don't mean to play it low key, because it's upsetting," she told me in a weirdly measured voice that freaked me out. "But at least it's an explanation. I can't change my genetic makeup. I love my mother and father, dearly, for who they were. This is the luck of the draw."

Hold up. What?

I hadn't even considered that anyone might blame their parents or think less of them for handing down a genetic mutation, never mind unknowingly. I could relate to the parental guilt in that equation, but not the reverse. Even when my mother and I had talked about curses, the notion of holding her responsible for any of our troubles never occurred to me. Was I just being naïve? Would this, too, need to be factored into the baby equation?

Ugggh.

Suddenly, I understood what had given Nancy peace. She didn't want to blame her parents or herself for her disease, but she struggled not to. A mutation was a way out for her. It had been innocently handed down through the generations, progressing stealthily toward sometimes tragic conclusions that no one could have altered, perhaps until now.

Nancy had met the enemy, and the enemy was not us. That was a giant load off her mind.

Clearly, though, I wasn't my sister.

The same test results that she found comforting stood to be devastating in my case. I wasn't already sick. I had much more to lose by linking myself to a serious genetic defect, and nothing that desirable to gain.

For the next four weeks while I awaited my lab results, I refused to let my mind wander into the places where it seemed too scary to go.

Ha.

I tried. The demons found me anyway.

I tossed and turned over dreams that took place on Scottish moors, where fuzzy figures that I took to be my paternal ancestors rode around on beautifully groomed horses more suited to *Bonanza*, since that was my visual reference point, chased by a vague malignant presence that stalked them in the moonlight. Eventually they would always be chased up a hill that became a ramp, and the ramp would become so vertical that it resembled the side of a skyscraper, or the top half of the cracked *Titanic* that Jack and Rose rode into the icy sea. All the horses and riders would at some point tumble off this rugged ramp, which is when I'd realize that I was actually among them and would awake in a panic, my legs kicking so hard to break my imaginary death fall that James sometimes had bruises the next day.

I was always prone to dreams about heights, their residue about evenly split between anxiety-provoking and exhilarating. This one made me want to seek professional analysis, but instead I just consulted the internet, which suggested I might be concerned about a health issue or failing at something.

Duh. Or failing at everything.

James tried to provide reassurance, but how do you comfort and protect someone who doesn't even know what she's most afraid of? He inquired frequently about the status of the "broken" gene, which is what his ears heard whenever anyone mentioned *bra-cah*.

I thought that was a keen interpretation.

Finally, one June morning, we found ourselves back in a windowless room of the genetics clinic. I had come to Dr. Smith's office the same way I approached most scary medical moments: dressed to run.

After every angst-provoking mammogram, each ominous diagnosis in a relative too young and too close, complicated births and exhausting deaths, a good long run has been both my therapy and my escape. Now, my worn-out running shoes felt sutured to the floor.

Dr. Smith was repeating her jubilant words, in case my silence meant that I hadn't heard them the first time: "Your results are normal. You do not have the BRCA2 mutation," she announced. Then she waited, again, for me to respond. But I was lost.

Dr. Smith had just pardoned me from a harsh genetic sentence shared by all three of my living siblings. In the same breath, she had also upended my entire adult life.

Even if I wanted to run, I no longer knew from what.

Normal. That one word hung in the air the same way the imaginary quarter had when it was first set in motion four weeks ago.

When the doctor's words finally sank in, I felt my eyes well up. Then I exhaled deeply and muttered something incredibly unimaginative, like

"Wow." I didn't know what I was feeling. This was one of the scary places I hadn't visited.

I was prepared, I thought, for bad news. Bad news was my family's specialty. This was a novelty: good news, delivered in a hospital—the same hospital, in fact, where Patty and Jan had both died in 1984.

If I was under the impression that their story was also my story, my test results were proof that I don't exactly fit the family blueprint. As my mother made clear when she set her change-of-life baby apart from the rest, enjoying my upbringing in a way that applied to no one else, I am the golden child. That label has been both the mantle I strive to live up to and the unearned privilege I can't live down. Now, here I was, the first Page known to have emerged unscathed from the mutant gene pool.

Perfect.

The survivor's guilt that Dr. Smith had warned of was real. I began to experience it almost immediately, hand in hand with my squeamishness over the whole golden-child status reminder.

Why me? I wondered. *Why no lucky breaks for my sisters, all of whom have families?*

I pictured Patty's perfect smile and luminous locks, all tangled up in the giddy hugs of the two young daughters she left behind, and I felt an overwhelming need to apologize.

In the days that followed, a painful and disturbing sense of separation settled in. I had always shared everything with my sisters; now they belonged to a club that I didn't necessarily want to join but still hated being shut out of. While I didn't expect much sympathy for this reaction, I couldn't deny it, either.

Carol and Nancy set me straight, the way that only our big sisters can.

"You're allowed to feel guilty and embarrassed if you want," they said. "But it's kind of silly. You didn't do anything wrong. In fact, what you did was, you got us in the game."

I waved them off, but they stood firm, insisting that my result had given them hope. Perhaps I wasn't alone, they said. Maybe more of our clan could play the genetic lottery and win.

As familiar as we all were with the 50/50 coin flip concept, had I tested positive for the mutation, Nancy and Carol both admitted that they would have mentally thrown in the towel on the rest of the family, including their own children. Now, suddenly, there was reason to believe in the possibility of better odds, meaning any odds that were not zero.

This did ease my guilt. Somewhat.

Still, though, I felt unmoored. Who was I without the greatest of my carefully cultivated anxieties and assumptions?

I would have to relearn many of my most basic adult behaviors, starting with how to enter the shower without *Psycho*-level fear of finding a lump (not that I would, or should, stop looking). And, only half-jokingly, I thought: Had I seen this rosier outlook coming, I would definitely have put more money into my 401(k).

But those were just the surface fears and conundrums. Hard behind them was the realization that now, suddenly, I had no excuse to delay living a "normal" life, as a person without reason or inclination to ponder her genetic fate.

Among other things, I felt almost a duty to go forth and multiply. How odd, I thought, that genetic testing should have been the thing to set me on that path.

Left to my own devices, I never would have written such an ending.

CHAPTER 15

The Valley of Clomid

Perhaps because James and I are the youngest offspring of large families, we'd never felt pressure to procreate for reasons of heritage, tradition, security, or ego. As we entered the twenty-first century with a growing list of reservations, from selfishness to deep-seated fear, we weren't even sure we wanted children. If we did, though, there was no sense of urgency. The adoption option had spared me from getting too caught up in ticking biological clocks or feelings of regret. I figured if I wanted to be someone's mother, I could and would make it happen. Whenever.

But then, when I wasn't looking, I fell right into the Valley of Clomid.

Maybe it shouldn't have surprised me to wind up there, but it did. At thirty-eight, I'd been dumbfounded to discover that I was the only one of my parents' offspring to be declared free of a mutation that invited breast, ovarian, and other insidious cancers, and thus the one in my family best equipped to procreate. In a further twist of irony, I was the only one who didn't have any children to benefit from my genetic good fortune.

Given that one sister had died of breast cancer at thirty-four and another was doing her best to live with advanced ovarian cancer at fifty-seven, on some level it offended me that my unmutated genes might go to waste. A combination of guilt and duty told me to go forth and multiply. So, like half the women I know, I spent the next couple of years punishing my achievement-oriented psyche, trying to prove that I could have a biological child if I wanted one, rather than examining whether that had become what I really wanted.

My fertility journey began in the same hospital where nearly all my assumptions about a presumed genetic death sentence had ended.

As usual, I came dressed in sweats and sneakers. But this time it wasn't escapism that inspired my wardrobe. I wore my running clothes to the reproductive endocrinology offices at Tufts New England Medical Center because I expected to be uncomfortable in every other way.

James and I were there to have our reproductive body parts evaluated.

As anyone who has ever submitted to this process knows, it makes you feel more manhandled and judged than a farm-stand avocado. But you run with it because you will tolerate any amount of baby doctor bullshit to get to the end result: a baby. You hope. Sometimes the cutting-edge medical advice seems only slightly less of a crapshoot than old-school fertility diet tricks, like drinking milk and eating yams.

For us, the pregnancy forecast wasn't so bad. I had eggs, James had sperm—both were viable, if not the freshest in all the land. I'd kept my anorexia in check and maintained a healthy weight ever since Patty died—it was the least I could do for her—which meant that my menstrual cycle was back to something approximating normal. That's how I'd known I was pregnant when I didn't want to be, before our wedding, and why I had confidence it might happen a second time with more intention. We could see value in increasing the odds of success at our advanced ages, but we wanted to start with the treatment that seemed least radical and most affordable.

Our doctor suggested we try Clomid, a drug used to stimulate the release of hormones that tell the ovaries to make eggs. I could take it in pill form and cap the ten-day cycle with what's known as a trigger shot, which sadly did not involve tequila and would need to be self-administered by hypodermic needle to my thigh as a signal to my ovaries to prepare to get busy. James and I were instructed to have intercourse within a few hours of the shot and again a couple of days later.

You never imagine something this romantic when you decide to get married and start a family.

Of course, it only gets less sexy as you work your way through additional options. If the Clomid protocol isn't enough to surmount your infertility, you can progress to intrauterine insemination (IUI), in vitro fertilization (IVF), intracytoplasmic sperm injection (ICSI), egg donation, surrogacy, and so on.

"It's a matter of what you're comfortable considering; what feels right to you," the doctor told us.

His words sounded nice. But I wondered if he needed to be reminded that my mother had pushed six children out of her vagina. The way I saw it, comfort didn't count for much in matters of childbearing. Everything seemed scary, and nothing felt "right" to me—unless by *right* he meant slightly less insane than some other things. All those things made my head hurt.

Perhaps James had it right. Maybe this *was* the perfect time to go see the Chinese doctor.

We were still getting to know each other when I first accompanied James to a health-care appointment in Boston's Chinatown back in the 1980s.

The way you see Chinatown when you're a *lǎo wài* (老外, *outsider/foreigner*) who only goes there for dim sum and cheap Christmas stocking stuffers is very different from how you see it when you're falling in love with a Chinese man and his culture. Suddenly, you start to notice all the small businesses and living spaces that make this an actual neighborhood. You notice that above the jewelry store, there's a law office. Below the bakery, there's a travel agent. And just down an alley, through a side entrance that leads up a dark stairway to an unmarked door, there's a windowless room where people go to be healed without first being weighed or asked for proof of insurance.

This is where I discovered the medicinal properties of cupping. And scraping. And slender needles intentionally inserted into sensitive areas like spines. And faces.

Restaurant work is hard, with long days and crazy amounts of repetitive, intensely physical labor. It does a number on your back and legs. James's feet, which were flat to begin with, needed periodic cortisone shots to mute the constant aching. He submitted to those shots, and to other prescriptions by Western doctors, while also seeking out Eastern approaches that gave him more holistic comfort. Cupping, also known as *bá guàn* (拔罐), was supposed to improve blood flow, among other things. It was sometimes used to treat high blood pressure, which ran in James's family.

"Does it hurt?" I asked him the day I sat in on the cupping process for the first time.

"Nahhhh," he scoffed. "It just feels like squeezing and burning."

"That does not sound fun," I said.

"Oh, well. Because you're not Chinese," he shrugged.

He was right. Some of my unease was bred by unfamiliarity, also known as ignorance. As I saw it, cupping was like leeching, just without the parasitic worms.

James would lie on his stomach, nude except for his Calvin Klein boxer briefs. His physician would ignite what looked like a jumbo cotton swab that had been doused in alcohol, then insert the flaming stick into a glass vessel that resembled a miniature goldfish bowl. After a few seconds, the fire would be removed and the bowl flipped quickly onto the skin, trapping the hot, smoky air inside to create a suctioning environment that made grotesque scarlet knobs of the underlying flesh. This process went on and on until James's back and shoulders were covered in glass vessels, giving him the appearance of human bubble wrap.

After about ten minutes, the goldfish bowls came off. Large, angry welts remained for several days, turning from circles of red to dark purple to brown before fading completely, sometimes not for weeks.

"Why do this to yourself?" I asked James. So what if it was only temporary mutilation with no lasting discomfort; it was still ugly to look at.

"It pulls out all the bad stuff," he said with enough conviction that I wondered if it could be true. Was it really possible to light a fire, invite all your ailments and body toxins to the surface, and kiss them goodbye with what amounted to a deep-tissue massage by vacuuming? Boy, if only that worked for cancer cells. And negativity.

I loved that James believed in this kind of thing. I wished that I could be as open and unquestioning. Which is probably why, when he suggested acupuncture treatments for fertility in 2001, I thought it was about time I gave the Eastern ways a try. I mean, what did I have to lose? Maybe if I hadn't ventured deep into Chinatown about a dozen years earlier to witness my boyfriend's adventures in cupping, I'd have asked more questions before letting a strange man stick needles into my abdomen. But that experience, plus my encounter with the qi gong master aboard our Yangtze River cruise, encouraged me to contemplate whether the natural powers of the universe could now be harnessed to my benefit. Plus, we found a Chinese acupuncture clinic less than a mile from our condo in Brookline. In a strip mall, with free parking, no less. That's destiny.

I was fully aware that acupuncture could be used to treat just about anything, from tennis elbow to addiction, chronic pain, and advanced disease. I knew several women who'd tried it for fertility, with varying degrees of success. Less convinced than curious, I did harbor some hope as I entered the clinic for my initial visit. The doctor took my pulse and examined my tongue. I'd been here—without being exactly *here*—before. It was starting to feel very comfortable.

Again, when you take a person's pulse, there is touching. There is connection and tenderness that you can't get through a stethoscope or a clipboard questionnaire. It's really a wonderful way to say hello while also engaging in data collection. Ever since my scary trip to the hospital in China in 1999, I'd become a big fan of the tongue-and-pulse diagnosis. In that case, it had nailed my acute bronchitis. Now, it was all that my acupuncturist needed to tell me I had been pregnant once before—he had no medical records to suggest I'd had an abortion—and that conceiving again was "possible."

He didn't say "likely."

The treatments would take a few weeks to start improving our chances of fertilization. I'd visit once a week to have the slender needles inserted in the soft flesh around my navel, and a few more into my arms, legs, back, and (for tension headaches) lower forehead. In between appointments, I'd drink foul-smelling teas with strange ingredients like red clover and *dong quai*. They not only tasted awful; my body reeked of them. A musky brown cloud oozed out of my pores and trailed me wherever I went—at least, that's the *Peanuts*-style cartoon panel I imagined. I bathed multiple times a day but the Pig-Pen cloud of stink persisted in my nostrils. Then, I started getting pimples.

"This is a good sign," my acupuncturist said. "This is what we want."

Let's be clear. *I* did not want acne. I did not want it at thirty-nine any more than I had wanted it at seventeen. But I understood what he was saying. If my skin was responding like a teenager's, then maybe my ovaries were taking a trip in the wayback machine as well. Maybe having to restock my medicine cabinet with Clearasil was the precursor to buying diapers and onesies.

Of course, I wasn't entirely sure which came first: the Clomid, or the acupuncture, or the pimples. There was no clear cause and effect here. But *something* seemed to be stirring inside my body, so we kept going even when those stirrings didn't pan out. Every month, James and I followed the prescribed routine—pills, teas, needles, sex, repeat—and every month, after all that, my period would arrive like an editor's red line through a superfluous paragraph.

"I don't think you need this," I might have suggested to a reporter whose slack writing I was attempting to improve. Now, the cosmos was suggesting it back to me.

The dark denouement of fertility treatments can be similar to the grieving process. There's denial, anger, bargaining, and depression, though not necessarily in that order. There's also worthlessness and shame, because if you can't do, on demand, the most basic thing your body was built for, you kind of suck at life. It's that much easier to conclude this when you've been programmed with "have it all" expectations and boundless Catholic guilt. I'm not blaming feminism for my infertility. Not exactly. But I do think that many of us who grew up in the 1960s and '70s, thinking we knew "our bodies, ourselves," really didn't have a clue—despite the mounting evidence—about the choices we were making or the things we might be forgoing because of those choices.

At some point in most failed fertility journeys there is acceptance, which for James and me meant getting off the ride while we were still at the level of the Rocket Swing and Beep Beep Cars, before we'd progressed anywhere near the Giant Coaster. We never seriously entertained IUI, IVF, egg donation, or surrogacy. After half a year of intro-level fertility treatments, we told our doctors that we were closing up the clam shack, not just for the season, but for good.

When I finally stepped back from Clomid, acupuncture, strange teas, and other monthly ways to drive myself crazy, I realized that, while I was happy for women who'd made medical advances work for them, most modern fixes just weren't for me—and that went double for James, whose traditional upbringing didn't mesh at all with making sperm deposits in a cup. But the one important thing we'd decided over these many months of timed intercourse and emotional ups and downs was that we really did want to open our lives to a child. Ours would just be a different path.

In the spring of 2002, we scheduled an informational meeting at the offices of China Adoption With Love Inc. (CAWLI), located right in our home neighborhood of Coolidge Corner, Brookline. It made sense to adopt from China, not just because there was karmic balance to it but because our household already offered the language and heritage of that country. And we preferred a girl, which China's population-control policies seemed more than prepared to accommodate.

If James wasn't a chef-restaurateur, he would probably be a Chinese-history professor. In his early forties, he remained a voracious reader, blazing through several books a week, mostly biographies of leaders and analyses of key events that have shaped Chinese life. He knew all about the economic and cultural forces that have historically led girls to be valued differently (not always less, as is commonly believed) from boys. And he knew the realities of the one-child policy that was introduced by China in 1979, to restrict population growth, and would not be officially revised to a two-child limit until 2015.

Actually, "one child" has always been somewhat of a misnomer. In practical terms, the law—which could impose substantial fines, forced sterilization, and other penalties on parents who violated its dictates—promoted a "one son or two child" policy. This meant that couples who first gave birth to a girl were often allowed to try for a son, and it also meant that many of the girls in Chinese orphanages had an older sister (or three) whose parents wanted one more shot at a boy.

"China has lost its balance," James would sometimes lament, to no one in particular. Such is the everyday consequence of government logic.

Before our first adoption agency visit, we discussed these myopic population curbs, in case one day we needed to defend our role in the very system that might have led to our daughter's being abandoned by her biological parents. I knew we were adopting for the right reasons in theory, but I worried that we were in some ways helping to perpetuate a horribly misguided doctrine. Were we really just fueling a baby trade? The truth is, we couldn't be sure. But there remained a pile of excellent reasons for us to adopt from China, and we couldn't see ignoring those, or the plight of little girls lying in orphanages today, just because we wondered how history and hindsight might characterize us tomorrow.

From the latest US immigration data available in 2002, we learned that more than 40,000 Chinese orphans had entered the United States since China enacted laws regulating international adoptions in 1992 (the number rose to more than 80,000 before China halted foreign adoptions in 2024). At the time, with upward of 6,000 foundlings arriving each year, China had become the leading contributor to more than 21,000 international adoptions by US residents annually.

Reliable data from the Chinese government was harder to come by.

Even insiders, such as CAWLI director Lillian Zhang (no relation to Yù Yīng's bully), knew little beyond what went on in the few orphanages they were allowed to visit. For example, though Chinese officials claimed the number of foundlings was then around 160,000, experts guessed it could have easily been ten times that high.

Lillian advised that we shouldn't get hung up on the overall numbers. "We don't need to know certain things," she told me emphatically. "Bigger-picture things don't even matter to us."

And yet this great wall of secrecy was part of why Lillian, a slender, middle-aged, Nanjing-bred woman with measured speech and caring eyes, was forced to warn her clients of the many things that could go wrong in this process, from simple paperwork snafus to grave undisclosed medical conditions.

The Chinese had crafted an adoption system that stood as a model for this kind of tidy enterprise. Still, when problems arose, it was often in the shadows. What I got out of our informational meeting was to expect the unexpected and don't even sign up for the long, arduous international adoption process if you can't bring patience to the table.

We began by assembling the mountain of required paperwork, which includes financial statements, letters of reference, autobiographical essays, and doctors' assessments. There were criminal-background checks to pass, as well as social worker evaluations and one lovely morning of fingerprinting. James spent a full day in court discovering the merits of paying your traffic fines on time.

Seven months later, in August 2003, our paperwork finally cleared all the US hurdles and moved overseas. This important hallmark is known as the DTC date—as in, dossier to China—and it starts the clock ticking on a waiting period that at the time was ten to eleven months before resulting in the referral of a child. We expected assignment of a baby in June or July 2004.

Imagine our surprise when China replied in just fourteen weeks.

❧

It was nearly Thanksgiving 2003, and I was sitting at my computer wrestling with rewrites of a book proposal that I wanted to finish before surrendering to a spate of baby preparations in the spring, when I would have plenty of time to start preparing for first-time motherhood as I was turning forty-three.

The phone rang.

A voice identifying itself as a CAWLI representative said something like: "Referrals just came in . . . blah, blah, blah. Your baby . . . blah, blah, blah. Ten months old . . . There are three pictures here. Oh, she's a doll! . . . Blah, blah, blah. Can you come down to the office today?"

I laughed, it was that ridiculous.

Your daughter is coming now, instead of eight months from now. Oh. Okay. Never mind that we hadn't covered the radiators or bought child locks for the cabinets or painted the spare bedroom adjoining ours. I hadn't cracked one chapter in a growing stack of books on child-rearing and adoption. With this little lead time, how were we to be the neurotic, overinformed American parents our child deserved?

If there had been a comic book bubble above my head just then, it would have read "Surrender, Dorothy." Among other things, I had to accept that there would be no way to determine why our referral had been expedited: it may have been because James's grandfather was born in Jiangxi Province and that's where this grouping of foundlings was also from, or it may have been that they'd streamlined the process for an adoptive father of Chinese heritage, or it may have been completely random. We'll never know. And it doesn't matter anyway.

When I got off the phone with the adoption agency, I called James, who laughed even harder and more anxiously than I had. He cut his day short at the restaurant so that by afternoon we were sitting in a small room at the adoption agency, looking at already outdated photos of our ten-month-old daughter. The voice on the phone hadn't embellished: She was a doll.

"Oh, my," the adoption worker said as she leafed through our growing file. "Your DTC date is August? Well, no wonder you were surprised when

I called this morning." Then she added, with an edge of concern, "So, is this okay?"

Interesting question, and one that I might have answered differently an hour earlier.

Now, though, we had seen our baby's face.

Now, we had started to picture ourselves through her quizzical eyes.

Now, there was no easy turning back.

CHAPTER 16

Selipity Slope

I stared at her photograph every day, multiple times a day.

The mysterious tangle of our daughter's past was on my mind constantly in the many weeks leading to our trip to China in late January 2004, weeks made more stressful by travel delays and concerns ranging from lunar New Year holiday closings to bird flu outbreaks and SARS paranoia. When I wasn't wondering why this fascinating little girl had been abandoned by her biological parents, or how she was faring in foster care, I was worrying about whether I had the nerve to be anyone's mother.

And then there was "The Name Game" playing inside my head.

Janice, Janice, bo-banice
Bo-na-na fanna, fo-fanice
Fee fi mo-manice, Janice!

My dad used to sing this to me regularly when I was still his little buddy and it seemed that all the world was obsessed with Shirley Ellis's 1964 pop ditty. He thought it was cute. I thought it was just another reason to hate my name.

Fanice.

While it wasn't Mitch or Chuck, which resulted in actual profanities, or Bart, the jackpot for "Name Game" bathroom humor, Janice had a payoff that was subtler and more unexpected. It delighted the older kids who deliberately ran names through the song's rhyming scheme looking for something to mock. *Fanice* was close to *fanny*. And *anus*. Or at least close enough to those minor vulgarities to tickle the amateur adolescent pop music critics in my neighborhood, who weren't trying to be mean. They didn't know that I'd never liked my name.

I was told that my father had decided it on the spot, when he was asked to fill out a form in the hospital just after my birth. The only name my parents had prepared was Joseph, because they'd had three girls and then two boys, and I would obviously be a boy to even out the teams. Why my dad didn't just go with Josephine when he saw me swaddled in pink, I'll never know. But instead of being Jo, which at least would have made me a formidable Little Woman, I got Janice, which had no inspiration, literary or otherwise. It was simply the thing that popped into his brain. I could just as easily have been called Cheryl, or Penelope (Penny), or Mortadella—any of which I might have preferred.

Janice is the name you bestow on the most annoying character in your book, play, movie, or television show. She's the Updikean model of a pathetic wife in *Rabbit, Run*; the stereotypical equivalent of a space-age secretary smitten with the ship's captain in *Star Trek*; the mobster's scheming sister in *The Sopranos*; the sitcom shrill who cackles like a dolphin in *Friends*. You can shorten her name to Jan, but that makes it only slightly cuter and no less annoying (see: Jan Brady), and it wasn't an option for me anyway, once my future brother-in-law Jan Ostrum arrived on the scene. Janet, by the way, is on a whole other planet ("Dammit Janet").

My parents couldn't even manage to gift me with the cooler spelling—Janis—so I'd at least have rock 'n' roll swagger on my side. I got the version with "nice" shoved into it, as though commanded by Al Martino himself. My folks were completely oblivious, which makes it all the more pathetic that three of their six kids got stuck with show biz-adjacent names. Janis Paige, famous Broadway actress (and Auntie V on TV's *Eight*

Is Enough). Patti Page, famous pop and country singer ("Old Cape Cod," "The Tennessee Waltz"). Jimmy Page, famous rock guitarist (though, to be fair, Led Zeppelin wasn't around when my brother was born). All of us have spent decades answering to our recognizable names with a genial shrug. "I know. Hilarious," we'd tell the strangers who laughed when we signed up for things over the phone. "My parents are real comedians."

Of course, given names aside, simply inheriting the last name Page invites comedy that knows no end, especially in the classroom. "I bet your favorite book is the White Pages," the jokesters will quip. "Are you the last Page? Or are you the next Page?" "Oh my God, you guys. Someone please twirl her; we need to *turn the Page*." Never gets old. And if you want that humor to follow you into the workplace as though you're a Dickensian character, you become a legislative assistant, or a journalist.

But the funniest thing about all of this—and by *funniest*, I mean *dumbest*—is that my mother often talked about her own name as a source of shame. Growing up, she wanted to assimilate, as most first-generation immigrant offspring do. She didn't want to be the girl whose mother pecked at her in rapid Italian. She wanted desperately to be a Susie or a Mary, with fine blond locks and a house that smelled of Campbell's soup. Instead, she had the most beautiful Italian name imaginable: Yolanda. To me, it sounded like the intoxicating prelude to a whirling tarantella: bold, rhythmic, vibrant, full of personality. My father despised it.

Or maybe he was just afraid of it, which made him act like he despised it. We never really determined what the root problem was. We only knew that he refused to say her name in public unless there was no getting around it.

Imagine that. The given name of Jocko's wife was rarely uttered by him in their children's presence. Not at the dinner table. Not shouted across a playground. And never in the car, where they would be sitting right next to each other with all of us in the back seat listening as my dad swerved like a professional racecar driver to avoid saying her name in conversation, no matter how long the journey lasted.

At home, if he picked up the phone and it was for her, he would say, "Janice [or Jimmy, or Patty, or whichever of his kids was around], go get your mother. Tell her she has a call." This happened even when he had to summon us in from the yard to deliver the message to their bedroom, which was about eleven steps from where he was standing. On the rare occasions when circumstance or urgency dictated that he had to summon his spouse himself, he would do so in the most mocking tone possible. "Yo-LANNN-dahhhh," he might sing out in a made-up tenor that was almost a yodel. "The phone is for you-ooh-ooh!"

It reminded me of Nelson Eddy and Jeanette MacDonald's "Indian Love Call." It was both ridiculous and ridiculing, and my mother knew it. She told him it offended her, which he pretended not to hear, but if she had insight into why he did it, she never let on.

Some men only call their wives Mommy or Mother, which seems infinitely worse because those labels are intentionally reductive and unintentionally creepy. At least with my father there were no schmaltzy pet names and no apparent subjugation strategy, only the usual cocktail of insecurities. Perhaps saying her name somehow threatened his masculinity, making it of a piece with his refusal to buy sanitary napkins and his need to belittle those products with a childish nickname to justify keeping his distance.

All I know is that I have a hard time remembering people's names, even after meeting them multiple times or working alongside them for years, and I have to wonder if that's a product of noticing that my mother was sentenced to a marriage in which she was nameless.

Maybe I'm subconsciously trying to put her on equal footing with the rest of the world.

Or maybe I'm just really bad at names.

At some point in my mad dash to prepare for our soon-to-be-adopted child, I began to obsess over what she should be called.

I'd always liked Mia, which gained a few points when the trailblazing US soccer star Mia Hamm rose to prominence, though the downside was an uptick in its popularity on those foolish lists that expectant parents consult to be on trend. Still, I thought it suited the fireplug of a girl whose picture stared back at me so confidently all the way from China, and after running it through "The Name Game" song, it seemed safe as well as adorable—the opposite of Janice.

James didn't get it.

"Mia?" he said. "No."

"But it's cute, and sporty," I said. "She seems like a spitfire. Mia is a good name for a spitfire."

"It seems short," he said.

"Short? Well, it *is* only three letters, but it's two syllables," I said. "Or do you mean it seems like a short person's name, whatever that is?"

"I mean short like . . . just like nothing," he said. "It has no personality."

"Really? I think it has tons of personality. But, okay," I said. "What do *you* want to name her?"

"Selipity," he said without hesitation.

I tried to download it.

"Selipity?"

"Yes, Selipity."

"Where did you get that name?"

"You know. Like the TV show."

"American TV? It's a show?"

"Yeah. The girl with the hair. The one whose name means 'happy.'"

"Felicity?" I said after a bit.

"Right. Selipity," he said.

I remembered now. Years ago, while we were watching an episode of the J.J. Abrams drama that starred Keri Russell as a bright-eyed college student with long, iconic curls before they were infamously sheared, James had asked me about the title character's name. I'd explained that it's derived from the Latin word *felicitas*, meaning luck or good fortune—I might have also said happiness, because that's *felicita* in Italian. I could understand how perfect that must have sounded to James, and how it had lodged in his brain.

"I just want her to be happy," he reiterated now. "That's all I care about."

This was the antithesis of my father's cold-cut-platter approach to naming a child. Still, how would it work if we named our daughter something so foreign to James's vocabulary that he couldn't even say it? He was already prone to adding "the" before English names—a kind of verbal tic that filled the space when he couldn't quite locate the word he wanted to say—so he frequently called me "The Janice," which I honestly kind of preferred for its comic value, but which I reckoned would be just one more level of embarrassment for our kid. The Selipity? She could become our very own Yolanda, wishing she'd been given to parents wise enough to recognize that she was clearly a Susie or a Mary. She might rightfully curse us every time she suffered through an attendance roll call or tried to order takeout.

"You're the sweetest man alive," I said to James, not meaning anything patronizing by it. "I love everything you just said. But I don't think I can live with Selipity any more than I'm guessing you could live with me mangling the Mandarin word for happiness."

"Xìng fú," he said.

"Sure, *shinfoo*," I said. "That's not even close, right?"

"Right," he said. "It's *xìng fú* (幸福). *Xìng*, like *xìng*. *Fú*, like *fú*."

"Yeah, that's helpful," I said sarcastically. "Face it. I'm never going to get the tone right; I'm still working on the difference between *shuǐ jiǎo* (水饺, *dumplings*) and *shuì jiào* (睡觉, *sleep*). We need to be realistic, for her sake. So how about we try to think of a name that at least we can both pronounce?"

"Deal," he said, like a man accustomed to compromise.

There was just one problem: Where would either of us find such a name?

Every Chinese foundling is handed a name by the orphanage that she or he passes through. It usually starts with the institution's place of origin and then plucks from a made-up list of common attributes and items, like flora and fauna. In the case of our baby, the orphanage had branded her Yì Lì Gē (弋麗鴿, pronounced *ē-lē-ger, with a soft r*).

The surname of Yi was given to designate the county of Yiyang in northeast Jiangxi Province, where our adoptee was found abandoned near the gate of the local civil affairs office on January 24, 2003. From a one-page "growth report" supplied by the orphanage—all the background that most of these kids come with—we'd learned she was taken in on the morning after her birth and spent five weeks in institutional care before being placed with a foster mother. The English translation makes no mention of it but, in Chinese, the document also says she spent her first cold night of life outdoors, wrapped in a thin blanket nestled inside a small cardboard box. She was purple and half-dead from exposure by the time she was discovered. I guess it's just lucky for us that James reads the native language; otherwise, this precious piece of her limited history might have gone unknown, as it probably does too often.

Lì Gē can be translated as either "Beautiful Pigeon" or "Beautiful Dove." I'd smiled at the pejorative difference in those two translations as I tried to fully take in the first images sent by the adoption agency. She would almost certainly want the record to reflect that she was named Beautiful Dove. Wouldn't anyone choose that moniker over [Irrelevant Modifier] Pigeon? And yet, from her picture, she seemed the perfect balance of both birds—one symbolizing lofty ideas about peace and love; the other as common, underappreciated, and resilient as any marginalized creature on the planet.

I'd decided that the best adjective for this little girl, whichever bird she most identified with in the long run, was *pensive.* She had alert, probing eyes that made me want to scoop her up and answer all her questions. In one photo she was propped up by a large stuffed tiger; in another, a ratty old car-seat cover cradled her tiny frame, made plumper by the layers and layers of clothing that no self-respecting Chinese baby is ever without. She looked healthy, if anything could be determined by snapshots, and I loved that at six months old, she already seemed skeptical.

I asked James if we should consider keeping at least part of the name that the orphanage had bestowed on her. Perhaps we should call her Li, I offered, though we'd have to constantly reinforce the pronunciation (lee). Or, what about Olivia, nickname Liv or Libby, so at least Li would be incorporated? No need, he said, "it's just a factory name," by which he meant assembly-line quality, born of expedience and necessity, devoid of personalization. I rather liked the name Olivia, but James did not. He also had no affinity for Tricia (after my sister, whose full given name was Patricia) or Patsy (another nod to my sister, but also to my favorite torch singer, Patsy Cline).

"Guilin?" I suggested hopefully. "It's a beautiful name and a beautiful city, and it has such a profound place in your family history."

"Nahhhh," he said. "Way too Chinese. She's growing up in America."

I hadn't anticipated this level of pushback. James was generally accommodating to a fault. It surprised me that he was so opinionated and invested in this one part of the process. That is, until I remembered his own experience with taking an Americanized name—the evolution of James, James Tseng.

After selecting that name, James had been startled to discover how often people took liberties with it. Among my family and friends, most took to calling him Jim. Customers at the restaurant seemed to prefer Jimmy, and it stuck (so much so that "Chef Jimmy's Specialties" became a top category on the Beijing House menu) before he'd had any chance to protest. I still called him Kao Shun, as did his own family, which meant that almost no one was calling him James, other than bill collectors and traffic cops.

None of which would have been a big deal, except that James worked in an Asian kitchen, where some of the help was Vietnamese. To those good men and women, hardworking and respectful but not devoid of humor, it just so happened that Jim sounded an awful lot like *chim*. And *chim*, in Vietnamese, is slang for "vagina."

Yes, I know. What are the chances.

Chim also means "bird," but no one employed at the 'Jing cared about that alternate translation; they were too amused by the colorful colloquialism. Calling a man the word that some people use for "pussy"—loudly and repeatedly, in the workplace where he is a boss—is definitely worse than calling a young girl something that kinda sorta sounds like *fanny*. I understood my husband's frustration and need to do better for his daughter.

TOP LEFT: Jocko and Yolanda as newlyweds in Quincy, circa 1942. TOP RIGHT: Jocko in his Navy uniform, circa 1943. BOTTOM LEFT: Yù Yīng and Qiáo Shēng in Shanghai, before fleeing the Chinese mainland for Taiwan in 1947. BOTTOM RIGHT: Qiáo Shēng in uniform as a member of China's Kuomintang Air Force, circa 1945.

TOP: Janice (age five) with Jocko in the living room of the tan ranch in Braintree, 1966. MIDDLE: (L-R) Patty and her husband Doug, Yolanda, Jocko, Carol holding Kristen (one year old), Jeff (two years old), and Janice (age ten) in front of the tan ranch in Braintree in 1972. BOTTOM LEFT: Tseng family photo in Taiwan in 1961: (L-R) the bottom row has Yù Yīng holding Kao Shun (a.k.a. James), Cháo Fēng, and Qiáo Shēng; the top row has Yǒng Míng, Chin Chin, and their eldest brother, Sān Guāng. BOTTOM RIGHT: Tǔ Xiù in China, circa 1959.

TOP LEFT: Benny Wu in the kitchen at Mandarin Garden in Braintree, circa 1979. TOP RIGHT: Yolanda sporting her cocoa-colored bathing suit at the beach in the 1970s. MIDDLE: Paragon Park, with its giant wooden coaster, in 1981. *Courtesy of Ly Y,* The Boston Globe. BOTTOM: (L-R) Nancy, Carol, Jimmy, Jocko, Yolanda, Jacky, high school graduate Janice (with a tragic disco perm under her mortarboard), and Patty in the backyard of the tan ranch in 1979.

TOP: Carol and Jan in front of the Hotel Vienna in London's Maida Vale neighborhood, where Janice lived as a college student while interning at the House of Commons in 1981. MIDDLE: (L-R) Janice, Patty, Yolanda, Carol, and Nancy pictured at a Cape Cod restaurant in 1980. BOTTOM LEFT: Tǔ Xiù and Yù Yīng reunite at an airport in China in 1987 after more than forty years apart. BOTTOM RIGHT: James in the Taiwanese army in 1979.

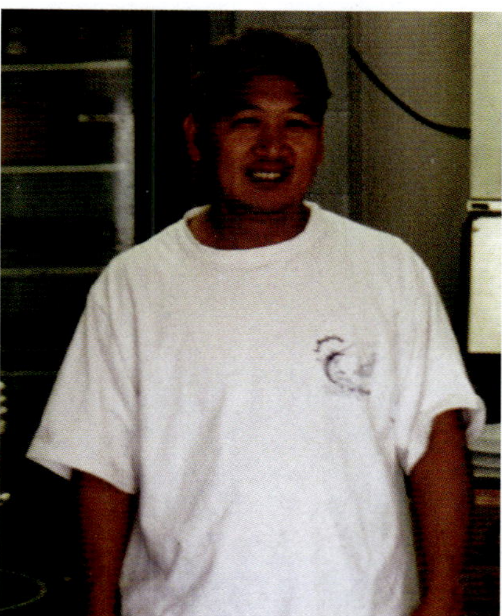

TOP LEFT: Janice in her office at *The Los Angeles Times*'s Orange County bureau in 1996. TOP RIGHT: James in the Beijing House kitchen in 1999. BOTTOM: Janice and James behind the bar at Beijing House in 1996.

TOP: (L-R) Cháo Fēng, Yǒng Míng, Sān Guāng, and Tǔ Xiù pay their respects at the gravesite of their paternal grandfather in China in 1987. MIDDLE: (L-R) James, Cháo Fēng, Chin Chin, Yǒng Míng, and Sān Guāng gather for the eightieth birthday of Yù Yīng (center) in Taiwan. BOTTOM LEFT: Yolanda walks Janice down the red-carpeted "aisle" of a cousin's backyard wedding in Norwell, Massachusetts, in May 1996. BOTTOM RIGHT: Yù Yīng and James share a moment at the wedding.

TOP LEFT: Janice on the Great Wall at Badaling during the first of her trips there in 1999. TOP RIGHT: The first photo of Zoe that was given to James and Janice by the adoption agency in 2003. MIDDLE: James and Janice meet Zoe for the first time, at the Gloria Plaza in Nanchang in 2004. BOTTOM: Not long after that chaotic, tear-filled first encounter with her new family, Zoe is all smiles in their room at the Gloria.

TOP: James, Zoe, and Janice at home in their Brookline kitchen in September 2004. *Courtesy of Mark Ostow,* The Boston Globe. BOTTOM LEFT: Zoe, about nine months old, with her foster mother in a Yiyang village near her orphanage. BOTTOM RIGHT: Zoe (age fourteen) reunited with her foster mother in 2017, back at the orphanage where they first met.

"Okay then," I said. "Here's one that I've always loved. It means 'life' in Greek. Ready?"

"Sure. Let's go. We're burnin' daylight," he replied in his John Wayne way.

I smiled.

"You're probably going to tell me it's too short, but anyway . . . Zoe."

"Zoe?" he repeated.

"Zoe," I said again.

He scrunched his face. "Not for me," he said. "Sorry, pardner."

I walked away, exhausted and out of suggestions, figuring that was that. Our child would be nameless, and when we needed to summon her we would have to get a search-and-rescue-trained labrador or something because we wouldn't have another child to do our bidding the way my father had counted on when he engineered situational workarounds to communicate with my mother. Luckily, my cynicism improved dramatically a few nights later, when James came home from the restaurant all excited, as though he'd had some kind of epiphany.

"Zoe!" he declared excitedly as he strode into the TV room.

"Rrrright," I said, confused. "What about it?"

"Zoe," he repeated.

"Yes, that's the name—Zoe," I confirmed, "but you said you hated it."

"No, Zoe!" he said again.

"I feel like I'm in an Abbott and Costello routine," I said. "Third base."

"I don't get that," he said.

"Never mind," I said. "What about Zoe?"

"Not Zoe," he said. "Zo-EE. Like *Zhōu* (周)—you know, the Zhōu dynasty—and *yì* (易), like 'easy.'" James went on to explain that the founder of the Zhōu dynasty (1050–221 B.C.E.) was King Wen, a heroic figure who is widely considered one of the most influential Chinese rulers of all time. Wen created the hexagram-based method of cleromancy known as the *I Ching*, the core of which is a divination text called *The Book of Changes* or *Changes of Zhou*, aka the *Zhōu Yì*.

"Sounds like a great guy," I said.

"Right. Very great," said James, explaining how he'd suddenly been reminded of a popular phrase used to acknowledge the king's most iconic attributes and accomplishments. "The phrase is four characters: *Zhōu lǐ yì lè* (周礼易乐)," he said. "Two of those characters make Zhōu Yì."

"Ohhhh," I said. "So you mean . . ."

"Right. Zoe, like Zhōu Yì."

It was a convenient combination that managed to draw a perfect line between the classic cosmological text of his favorite Chinese leader and the ancient Greek word I'd wanted for our child: life.

"I would like to name my daughter this. This is a very great name," he said.

I agreed. As did our adoption facilitator, Lillian, who, when we stopped by the agency to tell her, leaned back to size up the news, slowly nodded her head, and pronounced it "a big name for a little girl." Just what we wanted people to say.

Elated, James called Taiwan to tell his mother, who registered her enthusiastic approval. Perhaps she was thinking again of the daughter who'd grown up without her, the girl whose nickname—"Excellent Earth"—was as grand and significant as the one being given to Yù Yīng's newly adopted granddaughter. Yù Yīng could not have foreseen that she would leave one child behind in China, or that her family would gain another child who was born sixty years later under the exact same astrological sign. Even though Zoe's birth date was January 23, 2003, it fell within the 2002 lunar year. That made her a water horse, just like Tǔ Xiù, who was born in 1942. They were mirror images in a cosmic looping that happens only once in a typical lifetime.

It was an incredible coincidence if that's what it was. Not only did Zoe and Tǔ Xiù share a complex zodiac profile—derived from the same *Zhōu Yì* divination text that Zoe is named after (!)—the two also shared a defining destiny. Both were foundlings, at least for a time. In Tǔ Xiù's case, her nickname had allowed plausible deniability of her Kuomintang heritage, which had helped keep her safe from persecution. Somehow, her mother had known that she would need to be more than a water horse. She would also need the earth element to survive in the land of her birth after her parents had abandoned it, and her. Yù Yīng understood the importance of labels, and of surpassing the expectations they set.

"My mother says, *'měi míng sheng guò měi mào'* (美名胜过美貌)—a beautiful name is better than a beautiful face," James announced proudly upon hanging up the phone. In that moment, he was the personification of happiness. And that is how we came to have a child named Zoe, and not a child named Selipity.

CHAPTER 17

The Gloria

There were six chairs filled with Chinese babies when we entered the third-floor conference room at Nanchang's Gloria Plaza Hotel on January 31, 2004. Well, not babies exactly. They were almost all about a year old, give or take a few months.

The room was vast and functional, perfectly suited for an awards banquet or AA meeting. It had a recessed ceiling illuminated by columns of yellow light, which happily pulled focus from the dingy swirls of brown-on-brown carpet. A handwritten paper sign on the door as you came in read, in Chinese, "Today's event: clothes sale." It was false advertising. The order of business on this day was adoption. It would be nowhere near as tidy as a clothes sale.

"What kind of clothes do you think they were? Maybe we missed a good deal," I joked to James.

"I think made in China, same as me," he cracked back, throwing in one of his Santa Claus laughs: "Ahhh-ha-ha-ho-ho-ho!"

It was nervous, contrived banter not even worthy of the low-budget romantic comedies I could snack on endlessly when no one was watching. That's because, the more James and I looked around that modest hotel conference room in Nanchang, the more we had to be nervous about. Not one of the half a dozen kids on the row of padded metal chairs looked happy. They sat stiff-armed, packed tight in their winter clothing, even though it felt like a hundred degrees in the room. There was a lot of squirming and crying—by adults just as often as children—and while a line of nannies struggled to comfort the babies, more than sixty prospective parents strained from a respectful distance to determine who belonged to whom.

"Yì Lì Huá!" a social worker closest to one of the children shouted.

Silence from the onlookers.

"Ben and Flo Healy!"

"Over here!"

A couple in the back had leaped to their feet. Now they rushed to the chairs and enveloped their newest family member in a burst of hugs and tears. Another five names were called. Same reaction. The cacophony built as each expanding family retired to a corner to get acquainted amid *ooh*s and *aah*s and *ni hao*s. Then, the juggling act became a full-on circus.

The foundlings were being presented to us grouped by orphanage, but after the first batch cleared, the formality of the chair display was quickly abandoned to an overlapping cascade of youngsters arriving too quickly for any of us to process. As each child was brought into the room, her Chinese name was called out by one of our imperturbable tour guides, who would wait to see if there was recognition before calling for the adoptive parent by name. It seemed a kind of test, suggesting that if you couldn't recognize your kid's Chinese name, maybe you should get a toaster or a bootlegged video instead. Not that we needed any help feeling inadequate. Again, the name we were listening for was Yì Lì Gē, our "Beautiful Dove," which made me wonder if I should be looking for a baby with the angular features of a bird. Would she be cooing? I couldn't remember what she looked like. Jesus. *How could I not remember what she looked like?*

As screaming children filled the stuffy room, the urgency to hand them off increased, so that by the time they got to our Yiyang group, orphanage workers were bumping into one another scooting back and forth, depositing kids as unceremoniously as bundles of firewood. We thought we heard someone shout "Yì Lì Gē!" above the din, and the next thing we knew, she was there in James's arms, wailing so loudly that even in this noisy, chaotic soup, heads turned.

❧

It was incredible to think that it had only been a handful of hours since our plane touched down in Nanchang. Less than a week earlier, I was childless. Hell, just two days ago I was climbing the Great Wall at Badaling, alone in my thoughts and legally responsible for no one under the age of forty.

We'd flown into Beijing for a four-day pit stop, to shake off the jet lag and get in some frigid sightseeing before journeying on to meet Zoe in Nanchang, the capital of her home province of Jiangxi in southeastern China. The night markets and specialty restaurants of old Beijing called to us, instantly seducing James, who was steeling himself for the many tourist-tailored meals of gloppy sweet-and-sour pork he would have to endure once we became joined at the hip with our adoption group of thirty-three families. We ate and drank and shopped and drank some more, until karaoke seemed like a much better idea than it should have, so we crooned Everly Brothers duets in Mandarin and English until the wee hours of the morning.

The day I went to Badaling started off crisp and overcast. CAWLI was offering a tour; James elected to stay behind—"No thanks," he said. "I'm good."—because our visit to the wall in 1999, when we stopped by on our way to cruising the Yangtze and meeting Old Sister in Guilin, had confirmed every "tourist trap" assumption he'd stockpiled. Besides, he deserved a day in China that was free of programming. And I, too, was glad to have a few hours to myself as I boarded the tour bus and settled in by a window. It might be the last bit of alone time I would claim without guilt for quite a while.

Beijing is a fascinating city. Its mix of new and old smacks you in the face wherever you go. It's not just that the ultramodern skyscrapers dwarf a dwindling number of crumbling hutongs, and the streets are a near-miss collision of vehicles and pedestrians. Often, you see whole families loaded onto a single groaning motorized scooter. You see loyal disciples of the Mao era still sporting the drab uniform as they bicycle to work or the market. On the way out to Badaling, you see everything from urban street scenes to chocolate-colored oxen (or maybe water buffalo; I'm not sure) grazing farmland along the highway.

That's one of the many things I love about China: It wears all its faces with pride. For better and for worse, it's a country that makes few apologies. Critics can and do challenge its human rights record at length, but no one disputes that this is a land of astonishing riches, few of them having anything to do with economics or politics.

By the time our tour bus arrived at Badaling, the clouds had dissipated and the temperature had warmed. I departed the vehicle ready to climb.

The Great Wall is really a series of walls, commissioned by several emperors dating back to at least the seventh century BC. Though vast swaths of it are now gone, some archaeologists estimate the structure's total footprint spans more than thirteen thousand miles. Since this is a country that makes legends out of just about everything, I would have been sorely disappointed if they couldn't find inspiration in one of the most famous landmarks on the planet. I'd craved such a tale to punctuate our trek in 1999, and that's when James came through, as he generally does, with an on-the-spot recap of the legend of Mèng Jiāng Nǚ (孟姜女), widely known as Lady Meng.

There are many versions of this famous folktale. In James's version, Lady Meng is married to a slave laborer who dies during the wall's building and is dismissively buried under the blocks so that work can move on. When winter arrives, Meng comes to deliver warm clothes for her husband and learns that he has died. She weeps with such great force that a large section of the wall topples to reveal the skeletons of scores of workers killed during construction. Unable to identify her man's remains, she pricks her finger and bleeds over the pile, believing that only his bones will be penetrated by her blood—and it works!

But the emperor isn't thrilled with this nosy dame who has wrecked his wall. So, he summons her to his court, where he's so taken with her beauty, he demands that she marry him. She agrees, with conditions: Her dead husband gets forty-nine days of kingdom-wide mourning, a public funeral, and a princely burial, laden with treasures. The emperor doesn't guess that she's also plotting to have the last word, but of course she is. In the legend's dramatic, post-funeral denouement, Lady Meng does a fatal swan dive off the wall, presumably where it meets the Bohai Sea, as a coruscating denouncement of him and all the other callous, narcissistic rulers who arrive at their positions by abusing their countrymen (and women). Some even say that she haunts these megalomaniacs still—the dust of her bones is believed to have morphed into millions of tiny, silvery fish that continue to swim in China's waters today.

"There's a temple to her faithfulness and bravery," James explained. "Her story is so popular."

Of course it is, I thought. It's a patriarchal twofer: female sacrifice and eternal fidelity. What could be more honorable, or indoctrinating? But I didn't say that. "Cool," I said instead. Because it was. Cool. And moving, albeit also fraught, like so much of our human history and the myths that spring from it.

I knew so little of the vast catalog of Chinese folklore, I was in no position to comment on tropes. But it did seem to me that in the handful of legends I'd been introduced to, mostly by my husband, a lot of times the wife dies trying to make a point.

Hmm.

The first time I climbed it, the wall surprised me.

If you ascend only the opening section of this aggressively renovated site, you can come away underwhelmed, as James was. But if you commit to traveling the full 3.4-mile loop, which takes most folks less than a couple of hours, chances are that you will escape the vendors and the crowds and find a stretch to climb in solitude. Then it can approach something spiritual. Not to be flip, but if people can see the Virgin Mary imprinted on their grilled cheese sandwich or Jesus in a pierogi, it's certainly possible to find God while traversing an elevated ancient walkway that's visible from outer space. Far more possible than in the confessional of a Catholic church, for example.

I remember stopping numerous times along the stone walkway just to listen. There was only the sound of the wind and the birds, leaving open the possibility that this could have been any chapter in China's epic existence.

I'm the type of person who finds a quiet spot on the shore of Scotland's Loch Ness—just far enough removed from the tourists swarming the ruins of Urquhart Castle—and after a few minutes of squinting at the peat-blackened waters, I begin to glimpse shadows that could be . . . you know. Scotland has water horses, too. They're sometimes called kelpies, or nuggles, or shoopiltees, and according to legend they can shapeshift to trick and kidnap children. Even if Nessie was aligned with the darker side of water horse mythology, the idea of her seduced me just as much as Chinese water horses praised for their undeniable charm and fiery spirit. I can see monsters—and ghosts, imps, nymphs—in anything. At the mere suggestion of Lady Meng's legend, I felt her presence all around me. In the rustle of the wind, I heard her dress billow and her grief moan. I saw her lurking in the shadows of every turn and turret. She might be that hawk, or that butterfly. Was she hovering to get a closer look, sizing me up as I strolled? If anyone would recognize a woman on a mission, it was Lady Meng.

Feeling more empowered with every step, I wondered what it might be like to hike the entire length of the wall—what was left of it and accessible—perambulating the remote, rugged landscape and sleeping out under the stars, as I'd heard some people did when they could evade the government's patrols. You didn't have to be an adventurer to think like one here; all you had to do was look around. That's why I had impossibly high expectations for my second visit in 2004. And yet, the wall still delivered.

This time, I was acutely aware of being at a personal crossroads as I climbed. Every one of my steps seemed bound for a metaphor. I was on a path—to motherhood, to Zoe—and I would be as formidable as this fortress in protecting her. Though I was not rooted in this land, she was. And James was. And now it coursed through me in a way that felt like a gift. God help me, I was already thinking in Hallmark-speak.

Again, my mother-in-law popped into my head.

In recent days, whenever my musings had turned toward the anonymous woman who'd surrendered her newborn to the events that would finally make me a parent, I imagined something like the outline of a young Yù Yīng—the same silhouette that Tǔ Xiù struggled to summon adequately in the years after her abandonment. There was no reason to think the two women looked alike or had anything in common beyond a few probable demographics, but my mother-in-law was my reference point for the "primal wound" that some say accompanies all early cleavings of a biological mother and child, regardless of circumstance. I had deep empathy for both women, and so much gratitude. Zoe's birth mother's loss had been my tangible yet immeasurable gain, which felt incredibly wrong but also inevitable in a world that doggedly perpetuates its opportunity gaps. What Yù Yīng gave me was far less obvious, and just as life changing in its own way.

In the seven years since becoming aware of her story, I'd thought a lot about how Yù Yīng came to leave behind her firstborn child, if not exactly willingly then at least obediently, without realizing the long-term implications of what was unfolding. She may not have even clocked it as a goodbye; it seemed positioned as more of a "see you soon." Which is why I was thinking of her again now, as I arrived at this place with the unfathomable permission to claim and raise another woman's child as my own, because it occurred to me that together our journeys made a sort of wonky, jury-rigged, necessary circle—one large enough to encompass the ring of hell I'd reserved for abandonment traumas, and bold enough to challenge every winners' circle definition I'd been sold as a child. There were no winners here, only fighters, with varying degrees of success. Though I'd borne a considerable amount of loss in my life, I had to admit that Yù Yīng's story made my own family saga look like the work of a deity in training. And how she'd managed her losses, through a blend of stoicism, resilience, and casual acceptance, was a feat that I found immensely instructive. I'd gotten quite proficient at stoicism and resilience over the years; the acceptance part I still struggled with, even after I'd seen it played out so effectively between Yù Yīng and Tǔ Xiù in Guilin.

When you're on the Great Wall, it's natural to think about turbulence and pain. Every dip and bend reminds you of the country's volatile history, as well as your own. That's usually a recipe for my mind to turn on its camera, which in this case saw me as no bigger than the tiny black speck that famously appears on the horizon in *Lawrence of Arabia*, growing larger and more defined as it moves slowly into focus. In the beginning of that iconic scene, you can't guess what the speck—gradually evolving into a smudge and then a blob—will become, even with the sweeping desert sands for context. A vulture? A fox? A horse? Oh, wait, a camel? Yes. With a rider, enrobed in dark Bedouin clothing. The last thing you make out is the rifle, just before it's used to murder someone (Chekhov's Law).

I'm not insinuating that *I* was coming into focus. I'm not the speck in this admittedly overwrought analogy—that's Omar Sharif, playing deuteragonist Sherif Ali. *I'm* Peter O'Toole, as Lawrence, the stranger in a strange land who's trying to make sense of the speck, which in my case is obviously a baby, armed with all kinds of weapons I'm going to be powerless to counter.

I'm saying that none of it felt real; it all seemed like a mirage. Especially the infant on the horizon, who was right now making her way to us in a van that probably did not have safety-standard-compliant car seats, after being ripped from her Yiyang foster parents so she could be transported hundreds of miles to begin a new life with a whole other family she didn't ask for. It was an extended tracking shot that I could only imagine—and did, constantly. Which is why, when I think about the conversation that happened while I was navigating the wall that day, entertaining all manner of irrational thoughts, I picture it the way I'd write and direct that exchange now, with the benefit of distance.

EXT. GREAT WALL OF CHINA—AFTERNOON

On a remote section of the wall at Badaling, away from the crush of tourists, Janice, 42, sits alone, surveying the landscape but clearly preoccupied.

WOMAN'S VOICE

(off camera)

You sure look lost in thought.

JANICE

(looks up as the woman enters the frame)

Me? Oh. Yeah. I guess.

Enter Stacey, a gregarious, 35-ish woman wearing a lanyard and badge with the CAWLI logo—she's another of the about-to-be parents traveling with this adoption group.

STACEY

Janice, right? I called out to you, but you didn't move. I'm Stacey, just in case you're as overloaded on names as I am.

JANICE

More, I bet. Good to meet you—or meet you again—Stacey. And, sorry for being so in my own head; it's that sort of place, I suppose.

STACEY

And that sort of day, with so much just around the corner.

JANICE

Totally.

STACEY

Are you nervous? About adopting, I mean.

JANICE

Umm. Yeah, kind of. I mean, I'm excited, for sure. But, yeah, I have some major butterflies. Not quite at the level of a deepening dread, but I bet I can get there.

STACEY

Well, you'd be crazy if you weren't terrified. I mean, what do we really know about these kids? They're a couple of sentences on a piece of paper, right? The few photographs we have are already months old. Let's face it, they could be demon spawn.

JANICE

(nodding and exhaling a laugh)

Do you have other children?

STACEY

One. We adopted two years ago, also from Jiangxi. It's been great, in all seriousness. She's four now, and she's amazing.

JANICE

Oh, that's awesome.

STACEY

Yeah. She really wants a little sister. My mom says if you can take care of one you can take care of two, so . . .

JANICE

I've heard that. Sounds a little over-optimistic. They don't say that about husbands, for example.

STACEY

Touché.

JANICE

Where are you from?

STACEY

Kentucky.

JANICE

Oh, nice. I've never been there, but I did once win a March Madness pool with your university's help.

STACEY

You're welcome. Where are you from?

JANICE

Boston.

STACEY

Beantown!

JANICE

Mmm. Not really a thing. Unless I'm trying to sell you a tricorn hat. Or giving you directions to the "*Cheers* bar" [motions air quotes], also not a real thing.

STACEY

Noted. And what do you do in Not Bean-town, Janice?

JANICE

I'm a writer. Well, a journalist. A writer was what I wanted to be when I was a kid.

STACEY

What's the difference?

JANICE

A journalist gets a regular paycheck. Or can.

STACEY

Ah. And that's important to you?

JANICE

More like it's expected of me—by me, mostly. What are you, a therapist?

STACEY

Close. Stay-at-home mom.

Janice presses her lips together and nods in Stacey's direction, mimicking a James-style affirmation.

STACEY

(continuing)

But let's pretend I'm an actual therapist. Getting back to the adoption thing, what are you afraid of?

JANICE

(a bit startled by her directness, but not unhappy with the question)

Funny you should ask me that, Stacey from Kentucky.

(beat)

Got time for a story?

STACEY

Duh. Always.

The dream that I found myself revealing to Stacey probably sounds made-up, because all dreams sound made-up, even when they're 100 percent true, at least as you remember them. This one was so true that it didn't even qualify as part of my internal movie, because that would just be too meta. To get to *my* dream, though, I first needed to tell her about a whole other dream—one that James had experienced—which was related but not causational, and equally true to its source.

A few weeks before landing in China to meet Zoe, there was a morning when James seemed oddly troubled for a person who greets most days by giving bear hugs to the many houseplants he pampers as though they're a forest of little emperors. I inquired about what might be wrong, and he explained that he'd had a bad dream. Did he remember it, I asked? He did.

"We are at a backyard party," he began. "A wedding, maybe. Everyone is in fancy dress. Then, *wasai!* A big, yellow snake—thick, like a python—slithers into a clearing where Zoe is standing. So, I take out my sword . . ."

I couldn't let that pass. "You had a sword?" I interrupted.

"Yes," he said simply, refusing to have his momentum impeded. "So, I take out my sword and I cut the snake's head off."

There was no mistaking the exhilaration in his words. I might have had other questions, but all I could think to add was "Whoa, good job." And then he went on, less energetically, which I thought was because the beheading had taken so much out of him.

"I look around for Zoe," he said, turning darker. "I don't see her anymore. She isn't there. [Long pause.] I search and search. I run through the house and the yard. I'm yelling for her: Zoe, Zoe, *Zoe*! It starts to get dark. I look so hard, but I never find her."

His voice just trailed off, as though he were going to leave it there.

"You never found her?" I said.

"Right," he said.

"Never ever?"

"Right."

I asked him if he was worried, in the dream. "Not exactly worried," he said. "It feels heavy. And empty, like something is missing. But I also feel it's something that's supposed to happen. And then, I wake up."

Very unsettling, but also intriguing, I thought. What did he think it meant?

"It means she will leave," he said.

"Leave?" I repeated, as though he'd confused it with another vocabulary word.

"Yes. No matter what I do, no matter how I protect her; one day, she will move out and make her own life. She will leave us."

Like discarded water that can never be returned.

"Seriously?" I said. "You believe it's that straightforward? And you got all that from killing a snake? At a party? In a dream?"

"That's what I think," he said with a shrug. "That's what I say."

I gave Stacey a moment to sit with James's dream, the way I had when he first told it to me, because it was a lot to unpack. Then I explained that my husband was a very deep thinker. Very wise. Very certain. *Verrry* pessimistic, but in a very accepting, matter-of-fact way. I, on the other hand, was having a whole different kind of nightmare.

"What's *your* nightmare?" she asked.

"Where should I start?" I answered, trilling my lips in a sigh. "I have so many."

But I knew exactly where I wanted to start, with the most vivid example: the one where I'm pushing a shopping cart around a grocery store—strolling, really, at a pretty leisurely pace because that's what my mother did when she wanted to get away from us as kids. In that seemingly anodyne dream, I'm just wandering down a random aisle when it suddenly dawns on me: Zoe. Oh my God, I left her back at the house, alone.

I'm panic stricken, of course, so I race home and run through the door, up the stairs . . . I search and search and search, going room by room until I find her. She's crawled under one of the radiators in our bedroom—because they didn't give me time to get them covered, obviously—and she's lying there, as red and shriveled as a sundried tomato. I pick her up to comfort her, but there's no sound and no movement.

She's dead.

Or sometimes she isn't dead, I tell Stacey after a pause for dramatic effect; she's just badly burned. Or she's calling for me, but I don't know how to get to her. Either way, that's when I wake up, usually sobbing and unable to shake it for a really long time.

Stacey doesn't say anything when I finish telling her the dream. She knows I'm not done. She knows there's more to say.

"So, let's review," I suggest, as though she has a choice. "While James is concerned that someday Zoe will grow up and move on to live a wonderful, independent life that doesn't much involve us, I'm worried about killing her before she even gets out of diapers. See the disconnect?"

Stacey has a sense of humor, but more importantly Stacey understands that in the many, many minutes it has taken me to tell her about the twisted dreams of my husband and me, I've really just been talking to myself the whole time.

"Oh my God, you're hilarious," she says, chuckling. "Relax. It's all normal. The more bizarre your thoughts are, the more they sort of make sense. That's adoption. It's a roller coaster. All you can do is hang on and scream into the wind."

And that's when my mind resumes its movie, which flashes back first to Yolanda and five-year-old me, sitting at the apex of the Congo Cruise in Paragon Park, about to make the ride's terrifying and thrilling final descent. As we go over, I hear my mother let loose with a squeal of delight.

End flashback. My camera picks back up with me and Stacey on the wall, because there's one more thing we need to do to get this scene right.

EXT. GREAT WALL OF CHINA—STILL AFTERNOON

Seated, Janice and Stacey exchange conspiratorial glances. Then, they stand and turn their backs to the camera as they look out over the vast wilderness beyond the wall.

JANICE

Ready?

STACEY

Yep.

JANICE

One. Two. Three . . .

JANICE AND STACEY

(yelling loudly, in unison)

FUUUUUUUUUUUUCK!

(beat)

JANICE

(still yelling into the wind)

GǑU PÌ BÙ TŌNG! (狗屁不通)

Stacey looks at Janice quizzically.

JANICE

(shrugs)

It literally means "dog unable to fart." [Beat.] It's the Chinese way of saying, "this is bullshit." [Beat.] Just something I picked up at a Chinese restaurant a really long time ago.

Back at the Gloria Plaza Hotel in Nanchang, Zoe was keeping up the volume and tone of her first impression, despite our efforts to comfort her.

She was flushed and hiccupping from all the crying. She was also sweaty, smelly, overdressed, and extremely pissed off. Our encounter wasn't

Hollywood movie magical, and there wasn't any love at first sight; in truth, as she remained inconsolable for the entire ninety minutes that we waited to get our stamp of approval from the Chinese authorities, I questioned the extent of my stamina.

Would she be like this all night? All week? Longer? I pulled out every toy and stuffed animal we'd brought. None tickled her fancy; some (you know who you are, Mr. Caterpillar) even made her discomfort escalate. I tried funny faces. I tried snacks. Nothing stopped her sobs.

Look, my inner critic said. *See that family in the corner? They're smiling! And over there, and over there . . . No tears. That baby actually looks happy!*

"Are we doing something wrong?" I asked James.

"You ask me, who I gonna ask?" he replied.

Most times, I delighted in hearing his catchphrase. I'd even hijacked it on occasion; it came in handy for gently but flatly dismissing questions with no answers. But I was less than delighted with its use in this moment.

"Ask *me*," I said sharply. "Ask me if I'm amused."

"No thanks," he muttered, looking away.

We were being motioned to a table at the far side of the room. That's where a trio of government officials sat stiffly, with stern faces, interviewing families and okaying critical documents when they were satisfied that every piece of paperwork was in order. The officials asked us three questions. Roughly translated, they were: (1) Did we promise to love and take care of her? (2) Did we earn enough money to provide for her? (3) Did we agree to send her to a good college? The correct answers were: Yes. Yes. Harvard.

But here's what I would have asked, if I were them: (1) What planet are you people from? (2) What makes you think you're remotely equipped to do this? (3) Are you high?

Apparently, we passed the quiz, because each document was stamped, with a loud bang, in red ink. And that's when the real panic set in. Seriously, *could* I do this? It wasn't a formidable French recipe or a page 1 story on deadline; it was a child. I had no reason to think I'd be capable of raising her—in fact, just the opposite. My own mother, a funny, well-liked woman with acres of untapped talent and intelligence, was tangible proof that parenting isn't universally second nature. She loved us, of course, but that didn't mean she should have had us. Some women are just better at being the faithful friend, the wacky/fun aunt, and yes, fine, the spinster. I frankly had always seen myself as one or more of those. Lend me your children for a day or two; I'd dazzle and corrupt them, then return them and go back to my cats, Pauline and Kael.

I'd heard the standard cautionary tales of nightmare adoptions. People who'd gone into this with the best intentions only to find that they were just not prepared, or the child came with so much baggage that it would have been impossible to prepare. Sometimes these families found a way through it. Sometimes they didn't, and the child was sent back, or passed along to another family, or institutionalized forever.

When your childhood includes seeing your mom in a hospital room after electroshock therapy for her latest "nervous breakdown," which your dad insinuates was probably caused by a house full of kids and kid chaos, you do wonder if you have the genetic code required for successful parenting. I'd always been labeled an overachiever, but had I finally taken on the one thing I wouldn't be able to micromanage into a relative success? For a control freak such as myself, this seemed the perfect prescription for insanity.

There is a concept in the Asian adoption community known as the Legend of the Red Thread. It supposedly binds us, from birth, to those we are destined to love. The imaginary threads "may stretch or tangle," goes the proverb recounted in numerous adoption-related books and websites, "but they will never break."

Despite obsessing over the word, I am not a believer in fate. If there is a preordained script for all the tragedies of the world, it doesn't point to any kind of omniscient authority I want to embrace.

But I do believe in serendipity.

While it was regular teenage money problems that led me to search for an additional summer job in 1979, and random luck, I think, that the want ads led me to Benny Wu, our friendship and the cultural benefits it offered were pure serendipity. No one could have foreseen the many layers they'd contribute to my life, including—by way of Chin Chin, who was one of Benny's most astute hires as he expanded management of his growing restaurant empire—a husband and a child I'd never have met otherwise. If people like me accept that nothing and no one is responsible for all the bad that befalls us, we should also accept that nothing and no one gets credit for all the good. Serendipity is when our best options find us, whether we recognize them as they're presenting, or not until much later, or not at all.

I thought again of my mother-in-law, and the child she'd abandoned in wartime—a water horse, just like this child I'd been entrusted to rear. Was Yù Yīng my permission slip for jumping ship on this adoption if I had to—my proof that real-world threads do, in fact, break? Or was her life a reminder that all we can do is endure our mistakes, and hope that it's never too late for mending?

And what about Zoe's birth mother? I'd tried not to romanticize her backstory: Yes, she could be a victim of the one-child policy, but she could also be an unwed teen desperate for a way out of an unwanted pregnancy. She could be too poor or too ill or mentally unfit to care for this child. She could be dead. I had no idea if she was somewhere pining for her lost child or relieved to have lightened her load, or both. What I did know was that her forfeiture, regardless of what precipitated it, stood to be our greatest windfall. That's a hard thing to celebrate, and yet, if everything went the way I wanted for this promising little girl and for us, each year would strengthen our bond, and I would find myself thinking with a deepening sadness and zero judgment: How could anyone have given her up?

The editor in me believes that all great wisdom fits inside a fortune cookie. If I'm right, I suppose that Yù Yīng's fortune might have read: *Confucius say, the flip side of serendipity is bad fucking luck*. The obvious follow-up question was: What did luck have in store for me and Zoe?

CHAPTER 18

The White Swan

It is astounding, and humbling, to bond with an adopted baby. As glad as you are for the speed and depth of the relationship, you do know that one set of parents can't just be switched out for another as easily as changing a disposable diaper. Even if you haven't yet heard the term *relinquishment trauma*, it won't surprise you to learn, however many years later, that the psychological impact of a child being separated from its biological mother can (but thankfully doesn't always) manifest in developmental, behavioral, and social issues. It also won't surprise you that in the immediate aftermath of being handed a screaming one-year-old who only knows she's not happy with the current situation, the one thing that matters is finding a way to make the wailing stop.

When we'd finally surfaced from the sea of baby gatekeepers and red-stamped paperwork demanded by Nanchang bureaucrats, we hightailed it back to our hotel room, where we discovered that all Zoe needed to improve her mood was a change of scenery, fresh clothes, and a bottle of warm formula. We wiped her down but dared not try a bath; what if some of her parts had never been submerged in water? In moments such as this, your choices are instinctual and rooted in survival, which you realize is the same for the child. The emotional whiplash can be dizzying, and it can be magical, too. Less than thirty minutes after we'd left that crowded conference room scared out of our minds, Zoe was lying on our bed, laughing. That's not adoption. That's parenthood.

My mother used to say that children aren't a thing you can plan. I thought she'd been wrong about that, among other things, but now I could see what she meant. She wasn't only talking about procreation.

Zoe had come to us as a thirteen-month-old with clear needs, wants, and habits that she was instantly comfortable revealing. She smiled frequently, babbled determinedly, and roamed the hotel halls holding on to our fingers. By the second night, she was sleeping twelve hours without interruption and waking up ravenous. Best of all, as the television in our room was broadcasting the New England Patriots' 2004 Super Bowl win in hyperventilating Mandarin, Zoe was pronounced "perfect" by one of two American doctors who'd accompanied our group on the trip. We'd seen enough of China's childcare system to know that good health wasn't a given.

Only the best orphanages even allowed nosy foreigners inside their walls. The one we'd gotten to see in Nanchang wasn't part of Zoe's story—she'd grown up in rural Yiyang, more than 270 miles from this teeming capital city—but it was presented as an example of the way most foundlings were raised. Endless rooms crammed with tiny beds, forceful smells, and circles of lethargic children parked in front of ancient TVs. As we toured, I said a silent thanks for the unknown foster family who we'd been told had taken Zoe in, shortly after her birth. International adoptions are almost always well-intended. That doesn't make them any less privileged.

Whenever our group had free time to venture out onto the streets, we were—as our Chinese guide put it—"like pandas in the zoo." The Nanchang locals had seen enough Americans pushing strollers at this point to stop viewing us as a novelty, but we were still a curiosity. They weren't shy about staring, or pulling at a child's pant leg if it rode up to expose a sliver of skin, and a few might have been heard muttering *"yǒu jīng shén bìng"* (有精神病, *insane*) as we ambled past.

I don't blame them. We must have looked ridiculous, parading around with their native daughters dressed head to toe in Baby Gap. Friends who lived in the southern port city of Guangzhou had told us that most Chinese are grateful to non-Asians who adopt those in need, but also embarrassed and angered by an exodus that might have been less necessary if China's domestic adoption system were better supported and promoted. Lillian had told us that official policies and attitudes were changing, slowly (the one-child-turned-two-child-turned-three-child policy would take more than forty years to spin itself out, finally becoming a no-child-limits stance in July 2021). In the meantime, outsiders going to China to adopt would continue to be seen with a broad mix of emotions, including—for good reason—amusement.

Though several in our group had other children at home or along for the trip, and a surprising number had been down this exact road before, there were always new opportunities to appear completely clueless. By the third or fourth day in Nanchang, many of us were wearing our mistakes on our fingers, sporting Band-Aids where we'd been reminded that these newbies often came with teeth. We were learning who our little people were, as well as where they were developmentally. I discovered that Zoe's left eyebrow curled into a tilde whenever she was puzzling over something. She liked sticky rice and eggs. She didn't like caterpillars. In true red-thread fashion, she seemed perfectly matched to us not just because she was the spitting image of James's own chubby-cheeked baby picture, but because she was curious, displayed an absurd sense of humor, and appreciated the sublime singer-songwriting of Aimee Mann, whose albums she'd unfailingly sway to when we had them looping in the background.

Part of what made Nanchang special was sharing our first days of parenthood with people who sometimes had very little else in common, hailing from places as disparate as Kansas City, Missouri, and Newburyport, Massachusetts. Though the group was in many ways too large (most of those handled by Lillian's agency were about half as big), it felt cohesive. Occupying two floors of the Gloria Plaza Hotel, we threw open our doors and mingled over snacks and baby toys laid out in the hallways. We gossiped, marveling that two of the adoptees in our group might be twins given without government apology to parents from different states, and empathizing when we heard about a prospective mother weighing whether to refuse a girl who'd arrived with undisclosed neurological problems. Many shoulders comforted another woman who wondered if she should go through with her adoption plans, overwhelmed as she was by exhaustion and doubt, just hours into caring for her new, high-energy toddler.

"I'm just not sure I can," she confided.

All I could think of was Yolanda.

It wasn't fair to compare them—this woman I barely knew and the mother I knew to be so readily suffocated by parenthood—but we don't choose our triggers, and everything about this situation encouraged comparisons. Even if the woman had better overall mental health than my own mother did, both struggled to believe in their capacity to nurture and enrich another life without killing the host organism. I'd grown to understand that impulse, and I could relate to the panic it incited, but I could also see important differences between my mother's circumstances and my own. Yolanda had felt cornered into having most of her children and flattened by the weight of raising them, whereas I'd traveled more than seven thousand miles for the opportunity to have a child on my own terms, a kind of power she'd never even contemplated. I'd previously aborted a pregnancy that didn't feel right, and I was okay with that choice. I hadn't once been struck down by lightning. Attitudes and conventions had changed, somewhat. And still, conflicted women everywhere, including those of us now baring our souls to relative strangers in the hallways of a humble Nanchang hotel, were proof that the struggle continued.

"It's okay," we told the new mother in crisis, and ourselves. "Whatever you decide, it's going to be okay."

Though no one had handed us a bullet-pointed list of risks this time, of course I'd considered these and other nightmare scenarios. The woman with cold feet was single and roughly my age. She thought she was ready for motherhood, but how could she—or we—be sure?

The repeat adopters among us knew that life might be easier, or at least more luxuriously appointed, when we got to Guangzhou, the exit point for all international adoptions, but it would never again be as intimately shared as by our thirty-three families. The rest of us were just anxious to see what awaited us at the crossroads of adoption in China: the White Swan Hotel.

On tiny Shamian Island overlooking the Pearl River, the White Swan Hotel sits just around the corner from the US consulate, a fortuitous location that has made the inn adoption central for thousands of American families with important personal business to complete. No matter which province an abandoned Chinese child hails from, they must pass through this floating nugget of Guangzhou to obtain documentation necessary to enter the United States. And the White Swan is famously ostentatious enough that most every family shuffles through its doors to get a look, whether or not they're overnight guests.

It's an odd place that has even inspired a children's book *(The White Swan Express: A Story About Adoption)*, which seems about right. If all you ever saw of Asia was Shamian Island and the inside of the White Swan, you'd think China was Epcot, but with more earnest service. Guangzhou, formerly known as Canton, was once the country's gateway to foreign trade and tourism. Most of the city is congested and bustling, but on quaint, clean Shamian Island, the architecture reflects European colonialism, and the steamy weather supports a casual pace. Everything else supports a modern lust for commerce.

"Best deal here for baby clothes," one shopkeeper after another insists from the open doorways lining the streets. Before you drop a single yuan, the merchants lend you a stroller and arrange to do your laundry. (In the age before smartphones, they might also snap a family photograph and transmit it over the internet to your loved ones back home, where news of a baby is always most welcome but exponentially more so in families battered by loss.) Some vendors will even write your new child's name in frame-ready calligraphy, presenting it to you as a gift.

Though it was still primarily a hotel geared to business travelers, at the time when we stayed there at least 20 percent of the White Swan's guests were adopting families—most visiting from the United States—who frequently exceeded its fleet of 180 cribs for 843 rooms. When they weren't stuffed into backpacks and strollers, kids who could toddle roamed the shop-lined corridors like some tiny drunken gang, stopping to climb over every stone Buddha and foo dog in their path. At breakfast, they filled up the hotel's one hundred highchairs before most sensible travelers were awake, and they drooled on the cereal buffet whenever Dad, child in arms, leaned in too close. Eventually, they'd be corralled for group photos by the lobby's towering waterfall and along a massive red couch, rituals that adoption organizations had turned into rites of passage.

Outside the hotel, many of the families in our group ate burgers and burritos in Westernized cafés and bartered for knockoff Polo suitcases to transport souvenirs. Our official business spilled into the international health-care center, where screaming-baby examinations were conducted near overmatched "Keep Quiet!" signs, and then we zipped past waiting Chinese throngs at the US consulate so that a functionary could end our swearing-in by announcing: "This concludes the world's most bureaucratic process."

He couldn't have been more wrong.

Nothing that happens on Shamian Island marks the end of a process. On the contrary, the world just gets odder and more complicated from there.

One of our most unexpected souvenirs from Guangzhou is a doll. It remains preserved in the packaging it came in, unplayed with since its arrival in 2004.

When the doll showed up in our hotel room at the White Swan, it freaked me out a bit, the way I'm unnerved by crawl spaces, cooked raisins, and any kind of elf on any kind of shelf. I never played with dolls as a kid. Again, I was supposed to be named Joe, so I played with bats and balls and other things that would always get you labeled as a tomboy back then, not that the labeling has evolved much since. Once, someone gave me a Barbie as a birthday gift. I stuck her head in the dirt and used her upturned legs as a football tee.

The Going Home Barbie that was given to us in Guangzhou is the mod-hippie version. Her long hair isn't Malibu blond but is instead the color of a wet sand dune, with a few strands pulled into a side braid that dangles down her famous plastic chest. She wears a tan suede-looking skirt and visor, an off-the-shoulder floral blouse, and (what else?) open-toed hot-pink heels. As always, in her hands she holds a Chinese baby.

I say "always" because, unlike other Barbie accessories—Corvettes, handbags, Ken—the black-haired bundle of joy isn't just another piece of interchangeable packaging. Though this doll has had annual fashion makeovers, she's defined by an androgynous-looking child held stiffly at her waist, which in all honesty makes her look even sillier than that time she attempted math. Our 2004 model looks particularly uneasy. "Motherhood is hard," I think she'd say if she could.

Going Home Barbie is a special-edition doll that Mattel began manufacturing in 2001. She couldn't be found in retail stores, and she was never hyped on Saturday-morning TV. Only about six thousand of her kind were made each year, and all were distributed free at just one location in the world: the White Swan in Guangzhou. To get the doll, you had to stay at the famous five-star hotel, and you had to check out with at least one more child than you had when you entered the country.

It should go without saying that no one adopts a baby to get a collectible doll.

James and I didn't even know Going Home Barbie existed before she showed up in our hotel room, along with fresh towels and an explanation that read in part: "This souvenir is presented by Mattel (HK) Ltd. to adopting parents of Chinese orphan children." By then, we'd come to expect absurd surprises from the adoption process, so it hardly fazed me to be suddenly likened—at age forty-two, no less—to a poseable beauty queen with perfect measurements and proudly vacant eyes. In fact, despite my ready cynicism and usually dependable feminist filters, I actually found Mattel's opportunistic marketing at least as savvy as it was unsettling.

Even *Sex and the City* had managed to work in a Chinese adoption for one of its characters before the raunchy comedy ended its television run. International adoptions were undeniably trendy at the time, which didn't make them any less genuine.

At the White Swan, Mattel didn't just hand out Barbies; the company also sponsored a playroom stocked with piles of its own toys and giant reminders of branding. Each corporate dollar spent told me how significant American adoptions of Chinese foundlings had become, and how prominent a role the White Swan played in hosting most of them. Still, try as they might, six thousand identical Barbies couldn't begin to embody six thousand unique adoption stories. Maybe that was the real reason our mod-hippie doll looked so uncomfortable.

The process that had begun when we wrote our first checks to CAWLI in December 2002 delivered both Zoe, the girl whose photo had caused an agency worker to exclaim "Oh, she's a doll!," and Going Home Barbie, the doll that I never gave to my daughter to play with. I wasn't keeping it from her—the package still sits on a shelf in the same room where we positioned her crib—and I couldn't care less about its commercial value since we'll never sell it, no matter how many hundreds of dollars it could fetch on eBay. Rather, it's been preserved because Barbie is a part of our story now. She followed us out of China, the same way Zoe had, hitching herself to the antonym of everything that Yù Yīng had unintentionally abandoned.

⁂

"How much you pay for her?"

That's a line from Julia Sweeney's theatrical monologue *In the Family Way*. First staged in 2003, it springs from the former *Saturday Night Live* star's protracted path to parenthood, and what happened when she finally brought her daughter home from China to live in Southern California. One day, while shopping in Los Angeles with her adopted toddler, Sweeney found herself fielding the astonishingly indelicate question from a Chinese dim sum vendor.

"How much you pay for her?"

If that sounds too blunt to be for real, you probably haven't walked in Sweeney's shoes. Or mine. People don't have much of a filter when it comes to multiracial families. They often say what they're thinking—or at least they used to, before embarrassing cellphone recordings became as ubiquitous in America as ignorance. In her monologue, Sweeney talked about how such encounters inevitably made her more tolerant, because she had to find the patience and compassion to educate everyone who came at her with a question, a comment, or a look.

"I thought of myself as those things before," she told me in 2004, when I interviewed her for a *Boston Globe* magazine piece. "But, boy, by comparison, I am *really* understanding now."

Boy, could I relate.

For us, China had faded quickly once we returned to Brookline and settled into our new roles and realities. Zoe was old enough and mobile enough to require near constant supervision, sustenance, and engagement. Not to mention laundry. Dear God, the laundry—how on earth did my mother do this with a basement washer and dryer accessed by a slippery outside staircase, every day for decades, times six kids? Anyone can tell you that the best way to understand your parents is to become a parent yourself. But James and I were surprised by how much and how quickly we had to learn to keep up with the remarkable, insatiable one-year-old who'd fallen straight into our laps and was already demanding every ounce of the energy and patience my mother was always chasing.

Had my mom still been around when we brought our daughter home, she might have rightly remarked that I had it easy: Zoe was a smiley, tantrum-free baby who rarely got sick, ate just about everything put in front of her, and excelled at sleeping. But that undersells the baseline difficulty of raising a child, especially when the manual you're referring back to has a bunch of missing chapters with notations that just say "Mother Checked Out." Yolanda and Yù Yīng were both so much more than their unintentional abandonments, and yet they also had to own them, the same way I'd have to own everything I did for and to my kid on our way to building a modicum of trust. Julia Sweeney, my go-to guru for charting my own family way, put it thus in another of her monologues: "I have to accept what is true, rather than what I wish were true."

Julia and I had this reverence for verifiable truth in common. We recognized that our mothers were well-meaning if highly flawed beings, and our tolerance increased dramatically when we became moms ourselves. "My new attitude about my mother is that she did the best she could," the comic concluded in *The Family Way*. I could not have agreed more.

Like any expectant mom, I'd fantasized about all the incredible memories I'd start building with my child from day one. We'd read and hatch stories together every night, *The Princess Bride*–style. We'd spend our Saturdays running errands all around town, just as I did with my dad, the make-believe mayor of Quincy. And of course, I would give her a greatest day of her very own, perhaps built around her era's "it" entertainment *(Hamilton)*, copious clam strips, and nonstop ice cream, but those details would matter less than the idea behind them, because if I'd internalized anything from my greatest day, it was that time is precious, and you never feel as special as when someone you worship says you're worthy of their attention.

From both Yolanda and Yù Yīng, I learned to prioritize being present for my child whenever we were together, since we rarely anticipate how much we might otherwise be absent. Yù Yīng certainly didn't expect she'd flee China without her kid, and Yolanda had no clue that one nervous breakdown would spiral into many. Zoe didn't get to prioritize the minutes she had with her birth mom before their relationship was abruptly severed. I could do better for her, maybe—it was a low bar.

Meanwhile, there were other things I shared with Julia. Both raised Catholic, we'd been open about our long-lapsed faith, our terminated pregnancies, our initial ambivalence toward motherhood. We were each in our early forties when we adopted, and we'd agonized equally over what to call the child. Dismissing her daughter's orphanage nickname (Mulan, which read to Julia as "I'm From China" Sweeney), she went with Tara—a moniker as meaningful in Buddhist China as it is in the hills of Ireland—until one day her toddler announced that she preferred . . . wait for it . . . Mulan. At which point Julia learned, as I had, that names are an art form and everyone's a critic.

Maybe the thing the *SNL* star and I had most in common was being thrown into a jarring identity shift late in life, from established career-woman with her own byline and credits to Is She Really *That* Kid's Mom? The confusion, external and internal, was as hard to predict and navigate in Brookline as it was in L.A.

Most days, I was feeling pretty good about our collective progress as a family, even as I continued to ignore my stack of parenting books. Still, whenever I pushed Zoe's unfashionably low-end stroller through town or stepped onto a gated playground, I could feel people sizing us up. If I had my husband along, we were just another mixed-race family in a progressive New England town. Maybe our child happened to look more like him or maybe she was the product of his first marriage, but either way a biological connection was assumed to be part of the equation. Whereas, if it was just me and Zoe, the opposite assumption prevailed: I must be the adoptive parent or hired caretaker; no way was I this kid's biological mom. In the second scenario, we almost always got stared at, and frequently the stares turned to verbalized interactions that started right in with "Where is she from?" That question might be followed by something innocuous ("She's adorable"), or incongruous ("I have a niece from Korea"), or inappropriately, maddeningly, laughably direct ("How much you pay for her?").

Sometimes, just as the person was rhapsodizing about how great adoption is and how the world needs more of "us," James would emerge from around a corner and the presumptuous stranger's face would fall. Oh, no! Had they made a horrible mistake? You could see their internal GPS recalculating the route, looking for any kind of graceful exit. I must say, though, it was hard for me to get too worked up about these encounters, since I'd likely have been met with many of the same inquiries if Zoe were our biological daughter. That is, even if she were only half Chinese, people might assume she was adopted when she was out with me alone. Either way, I was Going Home Barbie. Which I suppose is at least better than being Going Home Midge.

You make a lot of choices as an adoptive mom. All mothers do, obviously, but there's a bit more to be discovered and decided when your child did not spring from your loins with a fully formed origin story. As Zoe grew more curious and verbal, I wanted her to be empowered without being overwhelmed. So, I sprinkled the incomplete pieces of her history like breadcrumbs set out for a dove—or a pigeon—reasoning that she could go there if and when she wanted, and my primary role was to recognize, enable, and unconditionally support her lead.

Regularly, we would visit our local public library, where she would pick out books from the early readers section and I would throw in a few also, just for consideration. Remembering how much literature had expanded my world, even before my Beverly Clearys and Judy Blumes gave way to *The Good Earth* and so much more, I looked for things to challenge her developing brain: things that might involve science or Shakespeare or fairy tales that skewed a bit grim. Prioritizing those weekly trips to the library with Zoe, usually followed by errands and lunch at one of our spots, was—in a good way—knocking down a few of my greatest day building blocks by normalizing them. It was making shared experience into a routine, something I never really had with my mom, and only had with my dad until he canceled me from his Saturdays because, you know, puberty. Unlike all those times my mother went to the grocery store to escape her children, I wanted Zoe to see that she was part of my habits—and not just an obligation along for the ride, but a welcome, full-on participant who could sometimes also drive. So, we combed the library shelves with equal enthusiasm, applying a mix of verbalized and internal metrics to size up which books deserved consideration on any given day. When we had a pile of ten or fifteen candidates, she'd go through them to cull the five or six she wanted to take home. Not infrequently, one or two of my choices would have something to do with adoption, overtly or in passing, in case she showed any interest. Without fail, every time I did this, those would be the first books she tossed aside, without comment. I never asked her why. But it did make me wonder.

When do we begin to settle on the things that will shape how we see the world and our place in it? Is the process mostly innate, as large-scale studies report it is with gender (trans and cis alike), or is any of how we identify rooted in conscious decision? And what happens if your entire world is remade only minutes after your birth? Or even years after? What if you feel guilty about being here at all, when so many others—better others—are not?

Almost all my life, I'd been exceptional at narrowing—the act of putting my head down and powering through whatever I needed to control and perfect to survive and conquer. My great good fortune in meeting Yù Yīng was the lens she opened, starting with the way I saw my role in telling her story. Here was a subject who eluded my every attempt to simplify and master, and whom I found even more intriguing when the precisionist in me failed. Yù Yīng forced me to be less rigid and more resourceful, more creative, as a writer and as a human being who would eventually have to figure out how to mother another human being. My own mother had provided a loving image that I could model, but she also handed down her many hang-ups, in the tradition of so many middle-class families who don't have a summer cottage to bequeath. I didn't see Yù Yīng as a counterpoint, or as any kind of superior role model; I just liked the expanded view that she and her story offered—the way they allowed acknowledgment of personal failings and cosmic misfortunes without positioning them as sins that demanded atonement.

Now that I was a mother myself, I understood the way that job amplifies, well, everything. And I was beginning to understand intergenerational trauma: the psychological wounds that can imprint themselves on our inheritance as darkly as any BRCA mutation. We all know that trauma isn't a competition. But if it were, just as with my Tao of Three Wishes, we'd have to preface it by acknowledging the difference between events of mass-scale impact and more-limited traumas that take an outsized toll on individual lives. A wise person doesn't compare their family history to that of anyone else. They do, however, seize every opportunity to connect with and take comfort from stories of survival and the useful tools they impart. Among the many things I took from Yù Yīng was a new perspective on loss and abandonment—not as things that happened to you or because of you, but as things that just happened, all the time and everywhere, but mostly outside your first-world frame of view.

Abandonment comes in so many forms: my mother's mental illness, my father's emotional withholding, my siblings' early deaths . . . Yù Yīng's version presented to me initially as more straightforward—in some ways it was the textbook definition of abandoning a child—but it turned out to be way more complicated than I'd imagined, even with its seemingly happy ending. Because that ending, like most fairy tales, was too good to be true. Yù Yīng and Tǔ Xiù didn't recover what they'd lost or how they'd once known each other simply by coming back together later in life. Instead, they inadvertently discovered that the best they could do was restart. No one demanded "closure," as far as I could tell.

And yet, that turned out to be enough.

At some point in our long long-distance courtship, James had given me a painting by the Chinese artist Yang Ming Yi, whose powerfully muted work he'd been collecting for a couple of years. The 18×15-inch watercolor-and-ink rendering depicts a winter landscape—predominantly gray, with flecks of snowy white and thin black strokes assembled into a shroud of leafless branches. The painting's focal point is a brown door that stands tall against the blizzard and is decorated with twin red scrolls, inviting Lunar New Year prosperity.

From a distance, at least to a Westerner, those scrolls can seem more like slender, vertical windows that glow with the fiery light of the home's interior. The doorway is rooted in the barest outline of a stone wall, making it look suspended in the storm. And because you can't tell where the house ends and the sky begins, you don't immediately know whether the slathering of snow that crowns the scene marks a rooftop or a distant backdrop of pristine trails and ponds.

Even today, I look at this painting and I hear 1994 James saying, "After an earthquake, when you see it on the news, do you see rubble, rubble, rubble, doorway, rubble? Does that make sense to you?" I don't know whether he was conscious of that comment when he purchased this evocative artwork. What I do know is he'd paid close attention when I told him the thing I missed most about New England: It was the cupping. I didn't mean cupping in the way that James might employ the word—to describe the acupressure practice of *bá guàn* that had bruised and bubbled his skin. I meant cupping as in nestling, as in coddling and protecting against those elements that conspire to harden and deflate us.

As much as I hate Boston winters, living in Long Beach made me realize that my definition of home is largely sensory: its smells and sounds, of course, but most specifically the feeling of coming in from the cold and being enveloped by a *WHOOSH* of furnace-fed warmth, a lot like the splash that concluded the Congo Cruise. It's a sensation steeped in the profound awareness and unshakable faith that I'm being sheltered (*bì hù*, that close cousin of my gecko friend, *bì hŭ*). Opening the back door to our little tan ranch in Braintree was akin to being held in the palm of a hand that would never not be there. Or so I believed.

Over the phone in 1994, I'd told James that I needed the equivalent of a house hug. And somehow, listening in Massachusetts to the insane lament of a girlfriend who'd moved to Southern California to escape almost everything about New England—including its winters, its emotional ties, and its men—he'd not only summoned empathy; he'd also found the perfect expression of my words in Yang Ming Yi's brushstrokes.

What we bring to a work of art is often as important as what that artwork brings to us. Great art opens our receptors. It invites transformation and shifts in perspective. It exists from and for evolution.

What I originally loved about this painting was what it said about my relationship with James—how fully he "got me" and how much he cared about my emotional well-being. I still love that. But what I see when I view the work now is something else entirely.

I see the brown door as a gateway, not just to a place but to a journey.

I see all the ways that my narrow teenage life exploded when I first walked through the door at Mandarin Garden in 1979, setting myself on a path to so much of what I would one day hold most dear.

I see Yù Yīng, holding up more than her half of the sky.

And I see Zoe, whose knowable story literally begins on a doorstep, in a cardboard box placed just outside that local civil affairs office, and stands in poetic contrast to her adoptive mirror-image aunt, the water horse Tǔ Xiù—one child taken from the land where one was left behind.

The idea of home has changed so much for me. It's no longer confined to a tiny kitchen in Braintree, Massachusetts, where the Serenity Prayer hangs on a wall. Home now extends at least as far as China, which my parents used to recommend I dig to as they handed me a beach pail and the flimsiest plastic shovel money could buy. They didn't foresee that I would get there eventually, multiple times, and all my digging would lead right back to serenity—the model that's attained instead of granted, not as platitude but as creed.

My mother thought she'd failed to have "the wisdom to know the difference."

Bullshit.

She lived in a tunnel—the kind where you rarely know when, or if, the ride is going to open up, and when it does, you do your best to just hold on until the next dip in the track. I was granted a more expansive view, with the opportunity to discover that you can't in good faith accept what you don't feel worthy of receiving.

It's not necessary to see the house in Yang Ming Yi's painting. You need only to see the doorway to be transported.

Just as it's not necessary to know you are lost before you can be found.

AFTERWORD

Home

Yiyang is a complicated place.

It's where Zoe was born. Maybe. We think. But she could have been transported miles from her birthplace to this ruggedly civilized home of ancient operas and giant reclining Buddhas. There's a good chance we'll never really know.

We do know she was left here, in the cold shadow of a government office building on an inhospitable January night in 2003, before she was welcomed into the palm of a local orphanage. And we know what that orphanage looks like and who raised her there, for the first full year of her life, because in June 2017, just before I turned fifty-six, we traveled to Yiyang to unearth what we could of Zoe's roots.

I tried not to expect too much of the trip, but that was no easier than it had been keeping my mind from wandering into the scary spaces while awaiting results of my BRCA gene tests, or while sifting through the nightmares that questioned my parental fitness in the weeks leading up to Zoe's adoption. This excursion was about giving Zoe, now fourteen, a past.

No big deal.

Yiyang is complicated in the way that my parents' tan ranch was complicated, as a place where happiness and sadness collide, and in all the ways that accompany rampant global inequality, as a place where poverty too rarely meets opportunity and circumstance too often shapes lives. The widening opportunity gap was on display everywhere we went in the region, from its dusty downtowns to its expansive rural tracts dotted with small farms and humble structures, some barely habitable. Zoe cringed at the disparity in her before and after lives; she has a pronounced sense of fairness that started showing itself in preschool, when her teachers would remark on her impulse to comfort and help if a classmate was struggling. Water horses are known to be "tough cookies with a good heart and a terrific work ethic," according to what I read. Good job, internet! That's my kid, to a *T.*

On our way to Yiyang, we'd visited Taiwan to see Yù Yīng, who was well into her nineties. That was when I first started noticing similarities in how my mother-in-law interacted with the two water horses who'd come into my life. Though she barely knew Zoe, who'd only previously visited twice, including a month of Chinese summer camp when James made the trip without me in 2014, Yù Yīng delighted in her latest Chinese American grandchild. I'd often catch her looking at my kid with what seemed to be immense pride, reminiscent of the time she'd said of Tǔ Xiù, during our visit to Guilin in 1999, "My daughter is a survivor." One afternoon as we were all sitting together after yet another abundant lunch, Yù Yīng abruptly walked off to her bedroom and came back holding a substantial piece of jewelry more than half the size of her hand. The necklace had a woven cord attached to a thick rectangle of jade that was the most beautiful shade of mottled emerald I'd ever seen. Carved into one side was a dragon, and on the other was a *qí lín*—the mythical cross between a dragon and a horse. Both were set into lush landscapes bursting with the kind of vegetation traditionally depicted to signify an abundance of wealth and promise. The pendant was overtly regal, clearly made for a person with wisdom and influence, or perhaps for a person who had yet to grow into her influence, a person with "a big name for a little girl."

Without a word, Yù Yīng handed the necklace to Zoe, who received it with many sincere thank-yous, though she had no concept of its worth. James leaned into her ear: "This one is very old jade—it's real, real treasure,

Zoe. Nǎi Nai must love you a lot." Then he leaned into my ear. "She never gave *me* anything like that," he said, not with bitterness, but with wonder.

In the Hollywood ending to this story, I bring Zoe to Guilin to meet Tǔ Xiù, her astrological twin. The two water horse foundlings discover cosmic connections that no one would have suspected, linking them far beyond zodiac generalizations and childhoods shaped by abandonment. Perhaps, depending on what kind of movie I'm fantasizing, they each have mind control powers that, combined, unlock a superpower capable of ending greed, reversing climate change, and making governments around the world act like they care about people. Or, if not that, maybe they just forge a deep personal bond that amends and enriches their individual lives. I know my Tao of Three Wishes would be satisfied with either scenario. But I also know better than to expect a Hollywood ending in matters of real-world consequence.

By the time we got back to Guilin with Zoe in 2017, Tǔ Xiù had died. She was sixty-two, felled by the same hypertension that had claimed her father in his forties. James had only gotten in the one brief visit with his eldest sister in 1999, and Yù Yīng had again lost her firstborn, this time with no known hope of reunification. The best we could do at that point was relate Tǔ Xiù's story to Zoe secondhand, through her forty-four-year-old daughter, Lina, who lived about a hundred miles south of Guilin, in Liuzhou. I never expected to make a perfect circle of Tǔ Xiù's and Zoe's abandonments, but I did hope that Lina could help flesh out our rudimentary sketch of her mother's struggle—I suppose so Zoe might feel less alone in her own struggles, however and whenever they inevitably came, and so that I might not feel quite so powerless to help her through them.

Lina knew Tǔ Xiù as the nurturer that Yù Yīng had hoped she'd become when she equipped her with a nickname designed to make her more grounded and caring. "My mother lacked the element of earth, or soil, in her five-element scheme," Lina reminded us, "so the character of 'Tǔ' was added to her name because the fortune-teller said she didn't have enough earth. Chinese people believe that putting the character of 'earth' [土] in her name will turn her fate to a better direction."

Of course, a "better direction" is subjective—like "intriguing"—and hard to prove. It's an interesting word choice, knowing what we know about the trajectory of Tǔ Xiù's life. And Lina said another interesting thing during the time we spent with her: She said her mother was "adopted."

We knew the story: how, after Tǔ Xiù's paternal grandfather died, her step-grandmother remarried into a family with eight or nine children who had no interest in another young mouth to feed. Tǔ Xiù was kicked into the streets, where she remained homeless until a friend's parents took her in and raised her as their own. It's not the legal definition of adoption, and I'd stupidly never even considered it in that context, but it's the word that Lina uses *(shōu yǎng*: 收养, *to take in, to care for)* to describe those years of her mother's life.

I don't know if Zoe heard it, or understood it, when Lina deployed the word in conversation, but I hope so. Because I now think she had it exactly right.

The banner above the entrance to the orphanage in Yiyang read, in Chinese characters, "Welcome home, Yì Lì Gē."

Seeing it, as our overheating passenger van sputtered to a stop on a day that topped 105 degrees Fahrenheit and 80 percent humidity, was emotional enough. Then, the building's front door opened to reveal a petite older woman with a bony frame and a toothy smile.

"Yíyi," someone official-looking told us. "Mama Auntie" (姨姨), James translated: Zoe's foster mother.

We'd hired a Chinese man who went by Wayne (John Wayne?) to track her down, and in the process, he'd uncovered that Zoe was "fostered" not in a family setting, as I'd assumed, but mostly within the orphanage walls by this woman who'd come to live there for a year, taking charge of several babies and occasionally bringing one or two of them home to spend a weekend at her concrete farmhouse in the countryside. Zoe was a favorite recipient of those day passes, the woman told us; she was a bubbly, bright child who loved to dance.

James, who never even tears up, about anything, sobbed in dramatic, uncensored gulps upon meeting this woman. We all did. If the first year of a child's life is anywhere near as developmentally important as the research indicates, we owe her much more than we can quantify; we owe her everything we have, because she gave us everything we now consider important. And whatever fraction of that was registering as we stood outside the orphanage dripping in tears and perspiration, I'm pretty sure we would still be there weeping if someone hadn't ignited the longest, loudest strip of celebratory firecrackers we'd ever heard. At that point, all we could do was laugh, because nothing hijacks a solemn scene like absurdity.

I remember every detail of that day in Yiyang—how the mostly unoccupied orphanage, which we'd just found out would be demolished in less than a month, presented a bomb cyclone of surreal observations and feelings when we finally moved inside its doors. I remember standing in a dilapidated room that had once held Zoe's crib and toys, looking out through a murky window onto a neglected, overgrown playground and thinking: *This is where she was? For a whole year?*

It helped to think the place had not always been in such disrepair, and to watch the kind-faced woman who'd guided Zoe through those months dote on her even now, vigilantly shooing any insects that dared alight on her sensitive skin. She was in good hands. *She has always been in good, loving hands.* I know this for sure, because of the red letter.

We got a look at it that day at her orphanage, but they wouldn't let us keep it, which seemed so cruel, even though we didn't know it existed before we came. The conversation was moving along normally between our family and the orphanage staff, like we were just there to donate the trunkful of Pampers we'd brought along as an offering, and suddenly there it was, in a folder of otherwise unexceptional stuff they handed us to look through while we sipped tea and nibbled on fruit.

The letter isn't really a letter, I should say. It's a note. And the note is just notations, no sentences. It's information, not literature, and it was pinned to the baby blanket that swaddled Zoe in her cardboard box the night she was found. All told, it is thirty-three Chinese characters arranged in four lines, etched in black ink on a piece of paper cut from what appears to be a red envelope of the type used for Lunar New Year gift-giving. Translated into English, it reads like the scene descriptions in a screenplay:

> **BABY BORN: year, month, day, time**
> *Western date: 2003 January 23*
> *Lunar date: 2002 December 21*
> *Afternoon, 2 o'clock*

Zoe stared at the note, looking confused—like the rest of us who were coming to grips with its existence—and also troubled.

"What's wrong?" I asked.

"Nothing," she lied. "It's just . . ." The tears were gathering again, but she managed to choke out the words, softly. "Why doesn't it say . . . *more*?"

Such a reasonable question. She wasn't looking for a novel. She could have been happy with a line or two, or even a couple of words, so long as they were the right kind of words, the kind that expressed direct love and concern for the child whose chest they were pinned to. But this usually pragmatic and unsentimental young woman had also watched enough TV to covet a corny, heartfelt message along the lines of *Please take care of our baby. Give her the home that we can't. Love her, as much as we do. Forgive us.* She couldn't help but be crushed by how far this was from that.

I'm grateful for my gimlet-eyed husband in many circumstances, but especially this one, because he can read subtext and think on his feet, and he took immediate action to correct the record. "Hang on," he implored his despondent daughter. "Let me tell you what else it says.

"Okay, first of all, look at the paper. It's not ordinary, right? It's fancy, expensive, for celebration. And red color, for good luck. It's also delicate. Precious.

"Then, look at what they wrote: You know Chinese fortune depends on birthdate, right? Also, time of day. Very important. So, they are giving you everything you need—for the temple, for the fortune-temple book, like the one I use every year to see how lucky we will be. This small piece of paper has all the important information, without giving away too much—you know, because they could be arrested for leaving a baby. They are saying, 'This baby is treasure. We hope she has a good life, a good chance, good everything.'"

I could watch a million Marvel movies and never encounter a superhero as great as James (James Bond) was in that one off-the-cuff moment. He didn't just save the day; he gave Zoe something she wouldn't always be able to find as she grew up and the questions got harder. He gave her an answer.

Questions were all that I had when I first met James. Questions about who I was and where I was going and, yes, even "Who gets to live?" Now I had a daughter who would also have to learn—not today, but eventually—that most things just don't add up, or stand a chance of being put right when you don't have a superhero standing by. To get anywhere near acceptance, never mind serenity, you need to know the value of carrying the uncomfortable questions gracefully, and how to let them inform but not define you.

I think for Yù Yīng, all the way up until she died in 2024 at one hundred (or 101, if you apply traditional Chinese accounting to start from one at birth), the hardest of those questions was: What if I'd brought her?

For Tǔ Xiù, it had to be: What if I'd gone?

For Zoe, it will always be: What if I'd stayed?

And for me, while I'll never run out of confounding things to ponder, I keep coming back to how difficult it is for my inner control freak to admit that the answer to most things of consequence is James's eloquently simple, frustratingly on-point catchphrase. "You ask me, who I gonna ask?"

Acknowledgments

The hallmark of a memoir that was way too many years in the making is the insane number of people there are to thank. I could start with my teachers, my mentors, my babysitters, and easily go on for paragraphs just listing family members (a rollcall that begins with my surviving siblings, Carol Page Ostrum and Jimmy Page) who've been all those things and more to me. But they know who they are and how much I owe them, well beyond the names and events covered in this book. So, instead, I'll zoom ahead to some folks who directly enabled and nurtured *Year of the Water Horse*, helping to bring it across the finish line even in what is, by all accounts, a horrible market for memoirs by people not named Britney Spears.

My deepest thanks go to Jessica Case at Pegasus Books, who is that rare editor still willing to take a leap of faith and follow her heart. I'm so grateful for your enthusiasm and spot-on guidance, and for introducing me to the talented Kara Klontz, who designed this book's spectacular cover.

To Todd Shuster and Valerie Frankel, my extraordinary agents at Aevitas Creative Management: Thank you for your wisdom and patience (so much patience) and, above all, for your friendship. You kept my eyes on the prize and made this entire journey fun, mostly.

To my early readers—M.J. Andersen, Meredith Goldstein, Beth Teitell, Scott Helman, Julie Dalton, Ann Hornaday, Amy Hitt, Peter Marks:

Where do I start? Thank you for your time, your vision, your candor, and your kindness, which kept me going when I doubted my ability to find the door. And thanks to my unlicensed therapist Rena Sokolow, who got me *out* the door for much-needed walks around the pond (not a euphemism). I'm also deeply indebted to Xuping Zhu and Amy Torborg for translating interviews, texts, and drafts with care and diligence that saved me and my pidgin Mandarin from untold errors and embarrassments. *Xiè xiè nǐ.*

To Yaddo, the place and its people: My month spent with you in Saratoga Springs was life-changing, thanks in general to the staff and creative vibe and especially to the support and generosity of A.M. Homes, Rosanna Bruno, Kavitha Buggana, Amanda Nadelberg, and Alice Elliott Dark. I also owe a shoutout to the estate's original owner, Spencer Trask, for letting me borrow his room, where it was an honor to write and rewrite these chapters.

To my fellow journalists at *The Washington Post*, *The Boston Globe*, *The Los Angeles Times*, *The Providence Journal*, *The Old Colony Memorial* (again, newspaper, not funeral home), and every other publication I've worked at, contributed to, or just read and admired consistently: You inspire me every day. Please keep doing the work you do, with integrity and dedication that will never be properly quantified or rewarded. Every important and sustainable thing I've learned about writing I learned in newsrooms, from people whose values and priorities continue to guide me. I'll never not be proud of that, double negatives be damned.

And finally, I do have to circle back to family, because that's where this entire saga begins and ends. To every Page and Tseng and their offshoots around the globe through the generations: I'm aware that my story is a very small part of *our* story, and I apologize for everything and everyone I've had to leave out. As my uber quotable chef-husband is fond of telling me, "In *my* business, the chicken is done when the chicken is done. Cook it too much, no one wants to eat. Cook it too little, you might kill someone."

"The problem with *your* business is," he says about the magnificently masochistic craft of writing and editing, "the chicken is never done."

I'll leave it there.